THE CARDINAL PROTECTORS OF ENGLAND:
ROME AND THE TUDORS
BEFORE THE REFORMATION

THE CARDINAL PROTECTORS
OF ENGLAND

*ROME AND THE TUDORS BEFORE
THE REFORMATION*

WILLIAM E. WILKIE

CAMBRIDGE UNIVERSITY PRESS

Published by the Syndics of the Cambridge University Press
Bentley House, 200 Euston Road, London NW1 2DB
American Branch: 32 East 57th Street, New York, N.Y.10022

© Cambridge University Press

Library of Congress Catalogue Card Number: 73–82462

ISBN: 0 521 20332 5

First published 1974

Printed in Great Britain by
Western Printing Services Ltd, Bristol

CONTENTS

Preface vii   Introduction 1

PREFACE

The period with which this book deals actually runs from 1485 to 1539, that is, from the accession of Henry VII until the death of Campeggio, the last of the cardinal protectors nominated by the crown. However, the chief object has been to study the personal relationship of Giulio de'Medici (after 1523 called Clement VII) and Lorenzo Campeggio with Henry VIII and Wolsey. Everything else is meant to provide a context broad enough to make the full implications of this main story clear.

The treatment is for the most part severely chronological, but an effort has been made to gather into Chapters 2 and 5 some of the more tedious matters connected with provisions to English and Irish bishoprics. The chief source available has been the extensive surviving diplomatic correspondence of the period. It is folly to impose a sense of immediacy and urgency on letters most often received more than a month after they were written, and in an age with a much different sense of time from our own. While the point of view taken here is essentially new, most of the people and events discussed have long been familiar to historians. More recently, the solid and complete research of D. S. Chambers into the career of Cardinal Bainbridge has permanently linked their names; and whatever is sound in my own interpretation of Bainbridge's relations with the official cardinal protectors owes very much to Chambers' very careful and balanced assessment. Any historian working with the period of Henry VIII is constantly grateful to the editors who calendared the *Letters and Papers of Henry VIII*. In most cases the English summaries there have been compared with the printed or manuscript sources, but the originals are cited in the notes generally only when they amplify or correct the summary. Emphasis has been placed instead upon archival material less readily accessible to historians in England.

Great numbers of archivists, librarians and fellow scholars have offered kind assistance, often far beyond what could normally be hoped for, even from very generous persons. In a most personal way I should like to thank Professor G. R. Elton of Clare College, Cambridge, and Professor Heinrich Schmidinger, formerly of the University of Fribourg, Switzerland, and at present director of the Istituto Austriaco di Cultura in Rome.

Wm. E. Wilkie

Cambridge
1974

To the Master and Fellows
of St Edmund's House,
Cambridge

INTRODUCTION

Henry VIII's campaign to divorce Catherine of Aragon is surely one of the best-remembered episodes in history. His quarrel with the pope and his marriage to Anne Boleyn have been studied and described in ever-increasing detail. It is regularly remarked that the pope in question was Clement VII, and that an Italian cardinal called Campeggio came to England to serve as co-legate with Wolsey in opening the marriage case. It is often recalled, at least in passing, that Lorenzo Campeggio had come to England once before, when Wolsey's treaty of London was made in 1518. Some have even begun to suggest without much comment that Campeggio was cardinal protector of England. But Campeggio's long and close association with Wolsey and with Henry VIII has never been studied in detail. It was Cardinal Giulio de'Medici who was elected Clement VII in 1523, and he had then served for almost a decade as protector of England before Campeggio's long-expected succession to the title. This close relationship of de'Medici both with England and with Campeggio has been virtually ignored. Yet when English diplomacy and policy toward the Church are seen from the Roman and papal point of view, the twenty years before England's break with Rome in 1534 appear chiefly in terms of the relations of Henry VIII and Wolsey with de'Medici and Campeggio, the cardinal protectors of England from 1514 to 1534.

Beyond doubt it was Clement VII's dilatory refusal to declare Henry VIII's marriage with Catherine of Aragon invalid which occasioned the break with Rome, but this refusal must be seen in the context of more than thirty years of Anglo-papal diplomacy. Henry VII used the cardinals in England's service as protectors, first Francesco Todeschini Piccolomini and then Galeotto della Rovere, to obtain the marriage dispensation for his son as a special favour and as reward for his loyalty to the papacy. Henry VIII hoped to find the Cardinal Protector Campeggio and the former protector, Clement VII, willing to declare this same dispensation invalid, also as a reward for his loyalty. Even if the case had involved different circumstances and lesser people, the sentence would probably have been in favour of validity; but there was a strong case in canon law against validity which would in justice have required its admission to trial. From the beginning, however, Clement VII excelled even Henry VIII and Wolsey in emphasising the external and diplomatic ramifications of the case over its legal and moral aspects. Their long and intimate association with Clement VII had provided Henry VIII and Wolsey with thorough experience of his very secular frame of mind and his personal psychology. As the only consistently reliable supporter of papal diplomacy, Henry VIII had grounds for expecting special consideration. As delay followed delay in deciding the marriage case, the fact that the king and Wolsey so clearly understood what was happening served to intensify the king's exasperation and Wolsey's apprehension.

The election of Giovanni de'Medici to the papacy in 1513 as Leo X transformed the curial position of his cousin, Giulio de'Medici, and coincided with the period of Wolsey's rise to power in the government of Henry VIII. It also coincided with the emergence of the much more ambitious English foreign policy that had been gathering force in the four years since Henry VIII's accession. Wolsey's diplomacy and his own position in England as lord chancellor and papal legate were an expression of the underlying Anglo-papal cooperation which made the protectorship work. Following, but hardly subservient to the papacy, Wolsey sought to make England conspicuous and influential in diplomacy by revising the traditional English policy of opposition to France in favour of an independent bargaining position between France and the Empire. The two de'Medici popes, Leo X and Clement VII, seeking by this same tactic to assure the independence both of the papacy and of their native Florence, turned increasingly to Wolsey for support. This was not so much the invention of 'balance of power' diplomacy as it was a realistic response to the changed diplomatic situation in Europe, and to the epic Habsburg–Valois struggle which dominated it. In diplomacy as in all things, however, Wolsey was first of all the servant of King Henry VIII.

Although the old issues agitated over the Statutes of Provisors and Praemunire had never been resolved, the cordial working compromise between the English crown and the papacy allowed the existence of these statutes to drift into the background or to be deceptively glossed over. Alone in Europe, Wolsey had systematic success in exploiting a national use of papal power as a legate *a latere*; parallel efforts in Germany, Hungary, France and Scotland to obtain similar legatine commissions achieved very limited success. By shrewd manipulation of the canon law and the English constitution Wolsey managed to unite church and state in his own person.

It is, then, not merely coincidental that Wolsey's lifetime commission as legate was finally granted by Giulio de'Medici as Clement VII, or that Wolsey's legatine career began with Campeggio's crossing over to England from Calais in 1518 and ended with Campeggio's departure from London for Dover in 1529 after his second journey to England as legate. In the commission of 1518 Leo X and de'Medici were yielding at last, and under cover of parallel grants to France and Germany, to what was probably already part of Wolsey's plan in making de'Medici protector in 1514. The fall of Wolsey in 1529 was the beginning of the end of Clement VII's and Campeggio's special relationship with England. Despite Campeggio's reluctance to accept the break as permanent, the Act of Supremacy of 1534, which followed shortly after Clement VII's death, finished the work of severing England's ties with the papacy. Thus the cardinal protectorship of England between 1514 and 1534 took on an importance far beyond anything it previously possessed.

1

THE BEGINNINGS OF
THE CARDINAL PROTECTORSHIP
OF ENGLAND, 1492–1514

The cardinals in the Roman Curia
The emergence of the national protectorships of cardinals in the
Roman Curia during the fifteenth century coincided with the
emergence of national monarchies and of organised diplomacy in
Renaissance Italy. The circumstances which motivated the
development, however, had long been sensed. The College of
Cardinals had been brought into prominence during the reform
movement of the eleventh century by the naming of several non-
Italian cardinals who were active reformers. Its new importance
was confirmed when Pope Nicholas II's decree of 1059 gave the
cardinals alone the right to elect the pope. As a body of advisers
to the pope, the cardinals in Consistory found canonical precedent
in the relationship of a bishop with his canons or of an abbot
with his monks in chapter. The term *consistorium* itself was a
revival of that anciently used for the meeting of the Roman
emperor with his council of state; the term *senatus* for the College
of Cardinals, although largely literary in import, was likewise a
revival of the ancient Roman term. The growth of the practice of
papal provision to benefices gave a new importance to Consistory
through which the provisions were made. The Western Schism
and the Conciliar Movement gave new impetus to the canonical
and constitutional role of the College of Cardinals.[1]

Cardinal protectors of religious orders first appeared in the
thirteenth century, most notably Cardinal Ugolino (Gregory IX)

[1] S. Kuttner, 'Cardinalis, the history of a canonical concept', *Traditio*, III
(1945), 129–214; and B. Tierney, pt. I, ch. III, 'Pope and cardinals', and
pt. II, ch. II, 'The structure of a medieval ecclesiastical corporation',
*Foundations of the Conciliar Theory, the Contribution of the Medieval
Canonists from Gratian to the Great Schism* (Cambridge, 1955), pp. 68–84
and 106–31.

as protector of the Franciscans.[2] From the beginning these protectors not only served as powerful agents and spokesmen on behalf of the order but at the same time exercised a profound, often telling influence over the internal life and constitutional discipline of the order. St Francis of Assisi enunciated an ideal of the religious life; it was Cardinal Ugolino who fashioned his foundation into the Franciscan order. St Dominic possessed to an eminent degree the sense of constitutional order which St Francis lacked. It is not surprising, therefore, that the first protector of the Dominican order, Cardinal d'Aigrefeuille, should appear only in the second half of the fourteenth century and during a period of relaxed discipline within the order and of external difficulties with the Avignon papacy. Nor is it surprising that the first reference to him should mistakenly use the familiar title of *procurator* rather than that of *protector*.[3]

On the other hand, the cardinal protector of a nation was never regarded as having authority to interfere in the internal affairs of the nation or to direct its ruler. In Henry VIII's rather lofty phrase, the cardinal protector 'indueth as it were our owne Person, for the defence of Us and our Realme in al matiers [in the Curia]...touching the same'.[4] As one having the right to participate in the deliberations of Consistory, the cardinal protector's foremost responsibility was to refer the ruler's nominations to bishoprics and other benefices to which the right of papal provision was successfully claimed, and to see to the expedition of the bulls of provision. He was to defend national interests when these came into discussion in Consistory or elsewhere, and to assist ambassadors (*oratores*), procurators, solicitors, and other agents on business in Rome. This might involve accompanying them in audience with the pope or intervening privately with the pope or any of the curial officials such as the datary or the auditors of the Rota. He was a source of information and a means of enhancing the prestige of the nation of which he was protector, both by his own personal importance as well as by his organising

---

[2] B. da Siena, *Il cardinale protettore negli instituti religiosi, specialmente negli ordini Francescani* (Florence, 1940).

[3] S. Forte, *The Cardinal-Protector of the Dominican Order*, Dissertationes Historicae, fasc. xv (Rome, 1959), pp. 13 and 66, follows G.-G. Meersseman, 'Etudes sur l'ordre des Frères Prêcheurs au début du Grand Schisme', *Archivum Fratrum Praedicatorum*, xxv (1955), 217.

[4] *State Papers of Henry VIII*, viii, 485–6 (*LP* vi, 806).

or participating in functions and fêtes. In Conclave he was expected to work for the election of the candidate for pope, often himself, that his prince might favour.[5]

The existence of national protectorships of cardinals was first openly and regularly recognised only by Julius II (1503–13). His language presented them as something parallel to letters of papal protection or to the protectorships of religious orders, and thereby implied a certain filial subordination to a benignly disposed pope.[6] The protectorship of a secular ruler remained in effect, however, the commitment of a powerful member of a deliberative body to serve an outside interest in return for the recompense given him in fees and gifts, often including even his own provision to one or more benefices in the nation of which he was protector. In short it was not unlike buying a member of parliament, but without the odious overtones such a situation provokes in the modern mind. Before the development of the Consistorial Congregations in the Curia after the Council of Trent and the decline of Consistory itself, the great majority of the curial cardinals had few official functions other than presence at papal ceremonies and participation in Consistory. They were expected to live with large households in the style of Renaissance princes but, unless they were from great families with wealth of their own, with insufficient and unreliable sources of income. The employment and income from services as national protector in a sense filled a vacuum. The advantage of the position became increasingly apparent when the duty of referring nominations to benefices crystallised into a customary right, and the offering or *propina* made became fixed at fifteen per cent beyond the amount paid in consistorial taxes for the bulls of provision, plus an additional five per cent for the members of the cardinal's household who had seen to the gathering of the necessary testimony.[7] Under Julius II and

---

[5] J. Wodka, *Zur Geschichte der nationalen Protektorate der Kardinäle an der römischen Kurie*, Publikationen des österreichischen historischen Instituts in Rom, vol. IV, pt. 1 (Innsbruck, 1938), pp. 27ff.; and D. S. Chambers, 'English representation at the court of Rome in the early Tudor period' (unpublished D. Phil. dissertation, Oxford, 1962), pp. 34ff.

[6] J. Wodka, 'Das Kardinalsprotektorat deutscher Nation und die Protektorate der deutschen nationalen Stiftungen in Rom', *Zeitschrift der Savigny-Stiftung für Rechtsgeschichte* (Kanonistische Abteilung, XXXIII), LXIV (1944), 301–22.

[7] W. E. Lunt, *Financial Relations of the Papacy with England* (Cambridge, Mass., 1962), II, 257–8.

Leo X it became rather standard for a newly created curial cardinal to send to selected princes an announcement of his elevation together with an offer of services.

It is likely that the terms cardinal protector and cardinal procurator were used very loosely and sometimes interchangeably during the fifteenth century. The precedent for the cardinal protectors probably lies in the cardinal promotors of the fourteenth century.[8] Certainly the most effective curial spokesman for national interests during the fifteenth century was a national like Jean Jouffroy or, later, Jean Balue, both of whom came to Rome as procurator for the French king and continued to work in that capacity even after their creation as cardinals. It is interesting that the earliest reference to the first cardinal protector of England, in 1492, should have involved the same confusion of the unfamiliar term of 'cardinal protector' with the familiar one of 'cardinal proctor' or 'procurator', as has already been seen in the case of the first cardinal protector of the Dominican order. After the emergence of the cardinal protectors there were still national procurators who continued on in that capacity even after elevation to the cardinalate, and there is little that distinguishes the services of the one from the other except perhaps the national procurator's greater initiative and dependability. However, even though there was generally at least one French cardinal resident in the Curia during the first half of the sixteenth century, Louis XII and Francis I chose successively as protector of France three Italian cardinals in addition.[9] The object was evidently to develop as wide a base of influence as possible.

During the fifteenth century strong objection was regularly raised to cardinal protectorships of nations, as well as to national cardinals acting as proctors; for both were considered inconsistent with the obligations of cardinals to the papacy, and a means by which discussions in secret consistory were divulged to secular princes. In 1425 Martin V attempted to forbid them entirely. Under Pius II a reform draft of 1464 still saw a national protectorship as inconsonant with a cardinal's curial responsibility, except

---

[8] Wodka, *Protektorate der Kardinäle*, pp. 23ff. See also J. Vincke's review of Wodka's book in the *Zeitschrift der Savigny-Stiftung für Rechtsgeschichte* (Kanonistische Abteilung, xxviii), lix (1939), 516–20, which supports Wodka's view.

[9] Federigo Sanseverino, Giulio de'Medici and Agostino Trivulzio (Wodka, *Protektorate der Kardinäle*, pp. 98–9).

in so far as the protectorship served to influence nations to accept papal leadership in those matters relating to maintaining peace, Christian orthodoxy and the liberty of the Church. It was in the confused days of Innocent VIII and the easy ones of Alexander VI that the protectorships were first openly permitted by the pope. These popes were content to insist, ineffectively, that a cardinal have explicit, written permission of the pope before taking any curial position of service to a secular prince. By the time of Adrian VI (1522–3) the notion of national protectorships had become so well established that an unidentified cardinal could actually submit a reform plan to the pope suggesting the raising of the cardinal protectorship to a full and official position in the Curia, and making them the regular channel of relations with the various states.[10]

Kings had long been assigning national procurators to the Curia to see to the expediting of routine business, and the sending of *ad hoc* diplomatic representatives to the pope was a well-established practice. In the last quarter of the fifteenth century, however, procurators could and did acquire promotion also to the status of ambassador (*orator*), and papal reluctance to admit resident ambassadors to the Curia was relaxed.[11] One reason for this was certainly the growth of organised diplomacy in Italy at the time; but another is the parallel development of the resident papal nuncio from the office of papal collector, thus making the exchange of diplomatic representatives mutual. At least in the first half of the sixteenth century there was no limit of one nuncio or ambassador; two or even three resident ones are frequently found, along with special *ad hoc* ones. The return to Rome of a papal nuncio as an ambassador for the government to which he

---

[10] Wodka, ch. 1, 'Das Kardinalprotektorat der Länder in den kirchlichen Reformentwürfen des 15. und beginnenden 16. Jahrhunderts', *Protektorate der Kardinäle*, pp. 4–10; the documents themselves are printed at pp. 34–8. Wodka rejects as improbable Kalkoff's suggestion that the unidentified cardinal who submitted the reform proposal to Adrian VI was Cardinal Cajetan. Although Wodka does not suggest it, a better possibility might be Cardinal Lorenzo Campeggio.

[11] B. Behrens, 'Origins of the office of English resident ambassador in Rome', *English Historical Review*, xxxix (1934), 640–56. In 1477 John Shirwood was referred to simply as proctor but in 1478 as orator (ambassador), although as was usual he remained also proctor. See the constant references to *oratores* in J. Burckard, *Liber Notarum ab anno M.CCCC.LXXXIII usque ad annum MDVI*, ed. E. Celani, vol. I, A.D. 1483–96 (Città di Castello, 1906).

had been accredited was not uncommon, and on occasion the pope sent an ambassador home to serve as papal nuncio.[12] The word *orator*, the regular Latin word for ambassador, reflects his basic function of orating or speaking formally before a foreign prince in the name of his own. The word came into Italian and continued in use in the first half of the sixteenth century; it was regularly used, along with the proper Italian word *ambasciatore* which was replacing it, to mean any envoy, whether to the pope or to a civil ruler. The term *orator* survived in use longer in the Curia than elsewhere, and the use of the term *nuncio* in Italian for an ambassador from the pope became permanent. It is not merely coincidental that the participation of the papacy in this burgeoning secular diplomacy was shortly followed by the long-delayed papal acquiescence in cardinals' becoming protectors of secular rulers.

Among the alien elements in England during the fifteenth century the most influential was possibly that of the Italians, present as merchants and bankers, papal officials and diplomats, or as scholars. Through these Italians and through Englishmen in Italy developed the, at first, rather utilitarian English interest in Renaissance humanism. From about 1400 exponents of the new classicism in England, whether Englishmen or Italians, began to rise in the royal service, and to set the tone of Anglo-papal relations.[13] In 1485 England had no quarrel with the pope, and the groundwork had already been laid for the enthusiastic cultivation of the Renaissance papacy which would mark the Tudor court in England for more than forty years. The cardinal protectors of England were one of its manifestations.

Henry VII and the papacy

Who nowadays would think of Henry VII as an innovator? When Cardinal Francesco Todeschini Piccolomini became the cardinal protector of England in 1492, it was on the king's initiative; and Piccolomini was apparently the first officially approved cardinal protector not merely of England but of any nation whatever. Earlier Edward IV had employed in Rome the services of the

[12] D. Queller, *The Office of Ambassador in the Middle Ages* (Princeton, 1967).
[13] R. Weiss, *Humanism in England during the Fifteenth Century*, 2nd ed. (Oxford, 1957), pp. 181–2.

pro-Burgundian bishop of Tournai, Cardinal Ferry de Clugny, who had died in 1483.[14] In turning to Cardinal Piccolomini Henry VII was perhaps simply thinking to continue another precedent from the past. But the king's action also suggests the launching of a strategy which culminated in the adventuresome Anglo-papal diplomacy of his son, Henry VIII, under whom the protectors of England exercised a very significant influence.

When Henry VII succeeded Richard III as king of England and lord of Ireland in 1485, it was both logical and typical that he should correctly assess the value of cooperation with the papacy as a lever against both domestic and foreign difficulties. The three royal ambassadors who had been serving in Rome under Edward IV and Richard III were reinstated. On 4 February 1486 the king sent off to Rome his almoner and trusted councillor, the priest Christopher Urswick, to instruct the pope on the new order of things in England and to win his support.[15] Although Innocent VIII had only shortly before received the obedience of Richard III, he more than amply complied with the king's wishes. On 2 March 1486 he issued a bull of dispensation for the marriage of the king and Elizabeth of York, in which he carefully recognised Henry VII's own claims as king and the marriage as the source of peace in England. He followed it on 27 March with a clear and strongly worded bull, threatening excommunication of any who would attempt to upset the present succession or revive the animosities of Lancaster and York, and granting a plenary indulgence to any foreign princes or any of the king's own subjects who would resist such rebels. A final section addressed a stern warning to the clergy of all ranks, exempt or non-exempt, and granted if necessary,

---

[14] *Ven. Cal.* I, 478 (Venice, AS, Collezione Podocataro, Busta vII, no. 414), and *Cal. of Papal Letters*, xIII, i, pp. 235 and 242. On 12 January 1482 Edward IV wrote to Sixtus IV in credence for Ferry de Clugny, who had earlier arranged for the marriage of Edward's sister Margaret to Duke Charles the Bold of Burgundy, and who was about to go to Rome: 'Quod mea subditorumque meorum ac Regni et patriae negotia eius opera et consilio sub Vestre Sanctitatis gratia et adiutorio diriguntur.' Cited in D. S. Chambers, *Cardinal Bainbridge in the Court of Rome, 1509 to 1514* (Oxford, 1965), p. 2.

[15] W. Campbell (ed.), *Materials for a History of the Reign of Henry VII from Original Documents Preserved in the Public Record Office*, Rolls Series, 60 (London, 1873–7), I, 176–7, 275–7, 297 and 323; *Cal. of Pat. Rolls, Henry VII*, I, 36, 59 and 250; and *Archivium Hibernicum*, xxIII (1960), 64 (abstracts from Arch. Vat., Fondo Borghese 880, fols. 96ᵛ–99ʳ and 106ʳ⁻ᵛ).

previous papal legislation notwithstanding, the authority to invoke the secular arm against them.[16]

The next spring, 1487, Henry VII formed an impressive embassy to thank the pope for the marriage dispensation and to make his canonical obedience to the Apostolic See. The ten members included three bishops, Mylling of Hereford, Shirwood of Durham and Dunmow of Limerick; John Weston, prior of the Knights of St John in England; William Selling, prior of St Augustine's, Canterbury; Edward Cheyne, dean of Salisbury; Sir John Kendall, long in Rome as the representative of the Knights of St John; two lay knights; and Hugh Spaldyng, *custos* of the English Hospice in Rome. The group from England, after being joined by Shirwood, Dunmow, Kendall and Spaldyng, already in Rome, made its formal entry into the City on Tuesday 8 May and was received in public consistory on 14 and 22 May. The prior of Canterbury gave an oration before the pope in which he likened Henry VII to Aeneas in his struggle to gain the throne, and to the Emperors Theodosius and Constantine in acknowledging his subjection to the Church.[17]

The effort to win the papal confidence eventually bore further fruit. Several weeks after the Yorkist rebellion of Lambert Simnel had been ended in the fierce battle of Stoke on 16 June 1487, Henry VII sent the news to the pope. He told how a false rumour of his own defeat had spread to London, and how one John Swit, a criminal seeking sanctuary at Westminster, upon proclaiming the defeat as proof that the recent papal censures against rebels were powerless, fell instantly dead, and the body became immediately blacker than soot and could not be approached for the stench of it. The king failed to mention that the rebel John de la Pole, earl of Lincoln and nephew of Richard III, had died in battle along with a good many others of the Yorkist leaders, all likewise anathematised. He requested the pope to proceed against the archbishops of Armagh and Dublin, and the bishops of

[16] *Cal. of Papal Letters*, xiv, 1–2 and 14–28; and Rymer, *Foedera*, xii, 294, 297–9 and 313.

[17] Burckard, *Liber Notarum*, ed. Celani, i, 195–6; J. Gairdner (ed.), *Letters and Papers Illustrative of the Reigns of Richard III and Henry VII*, Rolls Series, 24 (London, 1861–3), i, 421. See also U. Balzani, 'Un'ambasciata inglese a Roma (Enrico VII al Innocenzo VIII, anno 1487)', *Archivio della società romana di storia patria*, iii (1880), 175–211; pp. 196–211 are documents.

Meath and Kildare, who had countenanced and encouraged the rebellion from its outset in Ireland. Bishop Shirwood was despatched from Rome 'on business of the Pope and himself' with a retinue of twenty-four on 10 October 1487; but it was only on 5 January 1488 that a bull was sent to the archbishops of Cashel and Tuam, and the bishops of Clogher and Ossory, instructing them to inquire into the rebellious activities of the four bishops of the Pale and to send report of their findings to the pope with a view to further action. On the same day a similar bull appointed Archbishop Morton of Canterbury and the bishops of Winchester, Ely and Exeter to inquire into the connexion of Bishop Richard Redmayn of St Asaph with the same Simnel rebellion. The affair of Bishop Redmayn was soon settled; but the king needed something more direct than a request for four Irish bishops from without the Pale, themselves of rather unstable loyalty, to crush the Yorkist loyalties of the Englishry within the Pale. Indeed, the situation was soon reversed. The bishops of the Pale made their submission and were included among the many pardoned on 25 May 1488. A new bull of 17 May 1488 expressly including Ireland within the terms of the excommunication, which some had claimed applied only to England, was formally promulgated under duress at a provincial council of Cashel at Clonmell.[18]

Henry VII's clear policy of using papal censures to strengthen the crown was coupled with an attack on the rights of sanctuary, which were being used by still active Yorkist conspirators as well as by common criminals to evade arrest. During the spring of 1486 the king had ordered Humphrey and Thomas Stafford to be dragged from sanctuary and imprisoned in the Tower of London. A civil court judged the right of sanctuary did not extend to treason and, as a matter of common law rather than canon law, permitted the Staffords to be brought to trial.[19] To induce the pope to modify a right of the Church already thus challenged was a delicate matter. The king himself wrote long letters explaining the abuses of sanctuary as a threat to peace and good order,

---

[18] *Cal. of Papal Letters*, xiv, 305; *Cal. of Pat. Rolls, Henry VII*, ii, 370; Rymer, *Foedera*, xii, 332–4, 341–3 and 634–5. From 11 June 1492 until September 1493 Walter FitzSimons, archbishop of Dublin, served as king's deputy in Ireland; and on 26 August 1496 it was David Creagh, archbishop of Cashel, who was among those granted a royal pardon for sedition.

[19] G. R. Elton, *England under the Tudors* (London, 1962), p. 21.

and the famous embassy of May 1487 discussed the problem with the pope.[20] On 6 August 1489 Innocent VIII issued one bull limiting the privileges of sanctuary and still another granting permission for rebels excommunicated by papal bull to be forgiven without recourse to Rome.[21]

The pope's willingness to cooperate was not only the result of representations made in Rome but stemmed in part also from the king's good relationship with the papal collector and nuncio in England, Giovanni Gigli. In spite of an association since 1476 with a Yorkist government, which had granted him English citizenship, Gigli came to an understanding with the new king very quickly and gave the pope a most favourable report of the realm. As a poet, Gigli had presented a long elegy in honour of the proposed marriage of Henry VII and Elizabeth of York and then served as a royal proctor at London in obtaining the canonical dispensation for it.[22] During the next few years Gigli, whom Henry VII praised to the pope, was much involved with both papal and royal business, especially with subsidies against the Turks, and English relations with France and Scotland. But for an attack of gout, he would have gone on a peace mission to France in 1488 as the king's envoy. The papal chamberlain Persio Malvezzi, sent to England with the sword and cap of maintenance for the king, stayed on and, together with Gigli, became much involved in royal affairs.[23]

Among the various other Italians working in England were several of Gigli's nephews, including Sebastiano, who was a merchant, and Silvestro, who succeeded his uncle in the royal diplomatic service, as well as the pope's nephew, Gianbattista di Girardo Cibò, who was made an English citizen in 1490.[24] Pietro Carmeliano of Brescia, another holdover from the previous

[20] Gairdner, *Letters...of Henry VII*, I, 94–6.
[21] *Cal. of Papal Letters*, XIV, 35 and 196; Wilkins, *Concilia*, III, 621–2. On 5 July 1495 Alexander VI by request of the king confirmed this modification of the right of sanctuary; on 11 July 1495 he issued a bull empowering the bishops of England to absolve persons who had incurred excommunication for sedition (Rymer, *Foedera*, XII, 541 and 573).
[22] Campbell, *Materials for a History of the Reign of Henry VII*, I, 198–9; Br. Mus., Harley MS 336; *Cal. of Papal Letters*, XIV, 3 and 14ff.
[23] *Ven. Cal.* I, 506, 520, 531, 535, 548 and 550; Br. Mus., Royal MS 12. E. xvi, fol. 176; Polydore Vergil, *Anglica Historia*, bks. XXIV and XXV, ed. D. Hay, Camden Third Series, vol. LXXIV (Camden Society, 1950), p. 32.
[24] *Ven. Cal.* I, 551 and 577; *Cal. of Pat. Rolls, Henry VII*, I, 293. At this time Silvestro Gigli was master of ceremonies to Henry VII.

reigns, became Latin secretary to the king, a position subsequently filled under Henry VIII by Andrea Ammonio of Lucca and the latter's nephew Piero Vannes. But other than Gigli himself, by far the most influential of Henry VII's Italian friends in England were the future cardinal, Adriano Castellesi, and Castellesi's future associate, Polydore Vergil, author of the justly celebrated *Anglica Historia*, whom he sent to England in 1502.[25]

Yet even in this climate of papal cooperation and diplomatic friendships Henry VII in 1492 considered it necessary to seek out a cardinal protector in the Roman Curia. Despite the general appearance of harmony and success in his dealings with Rome, the king had reason to see himself at a diplomatic disadvantage and to develop grounds for dissatisfaction. From the outset he made the influencing of papal provisions to bishoprics the foremost responsibility of his proctors in Rome.[26] John Morton of Ely, whom Henry VII had made lord chancellor and nominated to Canterbury upon the death of Cardinal Bourgchier, was the only one among the English bishops in 1485 who had been intimately associated with Henry before his accession. Despite their rapid submission, the king had reason to suspect that many of the bishops in England might hope for a restoration of the Yorkists to whom they owed their promotion; and in Ireland a major portion of the bishops were overtly Yorkist. Henry VII had no plan to deprive any bishops; but nevertheless this would have been a most inconvenient time for the Curia, with support of Yorkist sentiment among the clergy of England, to decide to revive its dormant claims to the free election of bishops, or even of papal nomination, as a price for papal cooperation in the securing of his dynasty. On the other hand, the continuation of the tacitly accepted practice of royal nomination would keep open essential means of consolidating his control over his own government and within his territories.

Still another issue injected itself into the problem of consistorial provision of bishops, that of money. The pope was aware of Henry VII's sensitivity in these matters. In 1491 he had directed

[25] On Adriano Castellesi in England see Pietro Griffo's short biography in Bib. Vat., Cod. Ottob. Lat. 2948, fol. 36 (Br. Mus., Add. MS 15386, fols. 235ʳ–237ᵛ).

[26] Campbell, *Materials for a History of the Reign of Henry VII*, ɪ, 176 and 323; *Cal. of Pat. Rolls, Henry VII*, ɪ, 36.

Peter Huse, an apostolic notary but an Englishman, to inquire discreetly in the pope's name whether the king would submit to taxation of the incomes of the clergy; and Huse was first to call on the archbishops of Canterbury and of York.[27] On 8 December 1491 a plainspoken letter of the king to Innocent VIII objected to the holding up of the provision of William Smith, whom he had recommended for the see of Coventry and Lichfield to succeed Bishop John Hales, who had now been dead almost twelve months. The king carefully explained how the consistorial taxes had been fixed and refused to allow what he considered a rise in them. The nominee had been forbidden to pay more on pain of not being granted the temporalities by the king. Although the king's position seemed clear and absolute, the vexed question was far from settled.[28]

The sharpest disappointment, however, was the pope's persistent reluctance to create John Morton a cardinal. Henry VII was most eager that this mark of papal approval be bestowed on the man who as archbishop of Canterbury and lord chancellor was the king's closest associate in civil as well as ecclesiastical affairs. On 10 November 1488 the king reminded the pope that he had written on the subject often before, and that the delay was contrary to his expectation and that of the kingdom, and a matter 'much to the inconvenience of the commonwealth'.[29] The awaited creation of cardinals, the only one of Innocent VIII's pontificate, had in fact already taken place ten days before, on 9 March. Of the eight new cardinals, two were the Frenchman André d'Epinay, archbishop of Bordeaux and of Lyons, and Federigo Sanseverino of Naples, a future cardinal protector of France. Morton had, for the moment, been passed over.

Just when Anglo-French relations were becoming increasingly hostile over the question of Brittany, it could not have escaped the king's attention that the creation of a third French cardinal in 1489 bore some relation to the residence of another, Jean Balue, in the Roman Curia. Indeed, Balue, who was even designated as the 'French protector' at Rome, had of all the cardinals been the one most often involved since 1485 in referring the nominations

[27] *Sp. Cal.* I, 39–40; *Archivium Hibernicum*, XXIII (1960), 19 (Arch. Vat., Fondo Borghese I. 34B, fols. 210ʳ–211ʳ).
[28] *Ven. Cal.* I, 614.
[29] *Ven. Cal.* I, 535, 537, 539, 540f., 543 and 551.

to English and Irish bishoprics.[30] This French cardinal was willing, for a consideration, to refer the nomination of Morton to Canterbury; he had no such enthusiasm, especially in the Anglo-French diplomatic climate of 1489, to support him as a candidate for the cardinalate.

The only other cardinal regularly involved with English affairs in the Curia, the worthy Marco Barbo, was the nephew of Pope Paul II and the curial patron of Bishop John Shirwood. Yet he and other cardinal friends had not been able to induce Sixtus IV or Innocent VIII to make Shirwood a cardinal, despite the urgent request of King Richard III in 1484. Henry VII had recommissioned Shirwood as an English ambassador in Rome; but he may well have hesitated to revive the efforts to gain Shirwood, once a Lancastrian, so powerful a position in Rome until quite sure his more recent Yorkist loyalties had been exorcised for ever. Giovanni Gigli as an Italian thoroughly committed to the cause of England might have been a better candidate to advance as a curial cardinal; but, after long absence in England, he had arrived in Rome as an English ambassador only a few months before Cardinal Barbo, his patron as well as Shirwood's, died on 2 March 1491.[31] When Cardinal Balue died as well only seven months later, on 5 October, it was urgent that the English king find at least one reliable friend among the cardinals of the Curia, and that he should not be a cardinal committed to the service of France.

Francesco Todeschini Piccolomini

That some new arrangement of English diplomatic channels to the Curia had been made in the months before Innocent VIII died on 25 July 1492 is strongly implied in Henry VII's letter of 6 September to the newly elected Alexander VI. After lavishly congratulating the pope, the king stated that his ambassadors at

---

[30] H. Forgeot, *Jean Balue, Cardinal d'Angers*, Bibliothèque de l'Ecole des Hautes Etudes, Sciences philologiques et historiques, 106 (Paris, 1895), pp. 129–38 and 238. A series of letters announcing some of these provisions made in 1486–8 is in *Ven. Cal.* I, 513f., 516, 525, 528, 536, 553 and 582; the original letterbook itself (Venice, Bib. di San Marco, Collezione Podocataro, MS Lat. 3624) includes similar letters relating to German, Spanish and Scottish sees, as well as French. During this period Balue referred the great majority but far from all the French sees (Wodka, *Protektorate der Kardinäle*, p. 42).

[31] R. Weiss, 'Lineamenti di una biografia di Giovanni Gigli', *Rivista di storia della chiesa in Italia*, I (1947), 390.

Rome, John Shirwood and Giovanni Gigli, were reconfirmed in their office and charged to yield canonical obedience to His Holiness in the king's name. The only other point of business in the king's characteristically brief letter was to beg His Holiness 'to receive with kindness and even with favour, out of regard for Us, the Most Reverend Father, Lord Cardinal of Siena [Francesco Todeschini Piccolomini], protector of Ourselves and Our Kingdom, whenever he shall approach Your Holiness in all affairs concerning Ourselves and Our Realm'.[32] The Sienese ambassador in Rome in reporting the obedience made in public consistory on 14 December 1492 noted that the English ambassadors had nominated 'our Cardinal' as protector.[33]

The actual selection of Cardinal Piccolomini as protector of England is described in a long letter, almost certainly written by Giovanni Gigli, to the king from Rome.[34] An introductory section, addressed to 'My most redowted Soveraigne Lorde', summarised the current diplomatic state of Italy, the reaction in Rome to the marriage of Charles VIII of France with Anne of Brittany, and

[32] The summary in *Ven. Cal.* I, 620, states ambiguously that the king 'requests the Cardinal of Siena may be received as his and his kingdom's protector'. The reading of the original (Venice, AS, Collezione Podocataro, Busta vii, no. 443) makes it clear that the arrangement with Piccolomini had been made earlier. Another letter of congratulation was sent on 1 March 1493 (*Ven. Cal.* I, 629). See also Arch. Vat., A. A. Arm. I–xviii, no. 2958, fol. 115.

[33] Fazio Benassai to the Balia of Siena, 14 December 1492, 'Questa mattina li ordinarii oratori del re de Inghilterra ànno exposto et prestato obedientia per commissione per lettere avute da sua maestà et nominato im protettore lo Reverendissimo Cardinale nostro' (Siena, AS, Balia VI, Carteggio 549, no. 77). This seems to be the first mention of the protectorship, which apparently came to Benassai's attention because it was announced in public consistory. The ambassador Mino de Celsa, whom Benassai replaced in August 1492, made no mention of the original arrangements (Carteggio 548).

[34] That Gigli, an Italian, should write to the king in English is not implausible in view of his long residence in England and his holding a degree from Oxford; and the copy preserved might even be a translation from an original Latin text. The reference to a relative Sebastian, whose timely intervention prevented the payment of the inflated taxes for the bishopric of Coventry and Lichfield, is the telling point. A Sebastian Gigli was made an English citizen in 1491 (*Cal. of Pat. Rolls, Henry VII*, I, 368); and in 1500 an Englishman was cited for defaulting a debt owed to John Gigli, Doctor of Laws, and Sebastian Gigli, merchant of Lucca (*ibid.* II, 185). Giovanni Gigli was a Doctor of Laws who claimed Lucca as the city of his origin; on other occasions Giovanni Gigli's relatives paid the consistorial taxes on behalf of English bishops.

the possibility of a marriage between Philip of Burgundy and Elizabeth, daughter of George duke of Bavaria. Then the writer continued:

> Also in meane tyme of this writing I receyved lettres from youre Grace direct of the pope's holynes concernyng the manere of your hyghnes and the promocion of the chirches of Baythe and Chester,[35] and *also for the chesyng of youre proctur', in which youre hyghnes has remytted unto me for to chese one of the iij. the which be named by your Grace, of which I have chosen my Lorde Cardinall' of Seen'* [Francesco Piccolomini], *which, at instaunce of youre said Grace, has accept the same.* As for the oyer ij., viz., my Lorde Cardinall of St. Peter ad Vincla [Giuliano della Rovere] and Askaneus [Ascanio Sforza], as the worlde goeth now me thynketh yai ar' not convenient, for my Lord of Saynt Peter ad Vincla has diverse gret benefices in Fraunce and the Legate of Avynyon, be reason whereof it is to be thought that he shulde have yaim in favoure. Also my Lorde Askeneus he is the Duke of Millian's uncle and the Lorde Lodewyke's broyer, which governeth holy the said Duke, and, as it is before wrettyn, the alliaunce betwene the Frensh kyng and the Duke of Milliane is renewed with grete triumph and festes. *Wherefor' me semeth noder of thes twoo so indifferent to do youre Grace service as my Lord of Seen' is.*[36]

The letter concluded with a long report of the finding of a relic of the Holy Cross in Rome, and of the Roman festivities at the news of the capture of Granada from the Moors.

It is possible to deduce from internal evidence that the letter

[35] The diocese of Bath and Wells, vacant since May 1491; and the diocese of Coventry and Lichfield, vacant since 30 December 1490.

[36] My italics. From the Register of Thomas Felde, abbot of Burton-on-Trent from 1474 to 1493, among the Middleton MSS now in the University Library, University of Nottingham; printed in W. H. Stevenson (ed.), *Report of the Manuscripts of Lord Middleton Preserved at Wollaton Hall, Nottinghamshire* (Historical Manuscripts Commission), p. 261; the whole letter is given on pp. 260–3, and its possible date is discussed on pp. 612–13. Although there are some other items connected with the royal court and with Anglo-French affairs in the register, the letter is rather out of character with the other items copied onto its fifty-five large folio pages. The heading given the letter, 'The copy of the kynges lettres of grete tythynges', would seem to indicate that the interest of the copyist lay in the news of the capture of Granada.

must have been completed and sent off to England some time
between 5 February and 12 March 1492. Whether the date of the
letter can be fixed between 5 and 8 February, the earliest possible
date, is not in itself important. The nomination of Bishop Fox to
Bath and Wells, to which the letter refers, had been referred in
Consistory by Cardinal Piccolomini on 8 February. However
remiss Giovanni Gigli may have been in getting the report of it
off to England, the king's 'proctur' or cardinal protector had
begun to function in the king's service before 8 February
1492.[37]

This man who was to serve as protector of England during the
eleven years preceding his election to the papacy had already
been a cardinal deacon for thirty-two years, since 1460. From
1476 he had been protector of the Camaldese Benedictines and
had helped the reform party win control of contested monasteries.[38] Among his colleagues in the Curia he had a reputation
for his personal integrity. Despite his own Sienese origins and his
kinsmen's traditional loyalty to the Aragonese dynasty in Naples,
he remained relatively aloof from the intricate intrigues of Italian
diplomacy. His profound friendship with the Germans and their
emperor had begun in his youth, and he seems most of his life to
have had a few Germans among the clerics in his household.[39]
As a consequence, he had been deputed in 1468, with Cardinal
d'Estouteville, to receive the Emperor Frederick III at the gates
of Rome; and in 1471 he was sent to the great Diet of Regensburg
as papal legate.[40] As his circumstances required, Cardinal
Piccolomini was a patron of humanists and lived in the style of a
Renaissance prince of the Church, yet there was always a certain
inner restraint and moral sense which curtailed both the brilliance

---

[37] For the king's letters of 8 December 1491, see *Ven. Cal.* I, 613f.
[38] See the series of letters in E. Martène and U. Durand (eds.), *Veterum
scriptorum et monumentorum historicum, dogmaticorum, moralium
amplissima collectio*, III (Paris, 1724), cols. 278, 1063, 1095, 1102, 1131f.,
1134f., 1138ff., 1142f., 1146f. and 1223. See also letters of Piccolomini to
the Signoria of Florence of 30 March, 10 July and 13 November 1498
(Florence, AS, Signori Responsive, Filza x, nos. 54, 198 and 274; and
Mediceo avanti il Principato, Filza LXVI, no. 206, and Filza XLVI, no. 571).
[39] J. Schlecht, 'Pius III. und die deutsche Nation', *Festschrift Georg von
Hertling* (Munich, 1913), pp. 305–28; reprinted separately the next year
with five pages of additions and corrections and an appendix of twenty-
eight letters exchanged by Piccolomini and various Germans.
[40] Bib. Vat., Cod. Vat. Lat. 384, fol. 22; and Cod. Vat. Lat. 10637, fol. 588.

and the lavishness of his own personality and of his Palazzo Siena, close by his titular church of San Eustachio. His influence in the Curia was considerable and constant but of an unobtrusive kind. There were always at least several cardinals more conspicuous than he. Both his rank as cardinal and the general pattern of his life and attitudes he owed to his brilliant uncle, Aeneas Silvius Piccolomini, whose example he had habitually followed. With a certain dedication and even enthusiasm the future Pius III (1503) seemed content to pass his life in the shadow of the memory of Pius II (1458–64).[41]

It is difficult to decide the exact official form which Cardinal Piccolomini's friendship with Germany and the Emperor Frederick III had assumed in the course of the years before 1492. Joseph Wodka, after a thorough consideration of the evidence, refuses to decide exactly when Piccolomini became the German protector in an official sense. For Wodka, Piccolomini's protectorship of England is the first official one of any cardinal which can be firmly established.[42] But, terminological technicalities disregarded, for many years Piccolomini had been doing for Germans and the emperor all those things which a national protector might be expected to do in the Curia. When he undertook in addition to serve the king of England, Cardinal Piccolomini understood exactly what was expected of him. Nor, as Henry VII well understood, was there any conflict of interest in Piccolomini's serving both the Empire and England. Apart from the Habsburg concern for the Turkish menace, it was hostility to France and the sealing of marriage alliances with Spain which were the two controlling objects of both Habsburg and Tudor diplomacy in the years that immediately followed. As the English king had made clear to his agent Gigli, the primary requirement in the candidate for the protectorship was his independence of France. In this, Piccolomini's German connexion could even be reckoned an asset.

After the death of Bishop John Dunmow of Limerick, Henry VII had in 1490 sent David William, his master of the Rolls, and Giovanni Gigli, until then papal nuncio and apostolic collector in

---

England, to serve as resident ambassadors in Rome.[43] David
William died in October 1491, and therefore it had fallen to Gigli
as sole ambassador in residence to initiate the new relationship
with Cardinal Piccolomini. For a time, however, Gigli, archdeacon of Gloucester, was surely overshadowed by Bishop John
Shirwood of Durham, who arrived back in Rome on 14 June
1492, apparently sent to replace the late David William. When
the two rendered obedience to Alexander VI for Henry VII on
14 December 1492, it was Bishop Shirwood who gave the oration.
Gigli was so inconspicuous that the Milanese ambassador mistakenly concluded that Shirwood, who was well known in Milan
as well as in Rome, was the sole ambassador from England.[44]
Despite his recent absence in England of almost five years,
Shirwood had been in the royal service in Rome continuously
before that for a dozen years. At least for a time, Shirwood had
rented a good house, one of the great many belonging to the
English Hospice and situated just behind Piccolomini's Palazzo
Siena.[45]

However close may have been the formal contact between
Shirwood and Piccolomini as ambassador and protector, and
there is little evidence to elucidate it, the contact was of short
duration, for Bishop Shirwood died during the night of 12–13
January 1493. The cardinal's reaction to the death supplies an
insight into his relationship with England. On 12 January
Piccolomini received news that his own brother Antonio, duke of
Amalfi, with whom he had always been close, had died suddenly
several days before. Yet on Sunday, only the next day, he wrote
to the pope to announce that the bishop of Durham had died the
preceding night and offered his private grief at his own brother's
death as the reason for his delay.[46] Although preoccupied with
receiving the many cardinals calling to offer condolences, Cardinal
Piccolomini the next day sent members of his household in

[43] *Ven. Cal.* I, 573, 576ff.; *Cal. of Papal Letters*, XIV, 54; R. Weiss,
'Lineamenta di una biografia di Giovanni Gigli', *Rivista di storia della
chiesa in Italia*, I (1947), 387.
[44] Burckard, *Liber Notarum*, ed. Celani, I, 319, 370f. and 381; *Milan Cal.*
461 and 466; *Ven. Cal.* I, 619.
[45] Rome, Archives of the Venerable English College, Liber 18, fols. 40ʳ and
92ᵛ; and Liber 232, fol. 27ᵛ. The same house was occupied some years
later by Giovanni Gigli.
[46] Venice, Bib. di San Marco, Collezione Podocataro, MS Lt. 3621, fol. 32
(*Ven. Cal.* I, 634).

Shirwood's funeral procession to the church of the English Hospice for burial there. The Sienese ambassador reported Shirwood's death to the Balia in Siena.[47]

Although Giovanni Gigli was now again the king's principal representative in Rome, his contacts with the cardinal protector during the next year must have been few. Piccolomini, one of several cardinals still chafing at the election of Rodrigo Borgia to the papacy, had retired from Rome in chagrin some time during July 1493 and remained away at Pienza and possibly at Siena, apparently until the end of the year.[48] In the circumstances Gigli was forced to make shift. When Christopher Urswick, dean of York, returned to Rome in June 1493 to seek papal confirmation of the recent treaty of Etaples between England and France, it was Gigli who accompanied him in presenting the matter to the pope.[49] Some months later Bishop Robert Morton of Worcester came to Rome; and in the next year Gigli and the English bishop, who had known each other in England, served jointly as the two *camerarii* of the English Hospice for 1494.[50] Three years later Gigli succeeded Morton as bishop of Worcester. Although the cardinal protector had returned to Rome by 13 January 1494, the first indication of his serving England was his referring of Henry Deane's nomination to Bangor on 4 July 1494.

In the course of the subsequent years Gigli and Cardinal Piccolomini apparently worked in close harmony. On 29 January 1497 Henry VII wrote a stern letter to the English Hospice stating that he had been informed by the cardinal of Siena, protector of England, and by Giovanni Gigli, his ambassador, that the Hospice was richly endowed and could support, under proper supervision, a number of students in addition to the members then in residence. On the basis of this report, the king ordered the strict observance of all matters previously agreed

---

[47] Fazio Benassai to the Balia of Siena, 14 January 1493, 'Hieri mori lo oratore ordinario delo Re de Inghilterra' (Siena, AS, Balia VI, Carteggio 550, no. 64); Burckard, *Liber Notarum*, ed. Celani, I, 394.

[48] Sigimondo dei Conti's observation of Piccolomini: 'Sub Alexandro, cui libertas recti sentientium Senatorum erat invisa, Senatu saepe abstinuit; utque id excusatius faceret, in Thuscos quolibet ferme anno secessit' (*Le storie de' suoi tempi dal 1475 al 1510* [Rome, 1883], II, 292).

[49] Rymer, *Foedera*, XII, 531.

[50] *Ven. Cal.* I, 632; B. Newns, 'The Hospice of St. Thomas and the English crown 1474–1538', in *The English Hospice in Rome*, The Venerabile Sexcentenary Issue, XXI, May 1962), pp. 155–6 and 267.

upon by the membership in consultation with Robert Sherborne, also a royal ambassador, and Hugh Spaldyng's replacement as *custos* of the Hospice for a term beginning in October 1496.[51]

The crowning evidence of the understanding existing between the protector and Gigli is in the successful efforts made by Piccolomini to induce the king to nominate Gigli to the vacant see of Worcester in 1497. Henry VII, who had perhaps only wished to seem reluctant to promote him, had already taken the initial steps in a campaign to have him created cardinal when Gigli died in Rome within less than a year.[52] As if prearranged, Giovanni Gigli's position, both as the king's representative in Rome and as bishop of Worcester, was assumed by his nephew Silvestro, then thirty-five years old, who had long been associated with his uncle both in England and in Rome. A letter of 15 June 1499 from Piccolomini to Henry VII shows the cardinal protector working on English business in cooperation with the new bishop of Worcester in the same spirit as he had worked with his late uncle.[53]

Some time after Bishop John Shirwood's death at Rome, Adriano Castellesi, who had been serving as apostolic collector and nuncio in England, returned to Rome, where he continued to serve the English interest and to exercise the collectorship through deputies in England.[54] His relationship with the cardinal protector is not clear. Piccolomini in his office as protector had

---

[51] 'Intelleximus iamdudum tam ex litteris reverendissimi domini Senensis [Piccolomini], regni nostri protectoris, quam ex domino Johanne de Giglis, oratore nostro, hospitale Anglicorum in Urbe Romana adeo splendide et honorifice dotatum ut una cum consuetis omnibus nonnullas personas quae divinis obsequeiis ac litterarum studiis incumbunt (modo recte gubernetur) ad Dei gloriam et nostrum ac regni nostri decus et commodum sustinere possit, quemadmodum in hospitalibus aliorum regnorum Romae existentibus factum est, quorum dos longe inferior dignoscitur' (Newns, *English Hospice in Rome*, pp. 158 and 179, where the full text is printed). To preclude a plea of ignorance as a future excuse, the king ordered the letter copied into the Hospice record (Rome, Archives of the Venerable English College, Liber 17, fol. 20^r).

[52] Br. Mus., Cleo. E. III, fol. 142^{r-v}; *Milan Cal.* 559 and 564. Gigli died on 25 August 1498 and was buried in the church of the English Hospice.

[53] Gairdner, *Letters...of Henry VII*, I, 112–109* and 110* (*sic*). The letter concerned the promotion of Thomas Jane to Norwich.

[54] He had been granted English citizenship (denization) on 29 June 1492 (*Cal. of Pat. Rolls, Henry VII*, II, 386). See Arch. Vat., Reg. Lat. 935, fols. 31^r–34^r, 34^{r-v}; 938, fols. 2^v–4^r; and 950, fols. 260^{r-v}; and also Arch. Vat., Reg. Vat. 873, fol. 25^v; and 875, fols. 70^v and 71^r.

arranged a special reception when Robert Sherborne had arrived on 17 June 1496, empowered as ambassador to join England to the Holy League against France and the Turks; but it was probably the pope's idea to have Castellesi preach at the solemn mass on 30 July to celebrate Henry VII's commitment to an Anglo-papal diplomacy modestly foreshadowing that of Henry VIII.[55] Three years later Castellesi and Bishop Silvestro Gigli, 'orators and procurators of Henry VII', were admitted together as members of the Confraternity of the English Hospice. Both were empowered on 10 February 1500 to treat in the king's name with the pope and envoys of other princes concerning the defence of Christendom against the Turks. The same two were empowered on 3 April 1503 to obtain the pope's confirmation of the treaties between England and Scotland.[56]

Nevertheless even from the beginning there seemed to be signs of the strained relationship between Castellesi and Silvestro Gigli which would later become an open hostility. Castellesi's splendid rise in the Curia was independent of any patronage the cardinal protector might offer. His charming, if mercurial, personality had captivated Alexander VI as it had Henry VII and the Emperor Maximilian I. By 1497 he had risen through the curial ranks to become papal secretary. Although there was some speculation in 1498 of his misusing proctorial funds, Henry VII nominated him to the bishopric of Hereford in 1502. When the provision was made on 14 February, it was, significantly, not Piccolomini who referred the nomination, but Alexander VI himself.[57] On 31 May 1503, with eight others, Castellesi was created cardinal; and, more significantly still, when Roger Leyburn was provided to the see of Carlisle on 21 June, the last English or Irish provision made before Piccolomini became pope himself, it

[55] 'Feria sexta, XVII junii, circa horam XXII, venit ad Urbem venerandus d. Robertus Scherbourn, archidiaconus Bockingamie, secretarius ill. Henrici Anglorum regis, orator ejusdem ad SS. D. N. destinatus, qui fuit ad instantiam r. d. cardinalis Senensis, protectoris illius regni, a familiis cardinalium omnium et pape receptus, et usque ad domum d. Jo. Gilii, ejusdem regis etiam oratoris, associatus, licet non venerit pro obedientia summo pontifici prestanda' (Burckard, *Liber Notarum*, ed. Celani, I, 614; see also p. 644).
[56] Newns, *English Hospice in Rome*, pp. 159 and 191; Rymer, *Foedera*, xii, 747, and xiii, 55.
[57] *Milan Cal.* 584; and *Ven. Cal.* i, 771. The relevant letters are in Arch. Vat., Reg. Vat. 868, fols. 50^r–53^r and 62^r–65^v.

was not Piccolomini but Castellesi who had referred the nomination. The new 'English' cardinal, handsomely installed in a palace still under construction which he later presented to Henry VII, had to all appearances eclipsed England's cardinal protector.[58]

In addition to the ambassadors, both resident and special, there were in Rome, of course, numerous English agents of lesser importance, often in the service of English bishops or religious houses. The one institution which drew the whole English colony together was, as has already become abundantly clear, the English Hospice of St Thomas of Canterbury. It served as a centre through which Englishmen in Italy, whether on business, or as students and pilgrims, tended to circulate. Englishmen resident in Rome, if not actually lodged in the Hospice, were most often at least members of its Confraternity. It was, then, fully to be expected that Cardinal Piccolomini as protector of England should also identify himself with life at the Hospice.

The celebration of the patronal feast of the Hospice during Christmastide 1502 illustrates this dimension in his relationship with England, then of just over ten years standing. The pontifical mass was offered in the Hospice church by the ambassador, Bishop Silvestro Gigli of Worcester. Elegantly presiding just at the right of the high altar on a simple bench was Cardinal Piccolomini, protector of England, archbishop of Siena, still in deacon's orders. Beside him and on the bench opposite were two of his young relatives, Alphonso Petrucci, then bishop of Suana, himself created cardinal in 1511, and Francesco Piccolomini, then bishop of Bisignano, the cardinal's nephew and namesake. The only other dignitaries present were the Protonotary Alexander Sanseverino, brother of Cardinal Sanseverino; the chaplains of Cardinal Piccolomini; and Johann Burckard, papal master of ceremonies. Afterwards the papal choristers, who had sung the mass, were served dinner at the Hospice. The dignitaries were invited to dinner in the house of Bishop Gigli.[59] Few there would have thought that within less than nine months Piccolomini would be pope.

The election of Cardinal Piccolomini to succeed Alexander VI

---

[58] B. Gebhardt, *Adrian von Corneto, ein Beitrag zur Geschichte der Curie und der Renaissance* (Breslau, 1886), pp. 8–9.

[59] J. Burchard, *Diarium sive rerum urbanarum commentarii, 1483–1506*, ed. L. Thuasne (Paris, 1883–5), III, 228–9.

on 22 September 1503 was, however, more a testimonial to the shrewdness of the original choice of him as protector than a triumph of the English interest, for Pius III died on 18 October. The conclave which elected him was comprised of thirty-seven cardinals, of whom twenty-two were Italian, eleven Spanish, and four French. The Empire and England, supposedly with much to gain by Piccolomini's election, were represented only by Cardinal Adriano Castellesi, who did not vote for him.[60] In effect it was Piccolomini's neutrality which proved his best asset. A deadlock developed between the forces of Cardinal d'Amboise and Cardinal Giuliano della Rovere; and he emerged as the victorious compromise candidate, but even then ill and moribund. Pius III was pope long enough, however, to indicate that he aspired to peace in Italy and the reform of the Church, and, if Castellesi's account is impartial, to have acknowledged Castellesi in effect as his own successor as English protector.

Although the idea of an officially approved cardinal protector for any state may have been something new, Henry VII and Piccolomini were both essentially conventional characters. Their objectives were limited, and their style without flair. Indeed it is easy to overemphasise both the importance of Piccolomini's services and his dedication to pursuing England's advantage. Piccolomini did what was asked of him, but it is doubtful whether he was consciously and consistently striving to support any general policy. The driving force always came unmistakably from the king, and his ambassadors remained his principal instruments. Piccolomini's English connexion was never more than one facet of his life in the Curia, and to the very last it was overshadowed by his connexion with Germany.[61]

In the simpler days of Henry VII, a man like Piccolomini could succeed in serving as cardinal protector of two major nations. Cardinal Castellesi also continued to serve England even after succeeding Piccolomini as protector of Germany; his

[60] See the lists in Burchard, *Diarium*, ed. Thuasne, III, 269ff.
[61] An examination of the correspondence of both the Sienese ambassador in Rome and of Cardinal Piccolomini himself with the Balia of Siena and with the Consistorio there, has failed to produce any reference to the protectorship of England other than the one from 1492 already noted (Siena, AS, Balia VI, Carteggi 548–633, and Consistorio IX, Carteggi 2071–2088). On 2 July 1517 the newly created cardinal Giovanni Piccolomini wrote to offer his own services to Henry VIII and mentioned his uncle's service to the king's father (*LP* II, 3431, and *LP* III, 1932).

failure was due chiefly to his own faults of character and not to any substantial conflict of interest. In many ways the position of Piccolomini in serving both Germany and England, and even that of Castellesi, anticipate the much more splendidly scaled but similar position of Cardinal Campeggio in the next generation. As we shall see, what was readily possible for Piccolomini in the simpler days of Henry VII was a challenge beyond meeting in the more demanding days of Henry VIII.

The role of Adriano Castellesi

The election of Giuliano della Rovere as Pope Julius II on 1 November 1503 hardly threw the English interest in Rome into confusion, but it did produce a shift in forces to which successful adjustment was made only slowly. Della Rovere's pro-French outlook in 1492 had been the major factor determining the choice of Piccolomini rather than him as the protector of England. Since then Anglo-French relations had improved, at least officially; and in September 1503 della Rovere had failed of election chiefly through the concerted opposition of the French party of cardinals under the leadership of d'Amboise, who wished the papacy for himself, and who mistrusted della Rovere's courting of support from all parties. The new pope had no desire to alienate the Spanish cardinals, but he had not repented of his opposition to Alexander VI. The major representative of the English interest was Cardinal Adriano Castellesi, whose former position as a favourite of Alexander VI could now be reckoned only a heavy liability. England, however, in no way posed a threat to the Papal States, and Julius II responded quickly to Henry VII's signals of friendship.

Immediately after the election of the new pope, Cardinal Castellesi, although neither requesting nor mentioning the office of protector of England, certainly presented himself to Henry VII as the cardinal responsible for English affairs in the Curia. In a letter of 1 November, now apparently lost, he sent the king the news of della Rovere's elevation and followed it some days later with a fuller report.[62] He was flattered that della Rovere had

---

[62] N. Pocock (ed.), *Records of the Reformation: the Divorce, 1527–1533* (Oxford, 1870), ɪ, 1–4, who gives the date as December; but it seems from the content to have been written before 29 November 1503. See also *Sp. Cal.* ɪ, 394 and 414.

visited him at his residence before the conclave and had come
into his cell twice during the two-day conclave itself to speak
with him 'familiarissime et humanissime'. The day following the
election, Julius II received Castellesi and ordered the expedition
of the briefs confirming him in his office as apostolic collector for
England. Next day, Castellesi went with his good friend Cardinal
Carvajal to visit the pope and brought the merits of Henry VII to
his notice. Afterwards he returned to press for the granting of the
marriage dispensation for Henry prince of Wales and Catherine
of Aragon, about which the Spanish ambassador had already
spoken to the pope. Castellesi promised to continue urging his
cardinal colleagues and curial friends to work toward this object,
as he had done previously under Alexander. The expedition of
the provisions to Canterbury, Chichester and St Asaph, committed to him by Pius III, had been reaffirmed to him by Julius II,
who wished to honour the see of Canterbury by having it be the
first see provided in his first consistory.

However, Castellesi seemed to have suspicions that someone
unnamed, apparently Gigli, was seeking to discredit him with the
king. He wished the awaited obedience embassy to lodge with
him so that the whole Curia might recognise him as the king's
servant and 'ex toto Anglicum' until death. He begged the king
not to raise questions to others about his authority and loyalty in
the king's service.[63] Possibly Henry VII wished to assure himself
of Castellesi's exact standing in the favour of Julius II before
placing his full confidence in him. It was very much in Gigli's
personal interest to encourage doubts about Castellesi, his only
serious rival as the king's indispensable instrument in Rome. For
Gigli to have accepted Cardinal Castellesi as the patron on whom
his own future preferment depended would have been humiliat-
ing and even a bad risk.

In a generously desperate effort to fix the image of himself as
the one guardian of the English interest and to convince the king
of his unshakable loyalty, Castellesi invested Henvy VII with
legal title to his palace in Rome, the present Palazzo Giraud-
Torlonia in the modern via Conciliazione, and decorated it with
the royal coat of arms. The instrument of legal transfer, dated
March 1504, granted it, in view of the generosity of the king
toward him, to the king and his heirs absolutely for the use of

[63] Gairdner, *Letters. . .of Henry VII*, ii, 119.

royal ambassadors both temporary and resident, or for whatever use the king might wish.[64] The gesture was in effect an adroit attempt to secure his position. Having made his own residence, which he fully intended still to occupy, the official residence of the royal ambassador, Castellesi would be indirectly acknowledged as the king's chief representative in the Curia simply by occupying his own palace at the king's sufferance. Henry VII, however, even more adroitly accepted the gift without all the accompanying implications.

The obedience embassy became the triumph for Cardinal Castellesi for which he had hoped. In February 1504 the king had named six official members to it; Castellesi himself headed the list. The three who came from England were Sir Gilbert Talbot, a royal kinsman; Richard Beere, abbot of Glastonbury; and Robert Sherborne, dean of St Paul's. The other two, Bishop Silvestro Gigli of Worcester and Edward Scott, *custos* of the English Hospice, were already resident in Rome.[65] On Sunday, 12 May 1504, Gigli and Scott, together with the appropriate curial and Roman dignitaries, met Talbot, Beere and Sherborne at the gates of Rome. Talbot rode in the lead between Guidobaldo duke of Urbino, a papal kinsman and his newly elected fellow knight of the Garter, on his right, and the governor of Rome on his left. The embassy were solemnly escorted beyond the Castel Sant'Angelo to the palace of Cardinal Castellesi, who received them as his guests. A much modified group then escorted Gigli and Scott to their regular lodgings across the Tiber.[66] On Monday, 20 May, the five ambassadors with Cardinal Adriano waited in his own room in the papal palace for their summons into the public consistory. Although it was Sherborne who made the formal address to the pope, Paris de Grassi, newly named master of papal ceremonies, wrote of the occasion as the obedience of the king of England rendered by Cardinal Castellesi, 'qui erat dicti Regis Protector, et oratorum suorum hospes fuit'.[67] Two days later Duke Guidobaldo, captain general of the Church, was

---

[64] Polydore Vergil, *Anglica Historia*, ed. Hay, p. 140; PRO 31/9/62, fols. 135–7.

[65] *Sp. Cal.* I, 392.

[66] Burchard, *Diarium*, ed. Thuasne, III, 353–4; but Bernard André's account of the embassy in his *Annales* omits all mention of Castellesi (Gairdner [ed.], *Memorials of Henry VII*, pp. 84–5).

[67] PRO 31/9/62, fol. 52 (Bib. Vat., Corsini 38. E. 7).

invested in the pope's presence with the Order of the Garter, to which he had been elected in England during February.

It was soon evident, however, that Castellesi had been out-manoeuvred. On 6 June, the feast of Corpus Christi, some of the English ambassadors took dinner with the pope in the company of Cardinals Riario and Galeotto della Rovere.[68] In a letter of 6 July Julius II expressed his pleasure to Henry VII at the king's having chosen as protector of England the pope's nephew Galeotto della Rovere. The pope referred affectionately to Silvestro Gigli as his own kinsman, to Edward Scott as papal chamberlain, and to Robert Sherborne as ambassador.[69] Of the other presumably most favoured representative, Cardinal Adriano Castellesi, there was no mention whatever. Since possibly two months would be required for the necessary exchange of letters between Rome and England in arranging such a choice, it is clear that the initial steps had been begun even before the arrival of the obedience embassy in May. The king's informer in this deft short-circuiting of Castellesi was probably Silvestro Gigli. Ten years later the same pattern was to be carefully repeated by Gigli, then acting as agent for Wolsey and Henry VIII. Then the pope would be Leo X and the papal kinsman and new cardinal protector of England would be Giulio de'Medici.

Henry VII, apparently convinced that he now had two reliable routes to the papal favour, offered Cardinal Adriano as a consolation prize the wealthier see of Bath and Wells in place of Hereford, which he had held since 1502. Julius II rejoiced to the king in this promotion of 'Cardinalis ipsius Nobis acceptissimi'.[70] On 13 October the king restored the temporalities and sent on to Rome a long oath of loyalty to be received by Gigli, Sherborne and Inge as the king's delegates. The king expressed himself especially concerned that Bishop Gigli should be one of them.[71]

By this time the contentions among the royal ambassadors had damaged their own interests and the king's as well. In March

---

[68] Burchard, *Diarium*, ed. Thuasne, III, 359.
[69] Pocock, *Records of the Reformation*, I, 5–6; Arch. Vat., Arm. XXXIX, cod. 22, fol. 111; and PRO 31/9/1, fols. 3–4 (*Sp. Cal.* I, 396). Galeotto was bishop of Lucca, Gigli's native city; and their two families were related by marriage.
[70] PRO 31/9/1, fol. 5.
[71] Rymer, *Foedera*, XIII, 108–9.

1505 Gigli returned to England as apostolic nuncio, the position held until 1490 by his uncle and predecessor as bishop of Worcester. Whether this change was at the suggestion of the king or on the pope's initiative is not clear, but it was in effect to exile Gigli from his field of triumph and did not end the personal conflict.[72] Before Sherborne had left Rome, Gigli had helped him hurry the expedition of his bulls of provision as bishop of St Davids. Their authenticity was questioned by Bishop Richard Fox of Winchester because of an erasure inflating the income from Holy Cross Hospital, Winchester, which Sherborne had been allowed to retain. The matter eventually became a full-scale struggle between Bishop Fox and Cardinal Castellesi on the one hand and Archbishop Warham as metropolitan and Bishop Gigli on the other, with Sherborne vigorously protesting his willingness to do anything required to establish his innocence or to rectify the matter.[73] Apparently it had been Castellesi himself who had sent on the inaccurate report of Sherborne's having bought forged bulls. Urged on by Bishop Fox and by Bishop William Smith of Lincoln, in whose diocese Sherborne held the archdeaconry of Buckingham, he gleefully laid the matter before the pope, just before Henry VII quashed the whole affair. Castellesi, crushed, was again on the defensive. In a kind of aftermath in 1507 Gigli called upon Polydore Vergil, Castellesi's proctor in England, to act as intermediary in getting the cardinal to intervene in favour of Charles Booth, future bishop of Hereford, who was having trouble establishing himself as Sherborne's successor in the archdeaconry of Buckingham. The last word was with the king, who pointedly promoted Sherborne to Chichester, a see neatly lodged between Warham's Canterbury and Fox's

---

72 On 2 May 1505 Julius II had already addressed a letter to him as apostolic nuncio and ambassador (Arch. Vat., Reg. Vat. 984, fols. 167^r–170^r). In May 1514 Cardinal Bainbridge wrote dejectedly to Henry VIII that when Gigli returned to Rome in 1512, 'Pope Julie shewede me expresslie that. . . he shulde undoubtidlie within short space serve owdre your Grace or me or boithe as untreulies as he had oon hym' (H. Ellis [ed.], *Original Letters Illustrative of English History*, 2nd series [London, 1827], i, 226–32; *LP* i, 2926).

73 M. Kelly, 'Canterbury jurisdiction and influence during the episcopate of William Warham, 1503–1532' (unpublished Cambridge Ph.D. dissertation, 1963), pp. 45–56. To this should be added the letter of 16 October 1505 from Julius II to Archbishop Warham and to Bishops Barons of London and Nykke of Norwich (Arch. Vat., Reg. Vat. 984, fols. 127^v–128^v). Bishop Barons had actually died on 10 October.

Winchester. Yet the provision was made only on 18 September 1508, although Polydore Vergil had reported the rumour of it more than a year before.[74]

Whether in his imagination only or in reality, Cardinal Castellesi was not secure in the pope's friendship. Julius II seems to have been personally kind to him and twice defended him to Henry VII. The king had written to the pope some time later in 1504 or early in 1505 to accuse the cardinal of ingratitude and even disloyalty in remarks made to the pope and various cardinals at a time coinciding with the emergence of della Rovere as protector. The pope gave colour of truth to the charge by assuring the king that Castellesi may have been imprudent in his remarks but nothing more. On 14 August 1507 Julius again wrote to the king in spirited defence of Cardinal Castellesi against his unnamed detractors and praised his great industry and dedication to royal service.[75] Despite this the cardinal suddenly fled Rome without explanation on 1 September, even before the king could have received the letter. He was induced to return to Rome for a while, but during the night of 5–6 October he fled again. One explanation is that Castellesi, having angered the king by his imprudent remarks against him in the Curia, had sought to regain the king's favour by unwisely doing the opposite and writing to the king critically of the pope and cardinals, and that Bishop Gigli had sent the letters to the pope from England.

Whatever the truth was, Castellesi's influence had evaporated and efforts to arrange his reinstatement failed. The king, at first provoked, sought papal grace for the fugitive through the papal notary, Girolamo Bonvisio, who was acting as a royal solicitor in Rome. On 28 September 1508 Julius II wrote to the king to insist that Castellesi had no proper reason to fear to return to the Curia, and that the pope had explained to Bonvisio his attitude toward Castellesi's retention of the English collectorship. But on 17 October Polydore Vergil, who had been acting as Castellesi's subcollector in England, was commanded by the pope to cease sending any of the collected funds to Castellesi and to surrender both accumulated funds and the office itself to Pietro Griffo,

---

[74] Gairdner, *Letters. . .of Henry VII*, I, 246–52, and II, 169.
[75] 'Cardinalis praedictus apud nos nunquam honori tuo detraxit, nec apud alios, quod quidem sciamus. Esset enim non modo ingratus, sed imprudens' (PRO 31/9/1, fols. 15–16; see also fol. 81).

newly appointed apostolic nuncio and collector, whom he was sending to England.[76]

Cardinal Adriano Castellesi's voluntary exile lasted until the death of Julius II. He sought refuge first in Venice and then at the imperial court. He strengthened his earlier favour with the Empire; and when Julius II was thought to be mortally ill in 1511, he was made privy to Maximilian's wild scheme to combine the papacy and the emperorship in his own person.[77] Although Henry VII apparently continued to allow Castellesi to draw the revenues of his see of Bath and Wells, the king seems to have appropriated the London house of the bishop of Bath for his own use.[78] When Henry VIII succeeded his father in 1509, there were tentative efforts made toward a reconciliation of king and cardinal. On 3 August 1509 Castellesi sent congratulations from Trent in reply to the young king's announcement of his coronation and marriage, and offered his services in the imperial dominions. During the pope's illness of 1511 the rising royal councillor Thomas Wolsey even recommended Castellesi to the king as the papal candidate most favourable to England's interest. During the winter of 1512–13 Castellesi, though still considering Julius II his adversary, was commissioned by Henry VIII to encourage the peace between Venice and the Empire.[79] In March he returned to Rome for the conclave which elected Leo X and, as it soon proved, to resume the conflict with his old adversary Gigli, who since 1512 was once more resident in Rome as the king's ambassador.

The search for a protector: Galeotto della Rovere and Francesco Alidosi

As had already been seen, Cardinal Castellesi's role as quasi cardinal protector of England was cut short less than ten months after the death of Alexander VI, by the naming to that capacity of Cardinal Galeotto di Franciotti della Rovere, nephew of the recently elected Julius II. Galeotto was created cardinal with the

---

[76] PRO 31/9/1, fols. 117 and 119; and D. Hay, 'Pietro Griffo, an Italian in England, 1506–1512', *Italian Studies*, II (1939), 118–28.

[77] *LP* I, 880; and Wodka, *Protektorate der Kardinäle*, p. 17.

[78] Bernard André, *Annales*, in Gairdner (ed.), *Memorials of Henry VII*, pp. 112–23.

[79] *LP* I, 135, 1007, 1488 and 1574; *Ven. Cal.* II, 214; A. F. Pollard, *Wolsey* (London, 1929), p. 16.

pope's own former titular church, St Peter in Chains, on 26 November 1503, the very day of the pope's coronation and in the same consistory in which Cardinal Castellesi referred the translation of William Warham from London to Canterbury. On 29 May 1505 he was named papal vice-chancellor as well.[80] England's protector, though scarcely twenty-two years old, was ensconced in power. Henry VII had demonstrated his willingness to trim his approach to suit the person of the pope.

If the precipitous flight of Castellesi on 5–6 October 1507 had weakened the English interest in the Curia, the death on 11 September 1508 less than a year later of the cardinal protector at the age of only twenty-five threw it into confusion. There was no English representative in Rome who was both experienced and reliable. In 1504 Robert Sherborne, now bishop, had gone back to England; and Edward Scott had died in Rome. Since 1505 Bishop Gigli had been in England as nuncio, and Hugh Inge had apparently returned to England in February 1508. Of those active for the king in Rome, Girolamo Bonvisio was but recently named solicitor. His origins from Lucca and the pope's suspiciously enthusiastic pushing of him in the king's favour suggest that Bonvisio hoped to make himself a career on the model of that of Silvestro Gigli and saw the king's service chiefly as a means to that end. The only man on whose loyalty the king could truly rely was Christopher Fisher, who possibly had arrived back in Rome only in March 1507. He was named *custos* of the Hospice on 1 January 1508 and provided as absentee bishop of Elphin, Ireland, on 12 December 1508. Fisher, however, proved to be a sincere but ineffective administrator.[81] Against the thick ranks of seasoned professionals in the Curia, the king of England could set but a single, bumbling amateur. The nadir was reached with the death of Henry VII himself on 21 April 1509.

On the very day that Galeotto della Rovere had died, Julius II created Galeotto's half-brother Sisto della Rovere di Franciotti Garo a cardinal and conferred upon him the vice-chancellorship and the benefices held by Galeotto. Although he made no explicit mention of the English protectorship, Cardinal Sisto wrote to

---

[80] Eubel, *Hierarchia*, III, 10; Burchard, *Diarium*, ed. Thuasne, III, 391. Cardinal Ascanio Sforza, who had held the office since 1492, had just died.
[81] Newns, *English Hospice in Rome*, p. 162. Sherborne in 1528 implied that Fisher was in Rome in 1504 (*LP* IV, 5465).

Henry VII soon after this, obliquely declaring that he wished to maintain his brother's friendships, and hoping that the king would deign to consider the service of Galeotto not lost but rather renewed in himself. Some time afterwards, probably while Henry VII was still alive, Cardinal Sisto wrote to announce that he had accompanied Christopher Fisher in presenting to the pope a letter of the king dealing with some difficult but unspecified business. On 29 April 1509 Henry VIII, in announcing his father's death, took much the same tack as Cardinal Sisto had taken the year before by observing that the friendship and assistance of Sisto as one of the cardinals particularly close to his father were especially valuable to him. Even before this letter arrived, the cardinal had evidently received the news of Henry VII's death and wrote in sympathy to the new king. In offering his services, he referred Henry VIII to the testimonials of Christopher Fisher. Henry VIII's announcement of his marriage with Catherine of Aragon and their solemn coronation was sent to, among others, Cardinal Sisto as 'amicissimo nostro'. In another letter from this series from 1508–9 and addressed either to Henry VII or Henry VIII, Cardinal Sisto apologised for writing so seldom on the ground that he preferred to write about matters of business rather than tire the king with general news reports for which he already had better sources of information. He presumed upon the king's forgiveness in communicating with him through the bishop of St Davids rather than directly about several matters of minor importance. He suggested that the king benefice the cardinal's secretary Manilio, the king's loyal servant, who claimed England as his place of origin, whence he should one day like to return. The king's generous response would not only bind Manilio to the king's service but the cardinal to it as well.[82]

There is, however, no indication in this exchange that he was offered the protectorship of England. Cardinal Sisto, for all his protestations of wishing to follow in his brother's footsteps, was,

[82] Bib. Vat., Cod. Vat. Lat. 6210, fols. 4ʳ–7ᵛ, 13ᵛ and 14ʳ⁻ᵛ (see *LP* I, 101). These six letters are part of a series in a thin, middle section of a former letterbook, of which apparently the rest has been lost. The letters are clearly not in chronological order and have no relation to the rest of the codex. The bishop of St Davids meant in the last letter may be Sherborne, who had, however, been translated to Chichester on 18 September 1508, just a week after Sisto had been created cardinal. Cited in Chambers, *Cardinal Bainbridge*, pp. 10–11.

according to Paris de Grassi, scarcely of the calibre to do so. While the late Galeotto had been handsome, civilised and distinguished by largeness and liberality of mind, Sisto was given to the pursuit of wealth and was without letters, art or wit; he was in short a 'lignum rusticanum'.[83] Yet however unsuitable he may have seemed as a candidate for the protectorship, it would have been tactless to have bestowed it perfunctorily on another.

The man who seemed to fill the need in this delicate situation was Cardinal Francesco Alidosi, who had been a cardinal since 1 December 1505, and who was a favourite of Julius II in much the same way as Adriano Castellesi had been of Alexander VI. As early as 1503 Cardinal Adriano had recommended him, already papal treasurer, to the king's attention as a man of great influence with the pope. Alidosi, bishop of Pavia since 1505, was made papal legate to Bologna in the spring of 1508 and was thereafter frequently absent from the Curia dealing with the difficulties arising in the Romagna, from the Venetian occupation and then from the French invasion. When he actually became protector of England cannot be exactly established. The only surviving letters from him to England seem to be two, one of 15 July and the other of 5 August 1509, both to Henry VIII and both written at Milan, where Alidosi was on a special embassy to Louis XII of France. Neither mentions the protectorate. The first letter lavishly repeated recommendations of Girolamo Bonvisio made earlier by Alidosi to the late Henry VII. The second, acknowledging the king's letter of 8 July announcing his marriage and coronation, assured the king that Alidosi had praised him to Louis XII and the other princes at Milan, and made a great issue to them of his own special relationship with Henry VIII. When he returned to Rome shortly, he would bend all his efforts to Henry's service.[84]

It was not Christopher Fisher but rather Girolamo Bonvisio, eager to advance his standing in England, who probably established contact with Cardinal Alidosi. Yet this friendship of Alidosi and Bonvisio quickly proved to be of little value to England. Although Thomas Ruthal had been provided to the much dis-

---

[83] Pastor, *History of the Popes*, trans. Antrobus, vi, 222; Chambers, *Cardinal Bainbridge*, p. 10.
[84] Br. Mus., Vitell. B. ii, fols. 4ʳˉᵛ and 5° (*LP* i, 111 and 138).

cussed see of Durham on 12 June 1509, Bonvisio, who claimed
Henry VII had promised him the see, was sent by Julius II to
arrange a final settlement of the question of the use of its revenues.
In introducing his mission to the king, the pope begged him to
disregard bad reports made of Bonvisio. Shortly afterwards
Alidosi's letter from Milan recommended Bonvisio to Henry VIII
as the king's beloved solicitor, who had been reared from boy-
hood in England, and who possessed the favour both of the pope
and of himself. Alidosi vehemently urged that this worthy man,
whom he regarded as a brother, be rewarded at last by the
king.[85]

The first explicit mention of Alidosi as protector of England
comes only when both Alidosi and Bonvisio were on the brink of
disgrace. The agent of it was Archbishop Christopher Bainbridge
of York, who had been sent to Rome in 1509 with the specific
charge of pressing a reconciliation of Julius II with Venice, and
of countering the renewed French threat in Italy. Having just
been translated from Durham to York on 22 September 1508,
Bainbridge was well acquainted with Bonvisio and his involvement in the Durham question. Bainbridge soon developed deep
misgivings about him and his patron Alidosi.

Bonvisio's standing in England deteriorated rapidly. Julius II,
more eager than the king to promote him, issued Bonvisio with
general and special commissions as papal collector in England on
19 May 1511 and sent him off to England once more, this time
supposedly to solicit the king against the French.[86] Instead,
Bonvisio relayed all the discussions with Henry VIII on to the
French ambassador in London. Caught in the act, Bonvisio was
seized by order of the king and under threat of torture revealed
that he had been thus employed by Cardinal Alidosi.[87]

But by this time Alidosi no longer represented the English
interest. When he returned to Rome on 18 January 1510 from his
mission to Louis XII at Milan, Bainbridge had already sown the
seeds of suspicion against him in England. On 6 April 1510
Andrea Badoer, the Venetian ambassador, reported from London

[85] *LP* I, 100.
[86] Arch. Vat., Reg. Vat. 965, fols. 213ᵛ–214ᵛ and 256ʳ–257ʳ; PRO 31/9/1,
    fol. 155; *LP* I, 354 and 1234.
[87] M. Sanuto, *I Diarii*, ed. F. Stefani and others (Venice, 1879–1903), III,
    col. 333; *LP* I, 812 and 829, II, 3682; *Ven. Cal.* II, 109f.

that the king had dismissed Alidosi as his protector at Rome and conferred the post on Cardinal Sisto della Rovere Garo.[88] Whether the charge against Alidosi was warranted is difficult to discern. Although he was arrested and taken in chains to Bologna on 7 October 1510 on suspicion of conspiring with the French, he was given only eleven days later the administration of the see of Bologna in addition to Pavia. Although Alidosi was unpopular in the Curia and in Bologna, Julius II now refused to countenance the charges against his favourite; but he did show the treaties negotiated by Alidosi with Louis XII to Archbishop Bainbridge, who was firmly established in the pope's confidence and already being bruited for the cardinalate.[89]

During the ensuing war in the Romagna, which Julius II led personally, he relied most on Cardinal Alidosi; on Bainbridge, whom he created cardinal at Ravenna on 11 March 1511; and on his nephew Francesco della Rovere, duke of Urbino. As things went from bad to worse in the face of the French advance, Alidosi cautiously sought a means to peace through contacts with Bishop Poncher of Paris and Bishop Andrew Forman, a Scottish envoy, both of whom were then in Italy. After the loss of Bologna, both Alidosi and the duke of Urbino separately rushed to the pope at Ravenna to blame each other. Alidosi's party was the more successful in convincing the pope; and on 24 May 1511, when the two encountered each other in a street of Ravenna, the enraged duke slew the cardinal.[90]

If Sisto della Rovere Garo did become cardinal protector of England, either in 1510 or after Alidosi's death a year later, there seems to be no evidence of it. Although he died only on 8–9 March 1517, the next mention of the protectorship was in 1514, when Cardinal Giulio de'Medici was given the position, with no reference whatever to Sisto, to whose reputed baseness of character

---

[88] 'Perché il cardinal Pavia era protetor a Roma dil re, ma inteso è francese lo cassò e à dato il cargo al cardinal San Pietro in Vincula' (Sanuto, *I Diarii*, x, cols. 194–5, cited in Wodka, *Protektorate der Kardinäle*, p. 12; *LP* i, 421), and *Ven. Cal.* i, 59, where the second cardinal is erroneously identified as Galeotto della Rovere; *Ven. Cal.* iv, 1043, is correct.

[89] *Lettres du Roy Louis XII et du Cardinal Georges d'Amboise, avec plusieurs autres lettres, écrites depuis 1504 jusques et compris 1514* (Brussels, 1712), i, 282; ii, 80, 136–7, 139–41, 162, 216, 220 and 234; *LP* i, 674.

[90] *Lettres du Roy Louis XII*, ii, 216, 220, 246 and 248; *LP* i, 755 and 784; Chambers, *Cardinal Bainbridge*, esp. pp. 81–93, with two maps.

was added in 1510 the collapse of his health.[91] Out of deference for his title as vice-chancellor, he may have been given an empty title of protector in an arrangement of which no record survives. Andrea Ammonio, the king's Latin secretary, regarded Sisto as a friend; but it is unlikely that Cardinal Bainbridge would have had any enthusiasm for setting up a rival to himself. For the first time since the death of Cardinal Adam Easton in 1397, there was a cardinal of English blood resident in the Curia, and one who stood in high favour with Pope Julius II. There was no custom of according the title of protector to national cardinals living in Rome, but while Julius II lived it was Cardinal Bainbridge who filled the vacuum, real or in effect, in the protectorship of England. Then came Wolsey, and to Bainbridge's surprise and dismay the title of protector was given to Giulio de'Medici.

The career of Christopher Bainbridge

However his career as ambassador was to end, at least when it began with his impressive entry into Rome on 24 November 1509, Archbishop Christopher Bainbridge of York injected new life and purpose into the English interest in the Curia. Perhaps even Henry VII, who had so rapidly promoted him to the arch-bishopric of York, may have had this step in mind; but its spirit seemed to spring from the youthful and promising Henry VIII, who issued the commission at Knoll on 24 September 1509, just five months after his accession to the throne.[92] As king's councillor since 1499 and nephew of Thomas Langton, who was the immediate predecessor of Bishop Richard Fox of Winchester, Bainbridge was well acquainted with the men then most influential in the government. A former student of Oxford and subsequently associated with both Oxford and Cambridge as well as a member of Lincoln's Inn, he also studied law at both Ferrara and Bologna when in his later twenties. During 1493, having just become a Doctor of Both Laws, he lived in Rome in a house rented from the English Hospice, of whose Confraternity he became a member on 30 January, and of which he served as a *camerarius* for

---

[91] *LP* I, 949; Chambers, *Cardinal Bainbridge*, pp. 72ff. Giulio de'Medici succeeded Sisto della Rovere Garo as vice-chancellor in 1517 (*LP* II, 3015 and 3040).

[92] He was commissioned as 'Oratorem, Procuratorem, Actorem, Factorem, Negotiorumque Gestorem ac Nuncium specialem' (Rymer, *Foedera*, XIII, 264–5); *LP* I, 190(33) and 250.

that year. Possibly the career of the king's ambassador, Bishop John Shirwood of Durham, who died in Rome during January of the same year, served as one model for the later, more magnificently scaled one of Bainbridge. He may again have visited Rome in 1500 with his uncle, who had been ambassador in Rome during the reign of Richard III. In any case, when Bainbridge arrived there as ambassador himself in 1509 at the age of forty-seven, he was experienced and self-confident, immediately ready to pursue a vigorous policy in the interests of England.[93]

The English colony in Rome was dominated by Archbishop Bainbridge's presence. At first he installed himself and his household in the palace which the self-exiled Cardinal Adriano Castellesi had so generously given the king of England, but in 1511 he took over the Orsini palace on the via Papalis formerly occupied by Cardinal Caraffa. The three chief members of his personal staff, the humanist Richard Pace; John Clerk, future bishop of Bath and Wells; and William Burbank, were young clerics of impressive talents. On 3 May 1510 Archbishop Bainbridge assumed control of the English Hospice and, through these three men and others such as Thomas Halsey, effectively controlled its government. Christopher Fisher, who missed the promotion from royal solicitor to ambassador, saw his position as the most important Englishman in Rome vanish outright. On 1 May 1510 he yielded his position as head of the English Hospice to Burbank and was sent off to England with the Golden Rose which Julius II had on 1 April presented to Bainbridge for Henry VIII.[94]

With supreme assurance Bainbridge set out at once to establish his own personal influence in the Curia. Although Cardinal Alidosi, supposedly the English protector, and Girolamo Bonvisio, a royal solicitor in Rome, were openly favoured by Julius II, Bainbridge did not hesitate to attack this pair, whose loyalty he distrusted, and whose position as representatives of the king rivalled his own. Within a month of his arrival he wrote to Henry VIII in sharp criticism of them. That Julius II could abide this has a deeper explanation than his increasingly obvious common diplomatic interests with England. In Bainbridge, contentious

---

[93] Chambers, ch. II, 'Bainbridge's career before 1509', *Cardinal Bainbridge*, pp. 14–21; and Arch. Vat., Reg. Lat. 932, fols. 132^r–133^r.

[94] Newns, *English Hospice in Rome*, pp. 162–6.

and worldly, but forthright and single-minded, Julius II found a kindred spirit, and one whose forcefully held opinions came to blend easily with his own. This, coupled with his effective native talents and his fierce loyalty to Julius II, made his rise a rapid one. When he was created cardinal at Ravenna on 10 March 1511, it was an event long anticipated.

Bainbridge's consuming interest remained the unabashedly secular diplomatic policy he had been sent to Rome to implement, to reconcile Julius II with the Venetians and to counter the French power in Italy. In the spring of 1509 the Venetians found themselves both excommunicated after a quarrel with Julius II over the nominating of bishops and their encroachment into the Romagna, as well as threatened by the League of Cambrai, a general combination of most of Europe, designed to force Venice to disgorge the many territories she had absorbed at others' expense. The Venetian Andrea Badoer, who had come to England to seek aid of Henry VII, one of the few non-members of the League, was introduced instead to his son Henry VIII 'not ten days after his coronation'. Badoer claimed that he persuaded the new king both to write requesting the pope to absolve the Venetians from ecclesiastical censures and to send Bainbridge as his ambassador to Rome, 'who constantly took part with the Venetians against France'.[95] By the time Bainbridge arrived in Rome on 24 November, Venice had already been severely defeated by the French and papal forces acting independently; but Julius II was not yet quite ready to make his peace with the Venetians. That it was no longer Venice but France which formed the real threat to papal independence was clear enough to the pope, who readily perceived most things; but the intense activity of Bainbridge on behalf of the Venetians was certainly a factor in bringing about their solemn reconciliation with the pope on 24 February 1510. Even as the Holy League against France took shape the next year, Bainbridge was still concerned to finish undoing the League of Cambrai by working to reconcile the emperor with Venice.[96]

In opposing the French, Bainbridge's personal enthusiasm seemed to wax more quickly and to wane more slowly than that of the king he represented. His early unwise assurances to the

---

[95] *LP* i, 1307; Sigismondo dei Conti, *Le storie de' suoi tempi*, ii, 401.
[96] *LP* i, 250, 278, 286, 330, 373, 383, 669 and 1521.

Venetians of an effective Anglo-Scottish alliance against France
were belied when in January 1510 the French brought to London
the tribute due under the treaty of Etaples, and then on 23 March
even renewed the treaty itself. Bainbridge professed in April to
know nothing of this and gave renewed assurance of war between
England and France, if the French attacked the pope. During the
summer, in letters intercepted in France, both he and the pope
requested the papal nuncio in England to urge the king on in his
hostility toward France. In England there was hesitation at
breaking off a lucrative treaty until other members of the proposed league against France should commit themselves more
definitely. Accordingly, in September Bainbridge was sent what
must have been a personally embarrassing commission to obtain
papal confirmation of the renewed treaty of peace between
England and France. In the spring of 1511 Bainbridge, now
cardinal, took the field against France in the name of the pope.
After the loss of Bologna to the French, the Holy League com-
posed of Julius II, Venice and Ferdinand of Aragon was published
on 5 October 1511, with the hope that Henry VIII and the
Emperor Maximilian would soon join. Cardinal Bainbridge, careful this time not to overextend himself, finally received on
29 December the king's letter of 4 December, sent through
Germany, which ordered him to join England to the League.[97]

With Anglo-French hostility out in the open and the papacy
hard pressed by new French victories in Italy in 1512, Bainbridge
freely indulged his almost personal grievance against the French,
and now also against the Scots, who it was simply assumed would
come out in favour of their traditional ally. He prevented the
secretary of James IV of Scotland from making the Knights of
St John in Scotland independent of the Knights in England; and
he fought unsuccessfully to prevent Bishop Andrew Forman of
Moray, Scotland, from being promoted also to Bourges by
Louis XII, who wished to reward Forman's diplomatic services in
France. In 1513 Bainbridge, personally empowered by Julius II,
excommunicated James IV for violating the Anglo-Scottish treaty.
Against France Julius II drew up bulls, dated 20 March 1512,
which would have invested Henry VIII with Louis XII's rights as
king of France, including the title of Most Christian King, and

[97] *LP* I, 268, 326, 384, 432, 466, 553, 558, 572, 587(7), 873, 900, 965 and
1001.

sanctioned Henry VIII's coronation as king of France. However, despite repeated pressure from Bainbridge, he refused to publish them until Henry VIII had established effective control of France.[98]

When Leo X succeeded Julius II on 9 March 1513, the new pope's inclination to peace, despite all that the de'Medici had suffered in Florence at the hands of the French, was at first blocked by the simple necessity of continuing the war. Julius II had preserved the unity of the Church and frustrated the schismatic Council of Pisa by winning over the Emperor Maximilian, but at the cost of alienating the Venetians, who then turned again to France. It was now Henry VIII and Maximilian rather than the pope who had the more enthusiasm for a Holy League against France. After the Swiss defeated the French at Novara on 10 June, Leo X absolved the two schismatic cardinals, Sanseverino, protector of France, and Bernardino Carvajal. Cardinals Bainbridge and Schiner of Switzerland, who admired the sterner stuff of which Julius II was made, refused to attend the ceremony of submission and left Rome in anger. In August and September 1513 the English war came to a climax in the triumphs over the Scots at Flodden, and over the French in the battle of Spurs and the occupation of Thérouanne and Tournai. Before news of Flodden had reached Rome, Leo X spoiled Bainbridge's joy over the English victory in France by refusing to fulminate censures against the Scots and by even suggesting an Anglo-French peace, which Henry VIII, convinced he had fought a Holy War against the pope's enemies, rejected as premature.[99] Bainbridge futilely pressed for the promulgation of Julius II's bulls recognising the victorious Henry VIII as king of France in the place of Louis XII. On 31 January 1514, still fired with the old enthusiasm, Bainbridge wrote to tell Henry VIII that he had imprisoned under his jurisdiction two traitorous members of his own household who had thought to desert to service with the French.[100]

[98] Chambers, *Cardinal Bainbridge*, pp. 38–40, 50–1 and 75–6; *LP* I, 1391 and 1449; *Ven. Cal.* II 203. The copy of the bull of deposition in Arch. Vat., A. A. Arm. I–XVIII, no. 4063, is dated 15 March 1512.

[99] *LP* I, 2273; *Ven. Cal.* II, 314ff.; *Sp. Cal.* II, 141. On 20 September 1513, thirteen days after James IV had died at Flodden, Leo X wrote to Henry VIII that with the concurence of Bainbridge he was sending his secretary to James to arrange a peace. The news of Flodden eached Rome on or shortly before 1 October (*LP* I, 2288 and 2332).

[100] *LP* I, 2607.

But even then the now impoverished Henry VIII was moving toward peace with France, and the considerable talk of mounting an invasion of France may have been designed chiefly to strengthen his bargaining position. That Bainbridge misunderstood this was to be his undoing.

To say without qualification that Bainbridge was ambitious and contentious is to underrate his character. He sought power not merely for its own sake, but also because he saw so clearly what he wished to accomplish: to check the power of France, to exalt the papacy in a free Italy, and to seek his king's honour as a thoroughly devoted son of the Church. It was as much to assert these ideas as to establish his own position that he had successfully sought to discredit and remove his rivals, Fisher, Alidosi and Bonvisio. The Fifth Lateran Council marked the highest point of Bainbridge's power, but it also marked the end of his monopoly in representing the English interest in Rome. In the meagre opening session of 10 May 1512, attended almost exclusively by Italians, it was Cardinal Bainbridge alone who personified England's support of Julius II against the pro-French effort to gather an anti-papal council at Pisa. Of the original group commissioned to represent England in the council, only Bishop Silvestro Gigli seems ever to have got to Rome; and even he arrived only in October.[101] Although Gigli, after seven years' absence in England, had returned to serve again as a resident ambassador, it was among the cardinals that Bainbridge found his first new rival.

The death of Julius II on 21 February 1513 not only deprived Bainbridge of a mainstay of his policy, but also brought the immediate return of Cardinal Castellesi to Rome. In the conclave Adriano tactfully voted for Bainbridge on the second ballot, but the two cardinals quickly came into conflict as rival representatives of England. Although Castellesi had become also a thoroughly committed imperialist, he was reinstalled in his Palazzo Inglese, and as apostolic collector for England. Eager to rise with the peace movement then afoot in the Curia, Castellesi hoped to be sent as legate from Leo X to both Maximilian and Henry VIII.

On 25 June 1513 before the Flanders campaign Bainbridge was righteously reporting to the king, who was earnestly preparing for war with France, that Castellesi was boasting of access to

101 *LP* I, 1048, 1083(v) and 1170(i).

authentic information from Bishop Fox through Polydore Vergil, and claiming, quite wrongly, that the king had no real intention of going to war with France. In September, when it came to an issue of whether the pope should fulminate new censures against the Scots for violating their treaty with England, Cardinals Bainbridge and Remolines spoke out for England; and Sanseverino, protector of France, read letters from Louis XII in defence of the Scots as allies of France. 'My lorde the Cardinall Hadrian kepide silence and nodr spake for thoon partie ne thodr', even though he was actively claiming to be the protector of Maximilian I and Margaret governess of the Netherlands, both current allies of England; and 'he shulde have hade to have spoken by reason of his lyvelode within your realm'.[102] On a rare occasion when Adriano did show enthusiasm in reporting news of English affairs, Bainbridge objected to the king that he had bribed officials to get advance copies of the bulls in order to show 'his pretendide Diligence and goode service'.[103]

On the other hand, Cardinal Bainbridge and Bishop Gigli seem to have cooperated without conflict for over a year. With the election of Leo X, Gigli first emerged as a noticeable member of the partnership. The two sometimes wrote letters in common to the king; and Gigli, not surprisingly, warmly supported Bainbridge's attack on Castellesi. In the same letter to the king in which Bainbridge had opened his campaign against Castellesi he wrote that Gigli 'haith and doith dailie unto your said grace right goode service in all your causes here by reason of the verray good favors that he is in withe the popis holines'.[104] Although they were often referred to in common from England as the king's ambassadors, Bainbridge, writing of their joint efforts, spoke of 'me and my Lorde your Oratour here'.[105] Leo X himself, probably out of deference for the cardinal as being above a mere ambassador's position, made the same distinction. When Henry VIII, intoxi-

---

[102] Br. Mus., Vitell. B. II, fol. 53 (*LP* I, 2276); cited in Chambers, *Cardinal Bainbridge*, pp. 52–3. In writing to the Emperor Maximilian I on 4 June 1515, Leo X spoke of Castellesi as the 'Cardinalis Bathoniensis, nationis Germanicae protector, maiestatis tuae deditissimus' (Bologna, AS, AMC, 2nd series, 26/263).

[103] Bainbridge to Henry VIII, 12 September 1513 (Rymer, *Foedera*, XIII, 376–7; *LP* I, 2258).

[104] Br. Mus., Vitell. B. II, fol. 48 (*LP* I, 2029); cited in Chambers, *Cardinal Bainbridge*, p. 61.

[105] Rymer, *Foedera*, XIII, 376; *LP* I, 2436, 2355, 2436, 2517 and 2800.

cated with victory over both France and Scotland, wrote 'ex urbe nostra Tornaco' on 12 October 1513 to request the pope to reduce all the sees of Scotland to their pristine state as suffragans of Bainbridge's York, Gigli had no course open except to move for the moment with Bainbridge and his anti-French policy so inescapably in the ascendant in England.[106]

Gigli was soon to emerge, however, as an independent agent. He early made a favourable impression on Leo X and began to perform on his own routine tasks for the king and queen, and for Thomas Wolsey. On 31 December Gigli, in supplement to a common letter with Bainbridge, wrote to the king brashly claiming personal credit for the pope's gift of the sword and cap of maintenance.[107] By this time Gigli had the contacts and the issue which he needed. In England Wolsey, as Fox had long been, was now inclined to the peace favoured by Leo X; and through them the pope hoped to bring Henry VIII round. Bainbridge's firm resistance to a peace which he believed the king did not desire excluded him as intermediary. Gigli, untroubled by any such strong convictions, quickly filled the gap.[108]

The gulf between Cardinal Bainbridge and Wolsey at the beginning of 1514 was more than a matter of foreign policy. Neither Wolsey nor the king saw any point in yielding to the pope's desire for peace, until they had gained some advantage from it. In June of 1513 Leo X had most inopportunely informed Henry VIII of his consultations with Bainbridge and Gigli about a league against the Turks. On 11 October 1513, the same day on which Leo X sent the king congratulations for his victories in the field, Gigli under orders from the pope wrote to inquire whether Henry VIII would receive Cardinal Bainbridge as legate to arrange England's participation in such a league, indicating that Bainbridge would by no means accept until he knew the king favoured it. When the king in reply refused the offer, Leo X advised him that the Emperor Maximilian had requested Bainbridge as legate. The pope's design may have been to flatter

---

[106] Arch. Vat., A. A. Arm. i–xviii, nos. 4028 and 4035 (printed in A. Theiner [ed.], *Vetera monumenta Hibernorum et Scotorum historiam illustrantia, quae ex Vaticani, Neapolis, ac Florentiae tabulariis depromisit et ordine chronologico disposuit* [Rome, 1864], pp. 511–12; *LP* i, 2355); *LP* i, 2048.

[107] *LP* i, 1746, 1857, 1872 and 2530.

[108] Leo X to Fox and to Wolsey, 4 January 1514 (*LP* i, 2559f.).

Bainbridge into succumbing to the peace movement, but Bainbridge's unwillingness seemed to rest chiefly on the fear that it would be unpopular with the king. Bainbridge asked the emperor to write to Henry VIII to urge the matter, and it was probably from information supplied by Bainbridge himself that Leo X recalled that Henry VIII had earlier written Julius II to request Bainbridge as legate. Sir Thomas Cheney was sent off to Rome to head off the appointment; and the pope was advised that Bishop Gianpietro Caraffa, who had departed for England as nuncio in November, would suffice. Wolsey, supported by Fox, wrote to Gigli that because Bainbridge had been for so long the king's ambassador in the Curia and because he was the king's subject, Bainbridge's appointment as legate either to the emperor or to the king would raise suspicion that he was acting with royal assent.[109] The real reason was probably rather different. The Anglo-imperial negotiations about to begin would have considerable bearing on English policy toward France. Wolsey had no desire to give Bainbridge power to shape English foreign policy, especially in the role of legate *a latere*, one which he had begun to covet for himself.

Blocked from the commission as legate either to England or to the emperor, Bainbridge was at the same time being undermined in the Curia as well. On 30 September 1513 Giulio de'Medici, just created cardinal, wrote to Henry VIII a standard announcement of his elevation and offer of services. On 8 February 1514 the pope wrote to thank Henry VIII for having made his cousin Cardinal Giulio de'Medici protector of English affairs, and the pope's brother Giuliano de'Medici a knight of the Garter.[110] The parallel with Julius II's letter of 1504 thanking Henry VII for having made his nephew Cardinal Galeotto della Rovere protector, just after another kinsman Guidobaldo duke of Urbino had been made a knight of the Garter, could not have been coincidental.[111] Although he acted as the agent of Wolsey and

[109] Chambers, *Cardinal Bainbridge*, pp. 55–7; *LP* I, 2048, 2353f., 2436, 2448, 2512 and 2517.

[110] Rymer, *Foedera*, XIII, 378 (*LP* I, 2320); *LP* I, 2639f., 2642, 2644 and 2653.

[111] In 1514 Gigli recalled to Fox and Wolsey the part of Sir Gilbert Talbot and Abbot Beere in investing the duke of Urbino with the insignia of the Garter in 1504 and said he trusted that he would have a similar commission for the insignia of il Magnifico Giuliano (*LP* I, 2928).

Fox, the affair had been arranged by Bishop Gigli. He had short-circuited Cardinal Bainbridge in precisely the same way as he had Cardinal Castellesi less than ten years before. But this time he stayed on to reap the profits of it.

The immediate effect of the blow was cushioned. Wolsey, as yet neither cardinal nor lord chancellor of England, could not yet dismiss his rivals out of hand. Apparently wishing to test his standing in Rome, he enlisted the services of all three cardinals ostensibly in England's service, de'Medici, Bainbridge and Castellesi, in an unsuccessful attempt to obtain a reduction in the consistorial taxes for his provision as bishop of Lincoln. Despite a specific request from England, it was not the new protector but Bainbridge who referred the provision itself in Consistory on 6 February 1514. During the spring Polydore Vergil came to Italy on a visit to his home and to transact business with the pope for which he had been issued with a letter of credence by the king. Working with his patron Cardinal Castellesi, Vergil quietly undertook negotiations with Leo X to have Wolsey created cardinal 'in consideration of his great authority with the King'.[112]

It was Gigli, however, whose position as Wolsey's agent was as clear as his activities were obscure, who was really in charge of English affairs in Rome. As the prospects of an Anglo-French peace moved forward during the following months, references to Gigli in the correspondence between England and the Curia were as consistently frequent as the names of Bainbridge and Castellesi were consistently absent. Either from obduracy or from ignorance of the English government's true intentions, or possibly from both, Cardinal Bainbridge continued to support the fixedly anti-French policy which Wolsey was craftily dismantling. Although Gigli was informed that the much-advertised English plan to invade France in April 1514 had been called off and serious peace negotiations between France and England were under way, Bainbridge seems to have had no hint of it. Desperate, dejected and confused, Bainbridge wrote to the king at great length on 20 May to unburden his soul of Bishop Gigli's practices with the French ambassador and with Cardinal Sanseverino, the protector of France. What Bainbridge condemned as treason, however, was done at the king's bidding. On that very same day Gigli also wrote to Henry VIII, but to report

[112] Polydore Vergil to Wolsey, 21 May 1514 (*LP* i, 2932).

the latest steps taken by the pope and himself to further the peace with France. The real state of things dawned on Bainbridge at last. He forced himself to make his own personal *rapproche-ment* with his old opponent, Cardinal Sanseverino, and attempted to help shape the peace. But it was too late to retrieve the position long since assumed by Gigli. On 10 June Leo X wrote to England to urge the translation of Gigli to a richer bishopric, and on 19 June he made it clear that it was still Gigli on whom he was relying 'for furthering the papal projects for the peace and augmentation of Christendom'.[113]

After a short, severe illness Cardinal Bainbridge died in Rome on 14 July 1514. On the same day Cardinal Giulio de'Medici, acting in his role as protector of England, sent the news to England and indicated that he had at once gone to beg the pope not to dispose of Bainbridge's benefices without awaiting the wishes of the king. Cardinal Adriano Castellesi's letter, as laconic as it was tardy, was sent off more than a month later. Encouraged by the grieved and enraged Burbank, Pace and Clerk, who had shared Bainbridge's enmity toward Gigli, the rumour spread that Bishop Gigli had arranged to have the cardinal poisoned. Bain-bridge's chamberlain, an Italian priest who had formerly been in the service of Gigli, confessed in prison that he had been hired by Gigli to poison his master with a bowl of soup, retracted his written statement, stabbed himself, and then died reaffirming his guilt. Cardinal de'Medici, protector of England, appointed to examine the facts, instituted a trial.[114]

If the accusation against Gigli was false, he was never really required to prove it so to those who mattered. Pace, the chief mover of the accusation, soon perceived that neither Leo X and the cardinal protector in Rome, nor Henry VIII and Wolsey in England shared his sense of loss at Bainbridge's death or his anger at his alleged murder. On 29 September, before the trial had really begun, Leo X wrote to Wolsey and Fox of his annoy-ance at the sinister things written to them and the king about the bishop of Worcester by some of the late cardinal's household. Although he could not yet send the evidence of the whole case, the pope said, it already appeared that Gigli was free from all

[113] *LP* I, 2821f., 2927f., 3005f. and 3019f.; Chambers, *Cardinal Bainbridge*, pp. 58–9.
[114] *LP* I, 3076f., 3203f., 3220, 3261 and 3302ff.

blame or even suspicion of blame; and this they might communicate to the king in his defence. The king, without having seen the evidence or pressing for trial, assured the pope that he was satisfied of Gigli's innocence. The pope allowed the case to be completed in order to give no pretext to 'slanderers' and in December formally absolved him of the charge in Consistory.[115]

Gigli's early assurance that he would not be found guilty either strongly implied his innocence or implicated in his guilt those who had been using him, especially Wolsey. The indecent haste with which Wolsey was made Bainbridge's successor at York and Wolsey's cynical order to Gigli to seize even the personal goods of Bainbridge for him as Bainbridge's successor at York are as contemptible as Gigli's bid for the bishopric of Lincoln which Wolsey thereby vacated and his perfect willingness to carry out even Wolsey's meanest wishes.[116] Already on 12 August Henry VIII requested Leo X to transfer to Wolsey, 'secretissimum nostrum Consiliarium', the 'totum honorem' held by the late cardinal of York by creating him cardinal. The king had special praise for Wolsey's pivotal role in arranging the recently signed Anglo-French peace and no word of sorrow whatever at the passing of Bainbridge.[117] Wolsey, like the king, assured Gigli that he would punish his calumniators; but in fact within a month of the tragedy Wolsey had invited the talented Pace to come into his own service.[118] Perceiving that dogged loyalty to the memory of Bainbridge would only work their ruin, Pace and Clerk

---

[115] *LP* I, 3312, 3475 and 3574; *LP* II, 13; *Ven. Cal.* II, 543.

[116] Wolsey was given custody of the temporalities of York on 5 August 1514, that is, almost the instant the news of Bainbridge's death arrived in England (Rymer, *Foedera*, XIII, 412; *LP* I, 3226, ix). Cardinal Schiner made his own callous bid for York immediately upon the receipt of the news of Bainbridge's death. William Knight referred his request to Wolsey in a letter of 23 July 1514 from Bern, Switzerland (*LP* I, 3088).

[117] *LP* I, 3140 (printed in Theiner, *Monumenta*, p. 514, from Arch. Vat., A. A. Arm. I–XVIII, no. 4025). The letter implies that Henry VIII had already made this request even before Bainbridge's death, and thus the king's sanctioning of Wolsey's effort to prevent Bainbridge from upstaging him.

[118] Pace accepted the offer in his letter of 10 September 1514 and promised to support Wolsey's effort to become a cardinal (*LP* I, 3304). Burbank and most of the household had left for England soon after Bainbridge's death. Both Pace and Clerk returned to England within a few months and rose to prominence under Wolsey. Clerk was sent to Rome as ambassador during Gigli's declining days but arrived in Rome just after Gigli died.

relented. Early in the next year Pace and Gigli made their peace, and the affair was dropped.[119] Seven years later Gigli would die sacrificed to expediency as he himself had helped to sacrifice others, and Clerk would replace him in Rome as royal ambassador.

It is not necessary to seek poison as an explanation of Bainbridge's death. His death perhaps aroused but little grief even among the members of the English Hospice in whose church he was buried, and perhaps his fall from favour under Leo X was in some measure due to his own attitudes and personality. But whatever his faults he did not deserve the treatment he received from those whom he served. It was Wolsey who destroyed him, not by poison but by policy, with the connivance of the king and the pope, and using Gigli as the pliant instrument of his will. Because Bainbridge's influence in Rome was an obstacle to him, Wolsey undermined it. Because his return to England would have been intolerable to him, Wolsey prevented it. It was not only the smaller ambition of Gigli but the larger ambitions of Wolsey which brought final ruin to Bainbridge. The supple and wily insincerity which pervaded the Rome of the de'Medici popes encouraged Wolsey as much as it eluded Bainbridge. A humbler man could have survived, but Bainbridge's spirit was broken. Like Wolsey's his nature required power and pomp. Henry VIII permitted Wolsey to destroy Bainbridge, as Wolsey would one day be destroyed by the king himself.

[119] *LP* II, 151. 'The case against Gigli as instigator of a murder remains unproven, therefore. . .But on the available evidence he cannot be altogether cleared of suspicion' (Chambers, *Cardinal Bainbridge*, p. 139).

2

THE WORK OF THE
CARDINAL PROTECTORS, 1492–1514

England and Piccolomini
Securing the provision of the royal nominees to bishoprics, about
which Henry VII had earlier been so solicitous, was beyond doubt
the principal service of Cardinal Piccolomini as protector of
England.[1] As we shall see, Ireland presented a special problem,
but at least in the case of England Henry VII's and Henry VIII's
control of nominating bishops already existed before the cardinal
protectors began their work. The character of that control, however, was permanently changed.

In 1480, under the then prevailing haphazard system in the
Curia, four interrelated nominations to English and Irish sees
had, on the same day, been referred in Consistory, each in succession by a different cardinal.[2] Between the time of Henry VII's
accession in 1485 and Piccolomini's assumption of the protectorship in 1492, the eighteen provisions made to English and Irish
sees were referred by one or another of seven different cardinals.
After 1492, in the case of England, the situation was radically
changed. Of the thirty-eight provisions made to English sees
between 8 February 1492 and Piccolomini's election to the papacy
on 22 September 1503, thirty-four were referred by Cardinal
Piccolomini.[3] Although he continued to refer nominations for
other nations as well, particularly in Germany, of which he was

---

[1] Campbell, *Materials for a History of the Reign of Henry VII*, I, 176 and
323; *Cal. of Pat. Rolls, Henry VII*, I, 36 and 59.
[2] On 7 July 1480, when Thomas Rotherham was translated from Lincoln to
York, John Russell from Rochester to Lincoln, Edmund Audley from
Kildare to Rochester, and Edmund Lane was named to Kildare. The four
cardinals referring the nominations were, respectively, Marco Barbo, Jean
Balue, Raffaelo Riario and Giovanni Archimboldi (Arch. Vat., Arch. Cons.,
Obligationes 82, fol. 68; PRO 31/10/14, fols. 41–2).
[3] This enumeration includes the thirty-one listen in Wodka, *Protektorate der
Kardinäle*, p. 40, but supplies three omitted there: St Asaph (1495) and
Norwich (1499 and again in 1501) (Arch. Vat., Arch. Cons., Acta Cam. 1,
fol. 37ᵛ; and Obligationes 82, fol. 100ᵛ; PRO 31/10/40, fols. 50 and 63).

also protector, it was only in England that Piccolomini exercised a near monopoly.

That the candidates nominated to English sees by Henry VII were without exception provided is true; but papal provision was then by no means the automatic and subservient formality which, at least in England, the right of election by cathedral chapters had become. A cathedral chapter was, so to say, thoroughly exposed to the king's power; and the king, if he chose, could have his nominee elected by the chapter even after papal provision had already been made or, less prudently, simply ignore the formality of election altogether.[4] The Roman Curia, shielded both by distance and by the deference due it, possessed in its labyrinthine procedures an ingenius capacity for delay, counterpressure and compromise. It was such a delay in providing to the see of Coventry and Lichfield, vacant since the death of Bishop Hales on 30 December 1490, which provoked the king to address the strongly worded letter to Innocent VIII on 8 December 1491 in protest against the amount of the consistorial taxes being demanded.[5] To assist this vexed matter through the Curia was one of the first services asked of Piccolomini as protector. On 8 February 1492 Piccolomini referred the nomination of Richard Fox to Bath and Wells, which had been vacant for eight months. Hereford, vacant only since 12 January, was provided with Edmund Audley in Consistory on 22 June 1492. Only after the election of Alexander VI did Piccolomini succeed in getting the vacancy at Coventry and Lichfield filled; the provision of William Smith on 1 October 1492 came after a vacancy of just over twenty-one months. The consistorial taxes were arranged by granting Smith an *ad hoc* reduction of the basic tax for Coventry and Lichfield from the Curia valuation of 3500 florins to 2000. This was still considerably above the 733⅓ florins the king had demanded he should pay.[6]

[4] For example, Edmund Audley was papally provided to Hereford on 22 June 1492 and elected on 13 November following; John Blythe was provided to Salisbury on 13 November 1493 and elected on 20 November (LeNeve, *Fasti Ecclesiae Anglicanae, 1300–1541*, 2nd ed., completely revised by H. King, J. Horn and B. Jones [London, 1962–5], ɪɪ, 3, and ɪɪɪ, 3).

[5] *Ven. Cal.* ɪ, 614.

[6] See the three letters of Alexander VI to Smith, dated 1 October and 4 October 1492 (Arch. Vat., Reg. Lat. 933, fols. 266ʳ–268ᵛ). The reduction was also granted in 1496 and in 1503 as well as *ad hoc* for his two successors (Lunt, *Financial Relations of the Papacy with England*, ɪɪ, 228 and 244).

Perhaps the two clearest examples of telling influence of Piccolomini in the provision of bishops are the two, already mentioned, which were involved with the king's ambassadors in Rome, John Shirwood and Giovanni Gigli. When Bishop Shirwood of Durham died during the night of 12–13 January 1493, the cardinal protector wrote of it to Alexander VI the next day. With an evident note of urgency, he begged the pope not to consult or decide about filling the vacant bishopric, as he himself had already said to the pope and would explain still further, until the king of England had made his wishes known, as the see was of the greatest importance to the realm.[7] Since Shirwood had died *in Curia Romana*, the pope could, technically, assert the privilege of nominating as well as providing his successor. The fact that Piccolomini had already discussed the question with the pope suggests that Shirwood had been seriously ill for at least long enough to have alerted the curial vultures. But the bishopric of Durham was County Palatine of the North, and its bishop chiefly responsible for the securing of the northern frontier of England against the Scots, who were then actively supporting the Perkin Warbeck conspiracy against Henry VII's throne. The king, intent on restoring vigorous and direct government in Durham, nominated to the vacancy Bishop Richard Fox, who was lord privy seal and second in importance only to Cardinal John Morton among the king's ministers. On 30 July 1494 Piccolomini referred the nomination in Consistory, and Fox was duly translated from Bath and Wells to Durham. In the circumstances it is difficult to understand the king's delay in forwarding the nomination. Since the king was concerned to strengthen the northern frontier defences, he may have wished to direct to this purpose the considerable revenues of the see, which were his during the vacancy. Bishop Fox, king's councillor and already possessed of a see, would certainly have understood such a policy, especially since the pope had been induced to reduce the common service tax for his bulls from 9000 to 6000 florins, and the other consistorial taxes in proportion.[8]

---

[7] Venice, Bib. di San Marco, Collezione Podocataro, MS Lat. 3621, fol. 32. The summary in *Ven. Cal.* i, 634, does not make clear the extreme degree of urgency in the original.

[8] Not only was Durham allowed to remain vacant for more than seventeen months (12 January 1493 to 30 July 1494), but Fox was restored the temporalities only on 8 December 1494, an exceptional delay. On the

The providing of Giovanni Gigli to the vacant see of Worcester in 1497 shows Piccolomini exercising influence in reverse and illustrates perfectly the curial capacity for influencing a nomination in which there was sufficient interest. Gigli himself, possibly disappointed at not having been given Durham three years before, may well have been the instigator of the campaign of pressure on the king which was well in progress when Worcester fell vacant.[9] On 10 June 1497 Cardinal Piccolomini wrote to the king to acknowledge recent royal letters touching upon business with which both Gigli and the protector were busily engaged in the Curia and to press the king to nominate this deserving 'veterem curialem' to the see of Worcester. He deftly assured the king that Gigli's advanced age would allow him but brief enjoyment of the king's generosity, and that it was common for rulers so to honour and enhance the prestige of their ambassadors. He insisted that the pope had been most gracious and understanding about the needs of the king and of England, including the 'matter of Durham', and that it was now time for Henry to reciprocate.[10] The 'matter of Durham', as Cardinal Lopez, who wrote at about this same time, made clear, referred to the king's long-delayed nomination of Fox to Durham in 1494. The king had objected that giving an English bishopric to Gigli would be tantamount to surrendering control of it, since Gigli would die *in Curia Romana*, and the right to nominate a successor would, by custom, be the pope's. Three years before, Lopez argued, this very custom had been suspended at the king's request in the case of Durham; therefore, the king might yield in the present case in the peaceful assurance that his friends in the Curia would see to it that no innovations were made in the long-standing tradition of royal nomination.[11] Under such concerted pressure the king yielded, apparently satisfied that his interests were secure, and that there was more to be gained than lost by surrender. When Piccolomini referred the nomination to Worcester in Consistory on 30 August

reduction of the taxes at Durham *ad hoc* see Lunt, *Financial Relations of the Papacy with England*, ɪɪ, 229, 800–1 and 810–11.

[9] Cardinal Lopez to Henry VII, June 1497 ((Gairdner, *Letters. . .of Henry VII*, ɪ, 102).

[10] Br. Mus., Cleo. E. ɪɪɪ, fol. 142$^{r \cdot v}$.

[11] Gairdner, *Letters. . .of Henry VII*, ɪ, 103. In fact, Henry VII's suspicions were justified. Giovanni Gigli was the first of four Italians *in Romana Curia* who were provided to the see of Worcester, but in each case with enthusiastic royal consent or even initiative.

1497, Gigli had already been granted custody of the temporalities of the see on 18 July.[12] When Giovanni Gigli died in Rome on 25 August 1498, less than a year later, Silvestro Gigli was provided to Worcester within four months as the successor of his uncle 'in Romana Curia defuncti'.[13] But the king, reconciled to the new arrangement, may even have taken the initiative. Already on 1 December 1498 the king had granted to 'our beloved and loyal councillor, Silvestro Gigli, archpriest of Lucca, solicitor of our causes in the Roman Curia', the guardianship of the temporalities of the bishopric, with the power to collate to benefices and to appoint stewards and other officers.[14] In an informal consistory in the pope's private chamber before vespers on Christmas Eve, Silvestro Gigli was provided to Worcester. According to the Consistorial Acts, the nomination was referred by Piccolomini, one of the four cardinals present.[15] In fact, in 1502 Henry VII allowed his other Italian ambassador in Rome, the favoured Cardinal Adriano Castellesi, to be provided to Hereford.

There are two other examples, perhaps more typical, about which some detailed evidence survives: the provision of Thomas Jane to Norwich in 1499, and that of William Sever to Carlisle in 1495. Jane, who was then dean of the Chapel Royal in Westminster, archdeacon of Essex and a royal councillor, for some reason wished to retain the well-endowed canonry and prebend of Brownswood in the diocese of London, at least until after he had obtained possession of his see.[16] There is no other reason to believe that there was any objection raised to Jane's nomination to Norwich, but apparently on 15 June the translation of Thomas Savage to Norwich from London, possibly to make room for Jane in London, was under consideration.[17] However, the whole matter had already been settled according to the original plan on 14 June,

---

[12] Plenary restitution was made on 5 December 1497 (Rymer, *Foedera*, XII, 670; *Cal. of Pat. Rolls, Henry VII*, I, 111 and 139).

[13] Apparently Cardinal Lopez, contrary to the assurance given in the letter to Henry VII the previous year, tried to get the see for Bishop Gaspar Golfo, a member of his household, who went to England to speak to the king about it (*Milan Cal.* 584).

[14] Rymer, *Foedera*, XII, 704–5; *Cal. of Pat. Rolls, Henry VII*, II, 154. On Silvestro's later difficulties with benefices in Lucca, see Arch. Vat., Reg. Vat. 847, fols. 285ᵛ–287ᵛ; and 857, fols. 284ᵛ–285ᵛ and 285ᵛ–286ᵛ.

[15] Burckard, *Liber Notarum*, ed. Celani, II, 120–1.

[16] Jane relinquished both the archdeaconry of Essex and the prebend of Brownswood in 1499 (Le Neve, V, 11 and 22).

[17] LeNeve, IV, 24–5, based on Br. Mus., Cleo. E. III, fol. 112.

when Jane was provided in Consistory. After Piccolomini had read the letter from the king and explained the special arrangements requested, the pope ordered the bulls to be prepared in accordance with the written *cedula* presented by Piccolomini.[18] On the same day as the consistory Piccolomini wrote to the king. He made a special point of emphasising that the provision had been made precisely because of the king's recommendation and in view of the king's previous reputation for naming worthy candidates as bishops. He expressed the wish that other rulers would share the king's attitude. If this was a way of saying in veiled language that the king's will in nominating had prevailed over opposition, the reference was probably not to Jane and Norwich, but to FitzGerald and the king's will in filling the vacancy of Cork and Cloyne which was being hotly contested in Rome at this very time. Whatever the truth may have been, the cardinal protector and Silvestro Gigli had cooperated fully in implementing the king's wishes.[19] Jane, for all the trouble taken on his behalf, died the following year.

Although William Sever, OSB, abbot of St Mary's, York, was provided as bishop of Carlisle only in 1495, Henry VII had informed Piccolomini of his nomination to the pope on 18 May 1493.[20] There was, however, a twofold difficulty. The bishop of Carlisle, Richard Bell, also a Benedictine monk and still prior of Durham, was apparently unwilling to resign despite his old age and the offer of a reasonable pension to maintain himself. Secondly, the king wished his nominee to Carlisle to be allowed to retain his abbey in York, one of the very richest in England.[21] The provision, referred by Piccolomini, was finally made in the form sought, but after more than two years' delay, on 4 September

---

[18] W. M. Brady, *The Episcopal Succession in England, Scotland, and Ireland, A.D. 1400 to 1875* (Rome, 1876), I, 45; and Arch. Vat., Arch. Cons., Acta Cam. 1, fol. 75 (PRO 31/10/14, fol. 71).

[19] Cardinal Piccolomini to Henry VII, 15 June 1499 (Gairdner, *Letters...of Henry VII*, I, 112–109* and 110*). The letter begins 'Hodie...' but is dated 15 June.

[20] Rome, Bib. Angelica, MS Codex 1077, fol. 87ʳ.

[21] In the case of the relatively poor Welsh sees, the bishop was sometimes permitted to retain an abbey *in commendam*. Thus, Thomas Pigot (Bangor, 1500) was permitted to retain the abbey of Chertsey; Miles Salley (Llandaff, 1500) the abbey of Eynsham; David ap-Yeworth (St Asaph, 1500) the abbey of Valle Crucis in the diocese of St Asaph. Earlier Thomas Savage (Rochester, 1492) had retained his position as dean of the Chapel Royal. All of these provisions had been referred by Piccolomini.

1495. It is possible that John Harrington of York, who paid the consistorial taxes on 18 September, had been actively engaged as Sever's agent in Rome.[22]

The possible dissatisfaction of Bishop Sever with Piccolomini's services might offer one part of the explanation for the four exceptions to the practice of having provisions to English sees referred by Cardinal Piccolomini. The first of the four is easily explained. When Alexander VI's son Cesare Borgia, at that point a cardinal, referred the nomination of John Blythe to Salisbury on 13 November 1493, Piccolomini, who had not yet become fully reconciled to the high-handed Borgia style in the papacy, was absent in a kind of self-imposed exile in Tuscany.[23] Since the consistorial taxes for Blythe were paid by Silvestro Gigli, it is most likely that the nomination had been made through the ambassador Giovanni Gigli, who would hardly have ignored Piccolomini if he had been well and in Rome.[24] The second exception, the provision to Hereford of Adriano Castellesi, 'apostolic protonotary, and secretary and treasurer to His Holiness', is likewise easily explained. Adriano, well beloved by both king and pope, was provided on 14 February 1502 *motu proprio* by Alexander VI himself. Piccolomini's services would hardly have been needed or desired.[25] The third exception is the provision of William Sever to Durham on 27 June 1502. That it should have been referred by Cardinal Carvajal rather than Piccolomini might have many explanations; but one might be Sever's dissatisfaction with Piccolomini's handling of his provision to Carlisle seven years before. It could be purely coincidental that the provision to Carlisle of Sever's successor, Roger Leyburn, should be the last of the four exceptions to Piccolomini's otherwise perfect monopoly; for it was referred on 21 June 1503 by the newly created cardinal, Adriano Castellesi.[26]

What has already been said makes it clear that the scope of Piccolomini's role as protector went beyond questions of episcopal

[22] See the record of the tax payment in Lunt, *Financial Relations of the Papacy with England*, II, 798–9. Taxes were usually paid by Italians, either merchants or *curiales*.

[23] Pastor, *History of the Popes*, trans. Antrobus, V, 543; and Sigismondo dei Conti, *Le storie de' suoi tempi*, II, 292.

[24] Lunt, *Financial Relations of the Papacy with England*, II, 792.

[25] Arch. Vat., Arch. Cons., Acta Cam. 1, fol. 104 (PRO 31/10/14, fol. 77).

[26] On 31 May 1503; on Leyburn's previous activities in Durham, see Arch. Vat., Reg. Vat. 849, fols. 300ᵛ–301ᵛ.

provisions, but the meagre evidence available makes it difficult to discern exactly to what extent he became involved in other English affairs in the Curia. For example, on 8 February 1493 Henry VII's queen, Elizabeth of York, wrote to Piccolomini to urge him to renew his efforts to obtain papal grant of a plenary indulgence for the Hospital of St Katherine-by-the-Tower, of which she as queen was exclusive patron.[27] Her first letter of request, to which Piccolomini had made an unencouraging reply, must have been written shortly after he became protector. The implication is that such things were regarded as a regular part of his function. Presumably, it was to be an indulgence of the same character as the ones granted on 21 January 1497 to a similar, Cistercian hospital for the poor which Henry VII intended to found at Windsor, and to the Savoy Hospital, which he founded in London shortly before his death. Indeed, Henry VII had expended considerable effort in founding St George's chapel, Windsor, and in obtaining an indulgence for the Lady chapel he intended to build in it. When he later decided to build his burial chapel onto Westminster Abbey instead, he requested Cardinal Adriano Castellesi to ask the pope to transfer the indulgence to it; and the pope complied.[28] This suggests that Piccolomini did eventually succeed in getting the indulgence requested for St Katherine's, and that he might have had a hand in obtaining the others, since the first record of the king's turning to Castellesi is only after Piccolomini's death. But there seems to be no positive evidence of this, nor of any connexion of Piccolomini with the elaborate efforts of Henry VII to forward the canonisation of the Lancastrian Henry VI.[29]

So it is with the rest of the surviving evidence. In 1496 or before, Henry VII acknowledged Piccolomini's letter of 8 February recommending the Roman poet Nagonius, who had called at the English court; but there is no other evidence of Piccolomini's connexion with the Italian humanistic influences at work in

---

[27] Rome, Bib. Angelica, MS Codex 1077, fol. 13ᵛ.

[28] Arch. Vat., Reg. Vat. 873, fols. 16ᵛ–17ᵛ and 17ᵛ–18ᵛ; and Lunt, *Financial Relations of the Papacy with England*, ii, 501.

[29] Lunt mentions the grants of the Scala Coeli indulgence for the proposed St Mary's chapel made in 1497 and 1502 as well as the transfer in 1504. The original grant was apparently first made on 4 October 1494 (Rymer, *Foedera*, xii, 365). The other indulgence for the hospital was possibly first granted only in 1497. Lunt makes no mention whatever of St Katherine's-by-the-Tower.

England.[30] At his instance Sherborne was accorded a special reception on entering Rome in 1496, but Piccolomini's part in the English entry into the Holy League which followed remains a mystery. In June of 1497 Piccolomini had gone to the pope in private audience on secret business of the English king. Possibly it concerned the marriage settlement between Catherine of Aragon and Prince Arthur, but the secret remains.[31] In 1499 Piccolomini indicated to Henry VII some of the intense concern at Rome over the Turkish menace to Rhodes, but it is not known whether or not he influenced Henry VII's decision to negotiate the treaties with King Ladislaus of Hungary and Bohemia and with the Emperor Maximilian.[32] It would be expected also that Piccolomini would have been involved in the seeking of papal confirmation of the English treaties of peace with France and with Scotland, but again there is no evidence. The same is true of Alexander VI's renewal of Innocent VIII's bulls modifying the right of sanctuary in England and excommunicating rebels, and the negotiations surrounding royal control of episcopal provisions for Ireland.[33]

Almost as soon as he became protector, Cardinal Piccolomini seems to have been drawn into the struggle to extend the primatial rights of Canterbury. John Morton, supported by the king, had become deeply involved in a controversy with the monastery of St Albans in the diocese of London over his right of visitation. Innocent VIII had encouraged the development of the power struggle between the two in Rome by blandly allowing the issue of bulls supporting the position of each.[34] Both Innocent VIII and Abbot Wallingford died in 1492; and the king seized the occasion to institute a case in the Roman Rota, one of the very few English cases cited before it. The king's proctor, Jacobo of Piscia, called upon Cardinal Piccolomini on 16 October 1492 and obtained a

---

[30] Fragment of a letter of Henry VII to Piccolomini, 1494?–6?, printed by F. Wormald, 'An Italian poet at the court of Henry VII', *Journal of the Warburg and Courtauld Institutes*, xiv (1951), 118, from Br. Mus., Add. MS 45131, fol. 78ᵛ.

[31] Piccolomini to Henry VII, 10 June 1497 (Br. Mus., Cleo. E. iii, fol. 142ʳ⁻ᵛ).

[32] Gairdner, *Letters. . .of Henry VII*, i, 112–109* and 110*. For the treaties, see Rymer, *Foedera*, xii, 747; and xiii, 4, 5 and 9.

[33] Rymer, *Foedera*, xii, 531, 541–2, 573, 736, 762 and 765; xiii, 55.

[34] D. Knowles, 'The case of St Albans Abbey in 1490', *Journal of Ecclesiastical History*, iii (1952), 144–58; and also his *Religious Orders in England* (Cambridge, 1959), iii, 77–9.

formal citation of St Albans. Cardinal Piccolomini then sub-
delegated all his powers, excepting the definitive sentence itself,
to Bernardino Capotio, canon of Siena; but there is no evidence
that the suit proceeded further.[35] Nor is there evidence of Piccolomini's influence at work in Archbishop Morton's controversy
with Bishop Hill of London over the right to probate wills, or any
of the other aspects of the primatial struggle.[36] Even Morton's
eventual success in becoming cardinal owed little to the cardinal
protector.

The difficulty in assessing the protector's role stems partly from
the evidence itself and partly from the character of his position.
Little has survived either of Piccolomini's personal papers or of
the state papers of Henry VII, and that little is in both cases due
more to chance than to any selection. There is a similar dearth of
surviving letters exchanged between the king and his ambassadors,
with whom certainly he was in regular correspondence. However,
each English ambassador came to Rome with full oral instructions; and much, perhaps most of the business between the
ambassadors and Piccolomini was transacted orally. Certainly the
protector was involved in much more English business than the
direct evidence would indicate. But, on the other hand, mentions
of Cardinals Sforza, Lopez, de Costa and Riario suggest that not
only the archbishop of Canterbury but even the king himself felt
free to seek assistance from other cardinals, or to take action
without a cardinal as intermediary.[37] The strongest force for
England in Rome remained direct action taken by the ambassadors themselves.

It would be interesting to know what arrangement was made
to pay Piccolomini for his services. He was far from avaricious or
even mercenary, when contrasted with many of his colleagues
among the cardinals; but surely his service to England was sustained by more than altruism. If nothing else, the curial system
would have discouraged the precedent of his serving Henry VII
free of charge. Curiously, Henry VII gave numerous benefices to

---

[35] There is an appendix listing the surprisingly few English cases before the
Rota in Kelly, 'Canterbury jurisdiction', pp. 289–90. The reference to the
St Albans case is Arch. Vat., Arch. Rot., Manualia Actorum et Citationum
27, fol. 11.

[36] Arch. Vat., Reg. Vat. 873, fols. 9ʳ–12ᵛ, 26ʳ–29ᵛ and 124ʳ–136ʳ.

[37] *Milan Cal.* 559 and 564; R. Woodhouse, *John Morton* (London, 1895),
p. 225; Brady, *Episcopal Succession*, II, 257.

both his Italian ambassadors, Gigli and Castellesi, and eventually gave them bishoprics; Castellesi was even allowed to hold the lucrative office of apostolic collector long after he left England. Yet Piccolomini seems never to have received even a minor English benefice to complement his modest collection of German and Italian ones. Perhaps grants were made to him from proctorial funds, but even so they could never have equalled the generous 2000 Tours pounds given Cardinal Balue by the king of France for the year 1486. Between 1492 and 1503 the *propina* offered him for referring the nominations to English and Irish bishoprics could have reached a total even as high as 20,000 florins, perhaps even a fifth part of his income; but there is no way of establishing it as a fact.[38] Unless Piccolomini were offered an ample, regular retainer, there would have been a natural tendency to concentrate his attention on those services from which he derived his income.

Ireland and Piccolomini

If Cardinal Piccolomini exercised no such monopoly over provisions to Irish bishoprics as he did for English ones, it was because he was protector of Ireland only in the sense that Henry VII was lord of Ireland as well as king of England. Piccolomini's previous contacts with Irish affairs had been limited.[39] He doubtless had, at first, little knowledge of the intricate and fluctuating network of forces and counterforces constantly contending for control of the Irish church. Factions of Irish nobility or clerics competed with each other as well as in common against the English king, or, if it suited a present purpose, in connivance with him. Enterprising Irishmen might go to Rome to get themselves provided to some see without hope or even intention of taking possession of it. The popes, attempting a kind of neutrality, had by their want of firm principle merely given encouragement for further strife and had frequently through negligence, weakness or blunder granted authentic bulls of provision to several contending candidates.

[38] See the conjectural lists in Lunt, *Financial Relations of the Papacy with England*, II, 832–3. A list of the incomes of the forty-one cardinals in Pastor, *History of the Popes*, trans. Antrobus, VI, 91–2, gives Piccolomini's annual income as 9000 ducats; this is the median income of the group.

[39] On 21 February 1466 he had referred the provision of Nicholas Weston to Derry in the province of Armagh (Arch. Vat., Arch. Cons., Obligationes 82, fol. 1ᵛ; PRO 31/10/14, fols. 25–6).

On 21 April 1490 Cardinal Piccolomini, acting as substitute for Cardinal Caraffa, had referred such a disputed provision to Ross in the province of Cashel. Odo O Driscoll, canon of Ross, had been duly provided as bishop on 24 March 1473 at the resignation of a 'Bishop Donald', who continued, however, to meddle in the affairs of the diocese. When 'Bishop Donald' died some years later, Sixtus IV issued another complete set of bulls under date of 29 March 1482, appointing Thadeus MacCarthy, 'clerk of the diocese of Cork, by both parents of knightly race, in his twenty-seventh year', to be bishop of the same diocese of Ross. Both bishops were summoned to Rome and examined by Cardinal Caraffa. Decision was rendered at Cardinal Piccolomini's report of Caraffa's findings in favour of O Driscoll, and on the same day Piccolomini referred the provision of the loser, MacCarthy, to Cork and Cloyne.[40]

Henry VII, having at first no hope of a strong, direct control of Ireland, had carefully sought to avoid alienating irretrievably the powerful and pivotal Geraldine forces, led since 1477 by the eighth or Great Earl of Kildare, Gerald FitzGerald, and had turned his immediate attention to the rebels among the Englishry of Ireland. By 1492 the English Pale about Dublin had been purged of its Yorkist rebel spirit and, with papal support, its four bishops brought to submission.[41] Indeed, Walter FitzSimmons, archbishop of Dublin (1484–1511), who had crowned the pretender Lambert Simnel in Christ Church cathedral on Pentecost Sunday, 24 May 1487, was made king's deputy in Ireland five years later, despite or possibly even because of his Irish origins.[42] Octavian del Palacio de Spinelli, primate and archbishop of Armagh (1479–1513), had turned to cultivating the friendship of both Henry VII and the archbishop of Canterbury. John Payne, OP, bishop of Meath (1483–1507), who had been preacher at Simnel's coronation, was also preacher, in the same Christ Church, a year later at the solemn promulgation on 13 July 1488 of Innocent VIII's bull against the rebels. This English Dominican, although a less than docile suffragan of Archbishop Octavian, remained steadfastly committed to Henry VII. Kildare,

[40] *Cal. of Papal Letters*, xiv, 252, 259–61, 352, 743 and 783.
[41] Rymer, *Foedera*, xii, 332–3; Wilkins, *Concilia*, iii, 622–3; Gairdner, *Letters...of Henry VII*, i, 94–6; *Ven. Cal.* i, 519; *Cal. of Pat. Rolls, Henry VII*, ii, 370.
[42] On 11 June June 1492 (*Cal. of Pat. Rolls, Henry VII*, i, 376).

the only other see within the Pale, seems to have been abandoned by Bishop William Barrett, who died in 1492; and there seems to have been no resident bishop of Kildare during the next two decades.[43] Thus, Kildare excepted, during the whole period of Piccolomini's protectorship, no vacancy occurred in any see within the Pale, where the king's power to nominate was firmly established. Piccolomini's usefulness to Henry VII would be to assist him in controlling papal provisions to the other Irish sees, those without the Pale, as they fell vacant.

Sure of the Pale as a base of support, the king then began a short-lived but energetic effort to bring the government of Ireland, civil and ecclesiastical, under more direct control. In 1492 the Great Earl of Kildare had been deprived of his position as lord deputy, and two years later Sir Edward Poynings was sent to Ireland to conquer Ulster and to establish the rule of English law. Although the conquest degenerated into a system of buying loyalty, the Acts of Poynings' Parliament (1494–5) effected a legal subordination of Ireland to England which gave the king a new lever to use in controlling the land. The laws passed by this obsequious parliament at Drogheda may have proved over-ambitious and unenforceable; but they altered the ground, if not the nature, of the struggle itself.[44]

In so far as they directly concerned the government of the Church, the Acts of Poynings' Parliament had a twofold intent: to attempt to free church property from domination by the Irish lords, and to prevent the obtaining of papal provisions to Irish benefices, so to speak, behind the king's back. Pensions extorted from churchmen by force were declared invalid, and church lands misappropriated by various Irish lords were to be restored. A special Act repealed all grants made to the earl of Kildare by the sees of Armagh, Dublin and Meath. Three other acts sought to give Sir John Kendall, English prior of the Knights of St John, direct control over the Irish possessions of the order, whose prior there, Sir James Keating, was one of the few still unpardoned supporters of Simnel.[45] But of greatest import was Act X, which

---

[43] No provision for a successor to Barrett is mentioned in the Consistorial Acts. An Edward Lane, bishop of Kildare, died in London in 1513. The exact state of affairs between 1492 and 1513 remains in doubt.

[44] A. Conway, *Henry VII's Relations with Scotland and Ireland, 1485–1498* (Cambridge, 1932), pp. 42–143.

[45] *Ibid.* pp. 210 and 218–19.

sought to assure the king's control of papal provisions in Ireland by asserting the existing legislation, English as well as Irish, against papal provisions.[46] In England the good understanding between king and pope had left the Statute of Provisors in an unmenacing abeyance; but the Act against provisors, as it was intended to be applied in Ireland, unless most tactfully handled, could raise a storm in the Curia.

The part played by the cardinal protector in explaining the circumstances in Ireland, if any, is not clear; but it was soon obvious that the king had made a special effort to win papal support for his Irish plans. On 28 October 1496 Alexander VI, acting in response to a request presented in the name of the king, issued a bull aimed at the reform of church government in Ireland, especially in the intensely Irish civil province of Ulster.[47] The means chosen, a council of the whole Irish church summoned under the supervision of a committee of four bishops, was standard enough; but the four bishops selected were startling: Cardinal John Morton of Canterbury, Richard Fox of Durham, Oliver King of Bath and Wells, and Thomas Savage of London, all four English and all four intimately associated with the government of Henry VII. It seems unlikely that such a tactic could have been suggested by either Octavian as primate of All Ireland, or by Archbishop FitzSimmons of Dublin; for such an arrangement calmly ignored their metropolitan rights.[48] Despite the *post quod, propter quod* nature of the argument, there is an interesting relationship between the arrival of Robert Sherborne in Rome during June 1496 and the issue of the bull in October. That Sherborne should have been the one who explained the king's Irish policy, whether to the pope directly only or also through Piccolomini, is eminently logical. The king had gratified the pope by sending Sherborne to join England to a Holy League from which the king could draw little direct advantage. The king did,

---

[46] *Statutes at Large passed in the Parliaments held in Ireland, 1310–1786* (Dublin, 1786), vol. I, cap. v. The statute must have been enacted some time shortly after the opening of the Drogheda Parliament on 1 December 1494. Conway, *Henry VII's Relations with Scotland and Ireland*, pp. 78–80, argues convincingly that the laws have survived in chronological order and that Act xxiv must have been enacted before 27 February 1495.

[47] Rymer, *Foedera*, xii, 643–4.

[48] For the role of Archbishop Octavian in the Drogheda Parliament, see A. Gwynn, *The Medieval Province of Armagh, 1470–1545* (Dundalk, 1946), pp. 36–9.

however, have pressing difficulties in Ireland. It is unlikely that Henry VII's shrewd sense of politics would have failed him at such a juncture. It was hardly an opportune moment for the pope to accuse the English king of harbouring hostility to papal authority.

In the light of these developments, it is interesting to analyse Piccolomini's role in referring provisions to Irish bishoprics, both before and after Poynings' Parliament. During a period from 1494 until 1497, curiously coinciding almost exactly with the period from the opening of the parliament at Drogheda until after the papal bull on the reform of the Irish church, there is a strange silence in the Consistorial Acts about provisions made for Ireland. Of the seven provisions made, two were for absentee Italians in 1494 and again in 1495 to the really defunct see of Glendalough just outside Dublin. In 1494 Edmund Courci, papal collector and nuncio in Ireland, who had failed to get possession of his see of Clogher, was appointed to his native diocese of Ross; and shortly afterwards in the same year, James MacMahon was provided to Clogher, still actively claimed by Courci, and likewise failed to get possession.[49] Whether Cardinal Piccolomini had any connexion with these or the other three provisions from this period is not clear; and, even if he had, it would be difficult to interpret its significance.[50]

There is, however, a marked contrast between Piccolomini's role in the years 1492–3 and that in 1497–1503. On 22 June 1492, at the same time he had referred the nomination of Edmund Audley to Hereford, Piccolomini referred that of a Dominican, Richard O Guanach, to Elphin in the province of Tuam. Unfortunately, O Guanach was challenged by a predecessor, Nicholas O Flanagan, also a Dominican, whom the Curia had presumed dead in 1487; and the new bishop failed to get possession. Again Piccolomini had encountered something of the confusion existing in the Irish church. But it was three other cardinals, de Costa, de'Conti and Riario, who referred the other three provisions made in 1492 and 1493, although the latter two of these were of men who eventually served as suffragans in England.[51]

---

[49] Arch. Vat., Reg. Vat. 876, fols. 114ᵛ–116ʳ; and Gwynn, *Medieval Province of Armagh*, pp. 164–72.

[50] Three were in early November 1494, when Piccolomini was absent from Rome as legate to treat with Charles VIII of France.

[51] Piccolomini was probably not in Rome when John Bel was provided to Mayo on 4 November 1493.

When the Great Earl of Kildare, freshly restored to the deputy-ship, landed in Ireland on 27 September 1496, the king in effect indicated that the policy of vigorous enforcement of direct English rule was moderated. There is no evidence that any English-dominated council of the Irish church was ever held in accord with the pope's bull; but in Rome Cardinal Piccolomini emerged as the king's spokesman in Consistory in a spirited, if only partially successful, drive to establish control of papal provision for Irish bishoprics in the name of Henry VII. Of the ten provisions made between 1497 and 1503, five were referred by Cardinal Picco-lomini; and since one of the other five was of a Spaniard to the phantom diocese of Glendalough, referred in 1500 by the Spanish cardinal Juan Lopez, it might perhaps be more accurate to speak of only nine provisions.

Of these, the most important was the contested provision to Cork and Cloyne in 1499, which fully reflected the king's policy and Piccolomini's role in implementing it.[52] On 15 February 1499 Patrick Cant, abbot of the Cistercian monastery of Fermoy, was provided at the relation of Cardinal Pallavicini to Cork and Cloyne, said to be vacant by the death of Bishop Jordan Purcell. Apparently the objection had been raised that there was still a living bishop of Cork and Cloyne, and on 4 March unsuccessful pressure was still being exerted by Bishop-elect Cant, or his agent, to have the bulls expedited. Henry VII had some time just previously made an arrangement whereby John FitzEdmund FitzGerald, twenty-seven years old, should become bishop of Cork and Cloyne upon the resignation of a kinsman, Gerald Fitz-Gerald, who had been provided to the see in 1463. When word reached the king of the proposed provision of Cant, he took action both in Ireland and in Rome. In Consistory on 8 April 1499 Cardinal Piccolomini read a strongly worded letter from the king; and on 10 May he read still another, dated 4 April at Greenwich, which included and amplified the notions contained in the first. Just when he would have thought the desire of the two Fitz-Geralds had been satisfied, the king explained, he had learned

[52] Most of the relevant sections of the Consistorial Acts are quoted in the footnotes in Eubel, *Hierarchia*, II, 137; there is another set of the docu-ments containing the same information with only slight variations in Bib. Vat., Cod. Barb. Lat. 2876, fols. 40^{r-v}, 49^v–50^r and 56^v–57^r; 2932, fols. 21^r–22^v. Although Brady, *Episcopal Succession*, II, 81–4, gives no exact references, his account is based chiefly on the Barbarini MSS.

that some of his Irish subjects had affirmed to the pope that there was no living bishop of Cork and Cloyne, and that the earl of Desmond had recommended the abbot of Fermoy for the see. He was utterly amazed that more credence should be given to his subjects and to commoners than to the testimony of his own letter, and that a recommendation made by one of his subjects should be given more weight than his own. Indeed, the pope, having been apprised of the legitimate grounds, had already long before conceded the king the liberty of nominating to Irish sees and had freely allowed it in frequent subsequent letters. Now the king most urgently requested that the pope might maintain inviolate what he had once conceded and consistently confirmed.[53] But the matter was to be brought to Consistory twice again before being resolved.

On 19 June Cardinal Piccolomini, by this time impressively armed with documents, proposed in Consistory the provision of John FitzEdmund FitzGerald to Cork and Cloyne. He produced an original bull of provision of Gerald FitzGerald, which had been sent by Pius II, Piccolomini's uncle, to Edward IV of England under date of 31 January 1463. The letter of Henry VII read in Consistory the previous month was again presented, together with a letter dated 25 April from the earl of Desmond to Henry VII, which supported the king's position. Edmund Courci, apostolic nuncio and collector in Ireland, had written, also on 25 April, from his see city of Ross not far from Cork; and the dean and chapter of Cloyne had written from Cloyne on 27 April. All these letters, read out by Piccolomini, testified that the Gerald FitzGerald provided to Cork and Cloyne by Pius II had been duly consecrated and had been already thirty years and more in peaceful possession, that he had enjoyed the utter good will and obedience of all the clergy and of the chapter of the united sees of Cork and Cloyne, and that he was still very much alive. Cardinal Pallavicini, who in 1504 was considered the protector of Scotland, and who worked for most of the other rulers of Europe, Henry VII excepted, then reminded the pope and cardinals that he himself in a recent consistory had made a relation in favour of Patrick Cant to these sees, which were at that time declared vacant by the death of Jordan Purcell and not of Gerald Fitz-Gerald.[54] Then, much to Piccolomini's consternation, he recalled

[53] Eubel, *Hierarchia*, II, 137, citing Acta Cons. Miscel. 44, fols. 38 and 52.
[54] Wodka, *Protektorate der Kardinäle*, pp. 14, 15, 41, 43–5 and 109.

how Piccolomini himself had referred the nomination of a Thadeus MacCarthy to the same sees nine years before, and that they were then declared vacant by the resignation of a William Roche.[55] How was it possible, Cardinal Pallavicini asked, that Bishop Gerald FitzGerald could have been for thirty years in peaceful possession, when in the meantime there had been so many other bishops of Cork and Cloyne? Since the matter seemed 'satis intricata', it was put off until another consistory.

There is no reason to believe that there was any strong personal feeling between the two cardinals; but the interest represented by Piccolomini, that of the king, triumphed in the end. In Consistory on 26 June 1499 the pope received the resignation of Gerald Fitz-Gerald, 'bishop of the united dioceses of Cork and Cloyne, in Ireland, under the archbishopric and in the province of Cashel, in the territory of the earl of Desmond, subject of the king of England', and provided to the title John FitzEdmund FitzGerald, with a dispensation for want of canonical age and with permission to retain his other benefices. The Consistorial Acts made no mention whatever of Patrick Cant, whose episcopal aspirations were dashed in the triumph of the youthful but well-connected victor. In a kind of little sequel, of which neither cardinal may have been conscious, Piccolomini again triumphed. The next year, on 10 June, a coadjutor with right of succession, 'Andrew', referred by Cardinal Pallavicini, was provided for the diocese of Clogher in the province of Armagh. Edmund Courci, bishop of Ross, who still claimed the see despite his total failure to win control of it, failed also to win control for his coadjutor. Courci yielded his claim to Clogher; and on 24 January 1502 Cardinal Piccolomini referred the nomination of an Irish Augustinian, Nehemias Clonin, to the see. Although Clonin himself seems to have resigned the troublesome see within the next two years, Bishop 'Andrew' had been ignored in the provision and was not heard from again. Another unsuccessful contender for the see of Clogher, James MacMathghamma or MacMahon, provided in 1494, was provided, also unsuccessfully, to the diocese of Derry also in the province of Armagh, on 5 July 1501.[56]

[55] The provision had been made on 21 April 1490 before Piccolomini had become protector of England. William Roche, who had been archdeacon of Cloyne, seems to have based his claim on a resignation of Jordan Purcell in his favour.

[56] Gwynn, *Medieval Province of Armagh*, pp. 176 and 192–3.

The other three provisions referred by Piccolomini seem to have had nothing in common, except perhaps in the common confusion uncovered. On 30 April 1498 he related a Charles MacBriain to Emly, province of Cashel, said to be vacant by the death of 'N.', the previous bishop. Since the previous bishop, provided on 10 November 1494, had in fact been a Donatus MacBriain, there is a suggestion, unsupported by evidence, of a powerful Irish family interest at work as in the case of Cork and Cloyne. The translation of the Greek George Braua from Dromore in the province of Armagh, to Elphin in the province of Tuam, was occasion for an embarrassment for Piccolomini parallel to that of Cork and Cloyne. When the provision was made on 13 April 1499, Piccolomini reported the see of Elphin vacant by the resignation of a Bishop 'Nicholas'. Seven years earlier he himself had related the previous provision to the see, that of Richard O Guanach; and he had reported the see vacant then because of the death of a Bishop 'Cornelius'. But Bishop 'Nicholas', like Bishop Gerald FitzGerald, had proved to be still alive. If there was confusion connected with the provision of Thomas Clerke on 4 May 1500 to Killala, also in the province of Tuam, Piccolomini was at least not party to both parts of it. Piccolomini reported the see vacant by the death of 'Thomas', the last bishop. A bishop called 'Thomas' had been provided in 1471; but meanwhile, in 1487, Cardinal de'Conti had related the see in favour of John de Tuderto and pronounced it vacant by the death of 'Donatus', the last bishop.[57]

Henry VII was probably better informed about the Irish hierarchy than either Pope Alexander VI or Cardinal Piccolomini; and his policy in dealing with the Irish church, like his policy in dealing with the Great Earl, was aimed at the possible rather than any pursuit of principle. His insistence on the naming of a less than ideal candidate as bishop of Cork and Cloyne was clearly on his own initiative and represented an effort to cooperate with the Geraldines whom he had restored to power in Ireland. The forces backing Patrick Cant for the bishopric never clearly emerged. If indeed it was the earl of Desmond who first recommended him for the sees, the earl quickly withdrew that support. Cant may have been backed by a group sincerely seeking only the spiritual good of the Church, or Cant may have been a

[57] Probably Donatus O Conchobhair, op, provided on 2 December 1461.

solitary, unworthy intriguer. In 1497 the rebels supporting Perkin Warbeck had been under the leadership of Sir James Ormond, who was slain at Cork. The loyalty of Ormond's Geraldine rivals, the Great Earl of Kildare and the earl of Desmond, found recognition in the placing of a FitzGerald in the bishopric. To the king a contingent control of Cork and Cloyne seemed in the long run to be the most effective one.[58]

How the king's policy was applied to the remainder of Ireland is hard to discern because so few provisions were made to bishoprics in this period. It seems safe to assume that the other four Irish provisions referred by Piccolomini after 1497, if not of men whose nominations had been forwarded by the king, were at least of men provided to their sees with the king's knowledge and passive consent. Of the four bishops, Braua was a Greek who had been imported to Ireland by Archbishop Octavian, and Thomas Clerke was an Englishman, whose previous benefice, the archdeaconry of Sodor and the Isle of Man, raises doubts of any physical contact with Ireland at all. Either of these men, if he ever gained possession of his diocese, would have made an effort to serve the king. Of the other two, both apparently Irish, Clonin failed to gain effective control of his diocese, and MacBriain must have represented at best a compromise for royal authority.

It is the provision of Matthew O Briain, archdeacon of Killaloe, to Kilmacduagh on 8 March 1503, referred by Cardinal Carvajal, which most requires explaining. It is difficult to see Cardinal Piccolomini as a kind of watchdog in Consistory, waiting to challenge any provisions made to Irish sees of any man not approved by the king, but this provision would represent the single serious lapse of his attention in the years after 1497. Since Cardinal Carvajal also referred the nomination of William Sever to Durham on 27 June 1503, a nomination clearly made by the king, it would seem unlikely that the provision made to Kilmacduagh three and a half months earlier could have been contrary to the king's interest.

[58] The situation at Cork was somewhat parallel to that at Limerick. There was an English control of a sort over the city, but the countryside was controlled by the earl of Desmond. When John Dunmow, the king's ambassador in Rome, was made bishop of Limerick, the king issued mandates on 1 October 1488 to his kinsman Maurice FitzGerald, earl of Desmond, and to the mayor of Limerick to restore the temporalities to the new bishop (*Cal. of Pat. Rolls, Henry VII*, i, 250).

The one Irish provision which would have thrown the most light on Piccolomini's role would have been that to Tuam, the only one of the four metropolitan sees to fall vacant during Piccolomini's protectorship. Although William Seoighe (Joyce) had died on 20 December 1501, the vacancy was not filled until after the election of Julius II. If the years of the vacancy were marked by a struggle of the king to establish a man loyal to himself in this key position in western Ireland, his final solution was a failure. The man provided as archbishop, with the king's approval, was an Englishman, Philip Pinson, who died in Rome within three days of his appointment. However, in 1504 Maurice Fitz-Gerald was appointed successor to David Creagh as archbishop of Cashel in southern Ireland. The more realistic policy of compromise with the Geraldines begun so vigorously five years before at Cork and Cloyne was still alive.[59]

The cardinal protectors of England, let it be repeated, were protectors also of Ireland only in the sense that the king of England was lord of Ireland. Beginning with Piccolomini and Henry VII, conflicting provisions to Irish sees were gradually sorted out, and royal nomination of bishops became an established fact in Ireland as well. Like Henry VIII after him, Henry VII was never willing to expend the money and energy required to enforce the authority he claimed as lord of Ireland. He was able to achieve a worthwhile advantage at a minimum cost, however, when he sought the cooperation of the Roman Curia in attempting to extend English control over the Irish church. If the king's nominations to Irish sees most often represented a compromise with the Irish, this was because of the king's political realism, not because of pressure from the Curia. As we shall see, efforts under Henry VIII in the years after 1513 to use the cardinal protector Giulio de'Medici to influence the Scottish church and to gain control of the pro-French bishopric of Tournai were markedly less successful.

The protectorship in confusion

From after 1503 until 1514, that is from the end of Piccolomini's protectorship until that of de'Medici begins, it is not completely

---

[59] On Henry VII's use of Piccolomini to assist Anne of Brittany in maintaining her right to nominate to the Breton bishoprics against French encroachment, see *Ven. Cal.* I, 573, 597 and 613; and Eubel, *Hierarchia*, II, 198–9.

clear exactly how the protectorship functioned. The sudden death in 1508 of the talented papal nephew, Galeotto della Rovere, upset a promising arrangement. Neither his half-brother, Cardinal Sisto della Rovere Garo, who evidently wanted the position, nor the papal favourite Francesco Alidosi, to whom it was eventually given, developed into a satisfactory servant of the king. After Bainbridge's creation as cardinal in 1511, he became an effective cardinal procurator of the sort which Henry VII had earlier hoped to have in the unreliable Castellesi, but the completeness of Bainbridge's control until 1514 is presumed rather than proven. The consistorial records, which contain the names of the cardinals referring nominations of bishops, could throw considerable light on the problem. Unfortunately they are largely missing for precisely these years for which they would have been the most useful.

During the very brief pontificate of Pius III and immediately after the election of Julius II, Cardinal Castellesi assumed full responsibility with Bishop Silvestro Gigli in furthering English business. In a letter of 4 January 1504 he acknowledged receipt of a bundle of five letters from Henry VII, all dated December.[60] Of these, two were for the pope: one of congratulations on his election and the other concerned with the marriage dispensation of Prince Henry and Catherine of Aragon. Of the two addressed to Cardinal Castellesi and Bishop Gigli jointly, one recommended a candidate for the vacant Irish archbishopric of Cashel, and the other gave instructions for seeking the marriage dispensation. The last was directed to Castellesi personally. Gigli and Castellesi went together to the pope, and Castellesi read him the two letters. The dispensation, about which difficulties were raised, was entrusted to Cardinals Oliverio Caraffa and Giorgio de Costa, both of whom were then ill. Castellesi described at length the strenuous efforts of Gigli and himself together with the Spanish ambassador in pursuing the matter. Similarly, the pope was still reluctant to grant the bull requested by Henry VII touching upon the power of special confessors to absolve even from sins reserved to the Holy See, although Castellesi quoted at length from Henry VII's letters written during the pontificate of Alexander VI. The pope resolved to consult with Cardinal Riario of the Rota. Castellesi himself would speak with this cardinal, who was a good

[60] Gairdner, *Letters. . .of Henry VII*, ɪɪ, 112–24.

friend and whose room in the papal palace was near his own. Because the pope was new, he saw minor problems as great ones; nor ought it to be forgotten that Alexander VI had sent Christopher Urswick and the king's other ambassadors home without any bulls being expedited in another such case involving principle. The pope was gratified at news of the ambassadors appointed to render the king's canonical obedience, and Castellesi had invited them to accept lodging and hospitality with him.

Then Castellesi described minor business of a character associated with the work of a cardinal protector. The provisions to Canterbury, Chichester and St Asaph had been expedited; and the bulls were already despatched. Philip Pinson had come personally to Rome to see to his provision to the Irish archbishopric of Tuam. Because of the king's letters, and because he had served as suffragan in Castellesi's English diocese of Hereford, the cardinal was able to expedite the provision two days after his arrival. Unfortunately, Pinson died of the pestilence at Rome only three days later. In view of his death *in Curia Romana*, Castellesi wrote, an effort might be made in Rome to nominate a successor. Castellesi would do his utmost to forestall that but begged the king to make a nomination quickly. He further suggested that the king nominate some Englishman to serve as penitentiary in St Peter's basilica. The question of a successor had arisen in Consistory under Alexander VI, Pius III, and now Julius II. Castellesi had resisted efforts, especially of the Scots, to name a non-Englishman; and he had carried to each of these popes the bull of Eugene IV which provided for an Englishman as penitentiary who was also to hear confessions of Scottish and Irish pilgrims. Cardinal Pallavicini, protector of Scotland, and Cardinals Podocataro and Grimani had raised objection; but Julius II had ordered the datary to detain their supplications. The king's nomination should be made quickly in order to put an end to the struggle.[61]

Even after the choice of Galeotto della Rovere as protector in 1504, Castellesi still performed services for England.[62] It was he

---

[61] Hugh Inge, made bishop of Meath on 28 January 1512, became *custos* of the English Hospice on 4 November 1504 at the nomination of Henry VII. He was referred to as *Penitentiarius* in the record of it, so apparently he was named to fill this vacancy (Rome, Archives of the Venerable English College, Liber Instrumentorum I, fol. 12ʳ; PRO 31/10/8, fols. 13f.).

[62] PRO 31/9/1, fols. 19, 43–4, 47–8 and 61–4.

who presented to Julius II the petitions of the Lady Margaret, Henry VII's mother, for dispensations for Bishop John Fisher of Rochester to reside away from his see and to serve as her confessor. When the English were being called to task for failure to respect the papal monopoly in the alum trade and for having purchased it from the Turks, Castellesi, possibly in his role as papal collector for England, became involved. The vacancy in the Irish archbishopric of Tuam, which Castellesi had made his special charge in 1503, was finally provided with an Irishman, Maurice O Fihilly, OFM, in the consistory of 26 June 1506. There is no mention in the pope's letters of 10 July directed to Henry VII and to the chapter of Tuam of who O Fihilly's cardinal promotor had been; and most unfortunately, since O Fihilly, who apparently was in Rome at the time, seems to have been a candidate neither nominated by the king nor elected by the chapter. Either Castellesi had failed in his undertaking or had personally sponsored a man not nominated by the king.

However, the one great piece of business, the papal dispensation for the marriage of Prince Henry and Catherine of Aragon, had been secured through other channels. On 6 July 1504 Julius II had promised to send the bulls on to England with Robert Sherborne, whom the king had especially charged to see to it. However, shortly before the death of Edward Scott of a fever on 24 July, Sherborne, himself in bad health, left Rome without them. On 28 November Henry VII wrote to the pope in some impatience, asking him to send them with some of his other ambassadors. These were Cardinal Castellesi, Bishop Gigli and possibly Christopher Fisher, who was actually a solicitor rather than an ambassador. The pope's announcement of the granting of the dispensation and his acknowledgment of his nephew's assumption of the English protectorship were made to the king in a single letter of 6 July 1504. After more than seven months' further delay, Julius II gave the whole credit for winning approval for the dispensation to the new cardinal protector and to Bishop Gigli. On 17 March Gigli himself wrote to confirm the news earlier personally brought to the king by his merchant brother Gianpaolo, who had taken the pope's letters. Gigli left a few days later on his return to England as papal nuncio with the bull of dispensation and the sword and cap of maintenance for the king. The solemn presentation was made at Richmond in the presence of the Spanish ambassador.[63] Twenty-four years later Henry VIII would appeal to Campeggio as protector to assist in having the dispensation declared invalid.

Even before the granting of the marriage dispensation was complete, Galeotto della Rovere as cardinal protector had referred in Consistory the nominations of John Fisher to Rochester on 14 October 1504 and of Hugh Oldham to Exeter on 27 November 1504. The Consistorial Acts for the eight other provisions made to English sees during della Rovere's protectorship are missing, and of the seven provisions to Irish sees in these years, only that of Eugene MacCathmhail to Clogher is known for certain to have been referred by him. If, as is probable, the youthful cardinal protector referred most of these provisions after the pattern established by Cardinal Piccolomini, Julius II nevertheless did not hesitate to put pressure on the king to fill vacancies, and, at least in the case of long-vacant Tuam in 1506, to provide, after decent delay, without royal nomination. But royal nominees willing to pay their consistorial taxes seem to have encountered no difficulty.[64]

Evidence survives of several minor services performed by Galeotto della Rovere, evidently in his capacity as English protector. At his supplication a papal indulgence was granted on 21 June 1506 to John Mortymen, a chamber official of Henry VII.[65] Through him Robert Haldesworth of the archdiocese of York was made papal notary.[66] On Candlemas day 1508 Cardinal della Rovere ceremoniously accepted from the hands of the pope candles blessed by the pope which he gave to Hugh Inge, until lately *custos* of the English Hospice, to carry to the Lady Margaret, the king, Prince Henry, and the court.[67]

The last important service of della Rovere for Henry VII was in connexion with the king's effort to turn more and more of the revenues of the see of Durham as County Palatine of the North

---

[63] Pocock, *Records of the Reformation*, i, 5–8; PRO 31/9/1, fols. 17–18; and Gairdner, *Letters. . .of Henry VII*, i, 243–5. There is a bull of dispensation dated 26 December 1503 printed in Rymer, *Foedera*, xiii, 89–90, from the original in England, and which is the same as that in Arch. Vat., Reg. Vat. 984, fols. 39ʳ–40ʳ.

[64] PRO 31/9/1, fols. 9, 73–4 and 153; *Ven. Cal.* i, 840 and 876.

[65] PRO, SC 7/64/6, cited by Chambers, *Cardinal Bainbridge*, p. 9n.

[66] Julius II to Haldesworth, 18 August 1506 (Arch. Vat., Reg. Vat. 989, fols. 168ʳ⁻ᵛ).

[67] PRO 31/9/1, fols. 91 and 97.

to the needs of strengthening the frontier defences against the Scots. To his original tactic of allowing prolonged vacancies in the see and pressing for a reduction of consistorial taxes, the king sought in 1506 to make as a precondition to the provision of a bishop, permission to divert a substantial part of his revenues to the repair of fortifications. On 26 July 1506 Julius II granted approval to such an agreement for seven years, even before Girolamo Bonvisio arrived from England on this and other business. The new bishop of Durham, the future Cardinal Christopher Bainbridge, was at last provided on 27 August 1507, when almost immediately the problem arose again. The king claimed that if Archbishop Thomas Savage of York, who died just eleven days after Bainbridge's provision to Durham, had died sooner, he would have nominated Bainbridge to be metropolitan of York instead and wished to do so now. Now, however, he wished a precondition to run for eight years instead of seven, and to cover not only the repair of existing fortifications but new construction and the supply of war machinery as well. At this the pope balked, objecting that it was totally without precedent. In the hope of forestalling another artificially prolonged vacancy at Durham, he offered to compromise with a grant of permission for the eight years, but confined as previously to the maintenance or repair of existing fortifications. But on 26 July 1508, acknowledging the king's letter of 29 May, and crediting the entreaties made by Galeotto della Rovere as English protector and by Girolamo Bonvisio, whom the king had named one of his solicitors to please the pope, the pope gave way to the king's demand.[68] Before the translation of Bainbridge from Durham to York could be made in Consistory, Cardinal Galeotto della Rovere died suddenly on 11 September 1508.

There is little evidence to elucidate the period from 1508 to 1514, when Cardinal Alidosi and then possibly Galeotto's half-brother Sisto were supposed to have served as protector. There is no reason to think that the rumoured transfer of the protectorship from Alidosi to Sisto della Rovere Garo had actually been carried out by the king. Oddly enough, the only direct evidence of Alidosi's having performed a service for England is from after his supposed dismissal in 1510. In a consistory at fated Bologna on

---

[68] PRO 31/9/1, fols. 73–6, 105–9, 115–16, 153 and 155; Arch. Vat., Arm. xxxix, cod. 28, fol. 407.

30 April 1511 he referred the nomination of Thadeus O Reilly to the impoverished bishopric of Dromore, Ireland, and the consistorial *cedula* was duly issued in the name of the vice-chancellor, Sisto della Rovere Garo. The six provisions to English sees and the other five to Irish sees made in the less than three years between Galeotto della Rovere's death in 1508 and that of Alidosi in 1511, were all made before 1510; and none are noticed in any surviving consistorial records.[69]

The creation of Bainbridge as cardinal in March 1511, slightly more than two months before Alidosi's death, made it possible for him to act not only as proctor but directly in Consistory as well. During the next three years he sponsored requests for indulgences and dispensations, and in 1512 at his word the pope urged Henry VIII to settle himself a thorny controversy between Archbishop Warham and his suffragan, Bishop Fox of Winchester, over metropolitan rights in the probating of wills, in order to stop a suit these bishops had begun in the Roman Rota. Over the provision of bishops to English and Irish sees Bainbridge kept a careful and informed watch. In Consistory on 6 February 1513 he referred the king's nomination to Raphoe of Cornelius O Cathain; and on 30 May, with a dispensation from the common service fee, of his protégé Thomas Halsey as the continuously absent bishop of Leighlin, Ireland. On 18 June 1514 Leo X ordered the expedition of the bulls of Thomas O Mulally of Tuam 'without requiring payment for the united church of Annaghdown, which is certified by Christopher, Cardinal of St. Praxedes, to be so dilapidated and wasted by war that no fruits are at present taken there'.[70] The fact that Bainbridge referred the provision of John Young, the king's master of the Rolls, as bishop of Gallipoli *in partibus* on 15 April 1513 strongly suggests that he also referred that of Edward Birkhead to St Asaph on the same day. There is no record of the cardinal *referendarius* for the triple provision of 28 January 1512; but both William Rokeby, who was translated from Meath to Dublin, and Hugh Inge, former *custos* of the Hospice in Rome and who succeeded to Meath, were Englishmen dedicated to maintaining English control of the Pale in the face of a renascent

[69] PRO 31/9/62, fol. 67 (*LP* I, 747). One of these was the provision of Christopher Fisher to Elphin on 12 December 1508, during the lifetime of George Braua, who had been translated to it from Dromore on 19 April 1499.
[70] *LP* I, 3016.

Irish culture. The third, Desmond O Raighilligh, was provided to the thoroughly Irish diocese of Kilmore but eventually withdrew to the Pale. Whether seen to by Bainbridge or not, these were clearly royal nominations; and the only other Irish provision unaccounted for was that of Richard Barrett to Killala on 7 January 1513. If this too was referred by Bainbridge or at least a royal nomination, English control of Irish provisions was without exception.

The only other two provisions, both referred by Bainbridge, were in the end the most significant. On 24 October 1513 John Kite, an Englishman and servant of the rising Thomas Wolsey, was made archbishop of Armagh; and on 6 February 1514 Wolsey himself, dean of Bainbridge's York, was made bishop of Lincoln.[71] If there was a cardinal protector at this time, Cardinal Bainbridge was doing his work.[72]

[71] *LP* i, 2395; and D. Quinn, 'Henry VIII and Ireland, 1509–1534', *Irish Historical Studies*, xii (1960–1), 320–1, who sees the appointment as a first indication of a new interventionist policy of England in Ireland.

[72] Chambers, *Cardinal Bainbridge*, pp. 74–6. Part of Bainbridge's original commission was 'Promotionesque quorumcumque Anglorum, Wallicorum aut Hibernicorum Subditorum nostrorum ad Ecclesias Cathedrales cum vacaverint, per Nos Recommendatorum seu Nominatorum, solicitandi et cum effectu prosequendi atque ad debitum finem producendi' (Rymer, *Foedera*, xiii, 265).

intimates, Lorenzo Pucci, datary and later major penitentiary; Bernardo Bibiena, the pope's former tutor, who became treasurer general; and Innocenzo Cibò, a papal nephew. A week later de'Medici wrote to Henry VIII to announce his exaltation and to offer his services, indicating that 'others' had doubtless already passed on the news of it. During the following months, and while Cardinal Bainbridge was still alive, Bishop Silvestro Gigli made arrangements, as has already been seen, for Giulio de'Medici to become cardinal protector of England.[2] Thinking the official letters might have been intercepted en route and impatient to inaugurate the protectorship, Gigli used his own copies of the king's letters which had arrived to make the announcement. On 8 February 1514 de'Medici, avoiding, possibly from a sense of legal refinement, the actual use of the word 'protector' itself, profusely thanked the king. The same day Leo X wrote three letters to England. He thanked the king for having made his brother Giuliano a knight of the Garter and for having entrusted Cardinal Giulio with 'the patronage of English affairs'. To Bishop Fox of Winchester he expressed similar sentiments; and to Bishop Ruthal of Durham he announced the granting, at the intercession of Cardinal de'Medici and at the instance of the king, of the very unusual indulgence he had requested.[3] The protector-designate himself assured the king that he would have been happy to have referred the provision of Wolsey to Lincoln, made two days before, as the king had asked, except that the pope had wanted Cardinal Bainbridge to do it this time. But he did credit himself and Gigli with having obtained the indulgence requested and implied his own connexion with letters of greatest import sent off by Gigli four days before.[4] The presence of Gigli pervaded all four letters.

Ten days later the official letters themselves arrived and occasioned another surfeit of gratitude. Gigli, having a better sense of where the power lay, at least in his own case, had made

[2] Rymer, *Foedera*, xiii, 378 (*LP* i, 2320); possibly Sir Thomas Cheney, commissioned to Leo X on 10 November 1513 (*LP* i, 2437, 2732 and 2757).

[3] PRO 31/9/1, fols. 179–83 (*LP* i, 2639ff.).

[4] Br. Mus., Vitell. B. ii, fol. 64ᵛ (*LP* i, 2642, which erroneously suggests that de'Medici himself had written). An examination of the reports made by the Florentine ambassador in Rome and of the letters written by de'Medici to Florence has failed to produce any direct reference to the protectorship of England (Florence, AS, Mediceo Avanti il Principato, Filze lxvi and cv–cxlv; Signori Responsive, Filze xxxiv–xli; Otto di Practica, Responsive ii).

his report on 11 February to Wolsey. On 18 February Giulio de'Medici openly acknowledged his appointment as protector of the king and his realm. Next day Leo X thanked both Fox and Wolsey. To Bishop Gianpietro Caraffa, nuncio in England, he indicated that Giulio de'Medici, 'huius regni apud Nos et hanc Sanctam Sedem protectori', would write more fully about the plans for treating of peace and advised him to place special trust in Bishops Fox and Wolsey. Finally, on the day following, 20 February, the pope advised the king that his own kinsman and servant, Leonardo Spinelli of Florence, already acquainted with Henry VIII, was being sent to England with the sword and cap of maintenance blessed the previous Christmas.[5]

Against the obbligato of peace-making diplomacy, Wolsey sought to wheedle a reciprocal grant of honours from the pope: the cardinalate and a commission as legate *a latere*. Although the approach was made, neither was a real possibility so long as Cardinal Bainbridge remained alive. Even after Bainbridge's convenient death, the king's emphatic request of 12 August 1514 and Gigli's strenuous efforts produced no immediate success with either the cardinalate or the legateship. On 24 September de'Medici notified the king that Wolsey's provision to York was complete; and on the same day Leo himself explained that, as Gigli would clarify, the creating of Wolsey a cardinal was surrounded with difficulties, but that he would comply with the king's wishes at a suitable time. Gigli himself, expressing confidence of success, advised Wolsey against accepting a bull of promotion *in petto* as unnecessarily expensive and urged him to indicate as much to the Pope and to Cardinal de'Medici.[6]

The renewed French invasion of Italy in 1515 provided Leo X with the necessary pretext. In August, already assured by the pope that he would be created cardinal, Wolsey directed Gigli to press for the combining of the legateship with it and begged to be commended to Cardinal de'Medici. In Consistory objection was raised that the example of Bainbridge showed that Englishmen do not make proper cardinals, and that to make Wolsey cardinal without granting him the legateship he wanted would eventually turn him against the Curia and make him a supporter of Francis I,

[5] *LP* I, 2644, 2653, 2658ff. and 2664.
[6] *LP* I, 3132, 3140, 3300f. and 3496f.

instead of drawing Henry VIII to the pope's aid.[7] But on
10 September, in Leo X's second promotion of cardinals, Wolsey
was the only cardinal created. Protector de'Medici, although
absent in Bologna on papal business at the time, wrote to Henry
VIII from there five days later to claim his part in having brought
the matter to a happy outcome. On 5 November, once again in
Rome, de'Medici acknowledged Wolsey's letter of thanks for his
services.[8]

Although Wolsey was both cardinal, and since 24 December
1515 also lord chancellor, continued pressure on Rome to grant
the legateship *a latere* was resisted. Leo X objected that, if he
granted it to Wolsey, Francis I would demand a similar grant,
and the Emperor Maximilian would want the same for Cardinal
Lang; but he promised it, if Henry would undertake an expedition against the Turks. Wolsey used legatine commission held by
Cardinal Bakócz of Gran for Hungary, and by Cardinal Lang for
the Empire as precedents in asking Gigli to renew the request on
22 May 1516, apparently without knowing that Lang's earlier
personal bid in Rome to obtain such a commission had been
flatly refused in Consistory.[9] During much of the winter
de'Medici had again been absent as legate to Bologna in the wake
of the meeting there of Francis I and Leo X. On 28 January, from
Florence, he congratulated Wolsey on his becoming lord chancellor and assured both king and cardinal of his intention to see to
their requests; but neither on this occasion nor in later letters
from Rome, although he was in regular communication with
Gigli, does he refer to the question of the legateship. Indeed,
success came only two years later, after reintensified pressure,

---

[7] 'De facili non fiat aliquis Anglicus cardinalis, quia nimis opprobriose se
habent in illa dignitate, quod manifeste visum est in cardinal nuper
defuncto Anglico [Bainbridge]. Et etiam quod iste sit amicus regis intimus
non contentabitur de solo cardinalatu, ut ipsorum moris est, maxime
barbarorum, sed volet etiam habere legationem in toto regno Angliae; quae
si concedatur, Curia Romana destruetur; si non concedatur, ipse cardinalis
erit inimicus papae et omnium cardinalium, et per consequens inimicabitur
ecclesiae Romanae ac favebit regi Franciae' (Paris de Grassi, *Diarium*, in
PRO 31/9/15, fol. 309, from Rome, Bib. Minerva, MS xx. iii. 3). Paris de
Grassi was unfriendly toward Bainbridge on other occasions.

[8] *LP* II, 780, 910 and 1108. According to Wolsey's letter to Gigli, the
cardinals who had congratulated him, in addition to de'Medici, Castellesi
and Riario, were Bibiena, Carvajal, Pucci and Bandinello de Sauli (*LP* II,
894); and *LP* II, 893 and 1081.

[9] *LP* II, 966, 1876 and 1928; Pastor, *History of the Popes*, trans. Kerr, VII, 97.

and only after Cardinal de Boissy had succeeded in getting a similar commission in France. Cardinals Wolsey and Lang were both created legates in Consistory on 17 May 1518.[10] However, after Warham's retirement from the government in 1515, followed by that of Fox a few months later, both the king and the pope allowed Wolsey a predominating influence over affairs in the English church. When eventually the legateship did come, Wolsey was able to make much more of it than either de Boissy or Lang.[11]

In addition to the great volume of letters and Gigli's busy activity as intermediary, the lines of communication between de'Medici and Wolsey were supplemented by contact with such men of promising future in de'Medici's service as Gianmatteo Giberti, Geronimo Ghinucci and Friar Nicholas Schönberg. In a flurry of concern as protector, de'Medici even advised Wolsey of a French-supported plot for his personal overflow; but the mutual trust and cooperation affected was less than perfect in practice. As early as August 1514 Gigli was complaining that the protector had failed to give him sufficient support in a difficulty. De'Medici's responsibilities as legate to Bologna and to his native Florence required frequent and long absences. In 1519 in addition to being archbishop of Florence he assumed the whole responsibility for directing its civil government as well and spent more time there than in Rome. Even when he was in Rome, his very importance in the Curia exposed him to enormous counter-pressures, which restricted both his freedom and his inclination to give priority to England's interests. For all their supposed unity of action in foreign affairs, Wolsey and de'Medici failed in frankness at precisely the crucial moments, and the pope complained at the scarcity of letters from England. In 1520, when both England and the papacy were making approaches to the Emperor

[10] PRO 31/9/15, fol. 54 (Arch. Vat., Arch. Cons., Acta Cancel. 1, fol. 57).
[11] For example, in 1517 Archdeacon John Blythe of Coventry, acting in the name of Bishop Geoffry Blythe of Coventry and Lichfield, obtained letters from Henry VIII asking Cardinal de'Medici to intervene in their favour in a dispute with John Impingham, the Benedictine prior of Coventry. On 7 May 1517 de'Medici wrote to Wolsey: 'Paratus eram ei opem ferre quoad ius fasque pateretur, si opus fuisset, pro mea summa in Maiestatem suam devotione, necnon cura rerum suarum, sed intelligo fore, ut inter eos authoritate et egregia opera Dominatio vestra Reverendissima componatur, quod profecto laudabilissimum erit, mihique perquam gratum' (PRO, SP 1/15, fol. 116; *LP* II, 3213). See also *LP* II, 1519 and 2692.

Charles V, de'Medici complained to Geronimo Ghinucci, then in England, that both the emperor and the French king pretended to have England on his side and that Wolsey must reveal his true intentions.[12]

De'Medici and the Anglo-French struggle for Tournai

Even before his assumption of the English protectorship, Giulio de'Medici and the French had been in contact. He played a major role in negotiating the return of the de'Medici to power in Florence during the autumn of 1512 in the final months of Julius II's pontificate, and after the election of Leo X the diplomatic union of the Papal States and Florence encouraged both the French and the de'Medici to keep the avenues of understanding open. On 21 November 1513, following the death of Cardinal Guibé, Giulio de'Medici, already archbishop of Florence, was given the French bishopric of Albi, just when the French were hard pressed by the recent English successes in Flanders and the English had taken possession of Tournai. On 12 June 1514, during the Anglo-French peace negotiations so urgently encouraged by Leo X, de'Medici, protector of England since February, was also given the administration of the French see of Lavaur.[13] The peace itself, sealed by the marriage of Louis XII and Henry VIII's sister Mary, was celebrated in Rome on 3 September with a solemn mass at Santa Maria del Popolo, arranged by Cardinals Sanseverino and de'Medici, as the protectors of France and England, and offered by Bishop Gigli.[14]

The death of Louis XII on 1 January 1514 disturbed de'Medici's prospect of peaceful cooperation with both England and France. On 14 February he was given the far richer see of Narbonne in exchange for Albi; but Francis I's reconquest of Milan in Septem-

---

[12] *LP* I, 3197; *LP* II, 1928 and 3973; and *LP* III, 853.

[13] Eubel, *Hierarchia*, III, 113, 270 and 348. De'Medici's claims to Lavour were challenged by Simon de Beau Soleil.

[14] Paris de Grassi, who was personally consulted about the arrangements by Leo X two days before, and who attended, wrote: 'Papa dixit mihi quod duo cardinales, protectores regum Franciae et Angliae, volebant facere signa laetitiae propter pacem inter istos reges duos factam. . .Et factum est quod episcopus de Liliis, qui est orator Angliae, cantet missam, et quod duo protectores invitarent per suos scutiferos totam curiam, id est, cardinales et praelatos, et quod Papa det plenariam indulgentiam omni populo praesenti, quae publicaretur per tubicines in omni curia' (PRO 31/9/15, fol. 307, from Rome, Bib. Minerva, MS xx. iii. 3). See also *Ven. Cal.* II, 489; and *LP* I, 3236.

ber 1515 by the victory over the Swiss at Marignano placed the
Papal States and Florence at the mercy of the renewed Franco-
Venetian combination in northern Italy. Just several days before
Marignano, Wolsey had been specially created cardinal as a
pledge of the Anglo-papal understanding; on 14 December,
Adrien de Boissy, brother of the admiral of France, was specially
created cardinal at Bologna to mark the new understanding with
France into which circumstances had pressurised the pope.
Giulio de'Medici played an important part in that cordial confrontation of Leo X and Francis I in December at Bologna and
in the subsequent negotiations which resulted in the Concordat
of 1516. An indirect guarantee of the new order in Italy was to be
the Eternal Peace of Fribourg signed in the same year between
Francis I and the Swiss cantons, since it terminated their pivotal
role in opposing French control of Milan. The personification of
the Concordat was Giulio de'Medici himself; shortly after
Cardinal Sanseverino's death of 7 August that year, de'Medici
succeeded him as cardinal protector of France. This development
proved most inconvenient to England, for it was just then that
Wolsey was engaged in the long struggle to reap, through
diplomacy and with papal support, the fruits of the victories at
Flodden and in Flanders.

When Henry VIII made his solemn entry into Tournai on
25 September 1513, he came as conqueror to a great city which
since 1188 had been more or less subject only to the kings of
France. Reversing his style, Henry VIII had received its surrender
two days before as 'Roy de France et d'Angleterre' and had his
title on the coins struck similarly altered. The peace of 7 August
1514 between Louis XII and Henry VIII granted Tournai to the
English; but when Francis I succeeded to the throne, even that
pretence was dropped. Mary Tudor, queen of France for scarcely
two months, refusing to marry Francis I, secretly wed the duke of
Suffolk, whom she loved, and who had accompanied her to
France. Francis I, while negotiating the renewal of the peace to
gain time, began to lay his plans for the reoccupation of Tournai
as well as Milan.[15] To Wolsey, who had made his reputation with
Henry VIII in favouring and planning the Flanders campaign,

---

[15] A. Hocquet, 'Tournai et l'occupation anglaise, 1513–1519', *Annales de la
société historique et archéologique de Tournai*, new series, v (1900), 315–
316 and 327; for coins minted see pp. 466–9.

consolidation of English control of Tournai, which held ecclesiastical jurisdiction over all of Flanders, was even more a question
of personal prestige than for Henry VIII himself. Perhaps the real
intention all along was to barter Tournai away when it could
bring a diplomatically honourable return, but to allow French
intrigue among the pro-French populace of Tournai to wrest it
away under the very noses of the English garrison would have
meant loss of face for Wolsey both in England and abroad. For
the French to have papal support in doing it would have been
intolerable.[16]

The main struggle was ecclesiastical, and its circumstances
made Wolsey the very heart of it. On 8 June 1513, just before the
English occupation, Bishop Charles du Hautbois of Tournai had
resigned with a pension, in favour of Louis Guillard, then twenty-
two years old, in minor orders, and son of the second president of
the Parlement of Paris.[17] With the support of Cardinals Bainbridge
and Schiner of Switzerland in Rome, Margaret of Savoy, in whose
Burgundian territories much of the temporalities of the bishopric
lay, had tried to prevent it.[18] As a part of the English effort to
sever Tournai from France, the see was declared abandoned; and
Leo X obligingly gave administration of it to Wolsey, then bishop-
elect of Lincoln, until the 'return' of Guillard. It was even

[16] C. G. Cruickshank, *The English Occupation of Tournai, 1513–1519*
(Oxford, 1971), especially ch. VI, 'The battle of the bishops', pp. 143–87.
Cruickshank sees the struggle for possession chiefly as a physical one; he
does not remark de'Medici's particularly central position in the affair.

[17] Evidently Guillard's procurators had been in conference with the chapter
of Tournai during April 1513, and Guidon de Long took possession in
Guillard's name on 24 April 1513 (Inventaire des Archives de l'évêché de
Tournai, nos. 87–8). The documents themselves were destroyed with the
rest of the archive by World War II.

[18] Guillard was to be only administrator until he was twenty-seven (*LP* I,
2197). Adriano Castellesi was bitterly accused of remissness by Jacques
Annocque in a letter to Margaret of Savoy, 6 July 1513: 'Je croy quant
nostre Sire l'Empereur fera bien adverti de ce que esté fait en Consistoire
par le negligence dudit Cardinal Adrian je croy qu'il ne luy commettera
plus ces affaires, car s'il eut fait son devoir je croy que l'Evesché de
Tournay n'eust point esté maintenant en main des François car il eut bien
empesché la resignation qui est faite en faveur l'ung François, car nostre
Sainct Pere c'est declaré depuis, qu'il en eut servi l'Empereur s'il eut esté
requis. Pareillement Monsr. le Cardinal d'Albereth a esté restitué à la
coadjutorie et acces du l'Evesché de Cambray au dernier Consistoire
passé...Ledit Cardinaul Adriaen a esté accusé de ses propres confreres
qu'il avoit tres mal fait son devoir comme protecteur' (*Lettres du Roy
Louis XII*, IV, 170–1).

suggested, after the precedent of Calais, that Tournai be detached
from the province of Reims and placed in that of Canterbury. A
plot to surprise Tournai was organised by the father of the young
Bishop-elect Guillard, and it was claimed that Wolsey's promotion
to York had not included a dispensation to continue holding
Tournai as well. Leo X reconfirmed Wolsey in administration on
16 September 1514; but Wolsey's vicar general for Tournai,
Richard Sampson, still in his twenties, found himself in competi-
tion with a new vicar general appointed by Guillard, who had no
intention of abandoning his claim.[19] Sampson was continually
frustrated in his efforts to collect the revenues of the see, and
Wolsey was enraged at this loss of income as well as at the
English failure to control Tournai which it reflected.[20]

The new King, Francis I, assured Wolsey in February that
Wolsey should have the bishopric of Tournai 'and not only that,
but the best in France if ye would take it'; and a month later he
promised 'that he would make the other give it up to Wolsey in
all haste, and declared he would not stick with Wolsey for ten of
the best bishoprics in France'.[21] Yet one effect of the Franco-papal
rapprochement at Bologna after the battle of Marignano was
Leo X's restoration of Guillard as bishop-elect of Tournai at the
firm insistence of Francis I. The correspondence between England,
France, Tournai and Rome, already of amazing bulk, proliferated
beyond belief. While Sampson was busily engaged in enlisting
the support of Margaret of Savoy to impede Bishop-elect Guillard,
who arrived in person in August, from gaining possession of the
temporalities of the see, Gigli was desperately working to Rome
to have the restitution of the Frenchman quashed. The best Gigli
could get was a secret brief of restoration for Wolsey, which
under pain of excommunication was not to be shown until it was
clear that the pro-French party would not get the upper hand. In
Tournai contradictory proclamations and excommunications continued to multiply.[22]

[19] *LP* II, 824f.; *LP* I, 3004, 3284, 3331 and 3379; Rymer, *Foedera*, XIII, 584
   (*LP* II, 3140); and Arch. Vat., A. A. Arm. I–XVIII, no. 1901. See the
   competing letters to Margaret of Savoy from Henry VIII, 13 July 1514,
   and from Louis XII, 31 August 1514 (*LP* I, 3075 and 3217).

[20] LP I, 3287, 3296 and 3299; *LP* II, 262, 474 and 521.

[21] *LP* II, 176 and app. 7. Wolsey had earlier advised Sampson that the pope
   would not offend Wolsey for one thousand such as the elect (*LP* I, 3546).

[22] The bull empowering the restoration of Guillard from Paris was dated
   4 November 1516 (Inventaire de Archives de l'évêché de Tournai, nos.

Wolsey, too prudent to accuse Leo X and the cardinal protector of duplicity, had to be content with charging the English representatives in Rome with negligence. His wrath, nursed until January 1517, when it had become truly terrible, sought a ready second from the king and descended upon Bishop Gigli and Cardinal Castellesi. Gigli had already prevented Sampson from coming to Rome by objecting that it would be derogatory to his own mission; now the king threatened to dismiss him altogether unless he obtained a bull of revocation and showed more care in the future.[23] Castellesi, already under attack from the emperor for negligence in the matter of Tournai, had no desire to lose completely his seriously sagging reputation for serving England. The charges had the desired effect and sent Gigli, already frantically trying to satisfy Wolsey, scurrying to de'Medici and to Leo X in a paroxysm of pleading. Even Castellesi was stirred to action.

The pope and the cardinal protector had received milder letters of protest, but they were at last forced to accept responsibility for their action. On 5 February 1517 Leo X lamely protested to the king that, although Gigli had explained the king's displeasure more fully, there had really been no course open but to restore Guillard once peace had been made, and that he had not known the Elect would be pertinacious in refusing to swear allegiance or would endeavour to rouse the citizens of Tournai to rebellion. Therefore, Guillard's bulls of restoration were suspended for four months pending appeal. Cardinal de'Medici remonstrated to the king and Wolsey that despite his own effort there was actually little he could have done, since the pope had taken care of the matter personally, and defended Gigli's diligence.[24] The explanations given privately to Gigli made it clearer that the pope had acted out of weakness, considering the physically present pressure of the French more telling than the distant pressure from England. Leo X privately promised Gigli that he would restore the adminis-

89f.). Francis I had just previously sent three letters summoning the Archduke Philip to appear before the Parlement of Paris to answer for the conduct of his officials in resisting Guillard's efforts to gain control. See also PRO 31/9/1, fols. 241–2; *LP* II, 701, 2241f., 2289, 2695 and 2961.

[23] *LP* II, 2394 and 2871.

[24] *State Papers of Henry VIII*, VI, 52–3 (*LP* II, 2873); C. Guasti (ed.), 'I manoscritti Torrigiani donati all'Archivio di Stato di Firenze', *Archivio storico italiano*, 3rd series, XXVI (1877), 199; *LP* II, 2879f.

tration to Wolsey 'in amplissima forma', if the fortune of the French were to change, and sent Gigli to Cardinal Accolti to see what could be done to find a remedy 'per viam juris'.[25] Shortly afterwards de'Medici, feeling himself obliged to justify the situation to Wolsey yet again, claimed the pope had regarded justice first, and the honour and interest of the king and Wolsey only after it. Cardinal Castellesi insisted that, by the pope's own word, the restitution had been arranged at Bologna by the pope and Francis I without any witnesses. Finally, Leo X, wholly facing up to his chicanery, wrote to Wolsey on behalf of Castellesi on 21 February and of Gigli on 1 March, and frankly stated that there was no way that either could have known about the restitution.[26]

Meanwhile another related and aggravating issue was coming to a boil, the provision of a coadjutor abbot for the great monastery of St Martin's, Tournai. Abbot Jean du Bois, an absentee of poor repute, who had been living at the court of the queen of Denmark, had permitted the submission of the abbey to the English and the payment of the 3000 gold crowns which were its share of the 50,000 demanded by Henry VIII from Tournai. When the English began to consider the possibility of displacing him with an English partisan, however, he appeared in person some time during the winter of 1515–16 to rescue his position, and began to intrigue actively against the English. After the English gave proof of their determination to hold Tournai by beginning construction of a citadel, Abbot du Bois, acting on legal advice from professors at Louvain, sought to save himself by petitioning for the provision of some powerfully situated cardinal as coadjutor abbot. Leo X, grateful for the opportunity to benefice a kinsman, appointed his nephew, Luigi de Rossi, not quite yet a cardinal, and began the campaign to get him accepted. On 16 May 1516 the nomination of the coadjutor abbot, about which Wolsey had already been alerted, was communicated to Henry VIII by papal brief, with an accompanying letter in de Rossi's behalf from

---

[25] Gigli to Henry VIII, 8 February 1517 (Br. Mus., Vitell. B. III, fols. 112ff.; *LP* II, 2886). The letter, ten pages long and in English, is charged with emotion; Gigli, deeply hurt at the unfair charge of 'perfidie, infidelitie and negligens in this behalf', even offers to resign; 'his said holines made this revocation so craftly, secretly, and privatly, that it hath ben unpossibyll to come to my heryng'. To his friend Andrea Ammonio, the king's Latin secretary, he wrote that his grief at the king's accusations would shorten his life by ten years (*LP* II, 2890).

[26] *LP* II, 2947, 2961, 2965 and 2975.

Gigli, who had been advised from Flanders to stop it altogether. The same day Cardinal de'Medici, anticipating difficulty, wrote to Wolsey to plead for his help in getting the arrangement accepted by Henry VIII. Four days later the candidate himself made his appeal to the king and to Wolsey.[27]

Thus the struggle, in the main one between England and France for the grant of the bishopric, became in this respect one between England and the papacy over the right to nominate a coadjutor abbot. In November 1516 there was another full round of recommendations for the papal nominee. Leo X wrote to the king and Wolsey, stressing the fact that de Rossi was his kinsman; and de'Medici's language to Wolsey became markedly more urgent. Gigli, obviously under duress from the Curia, repeated his own earlier recommendations. In February 1517, in the very letter which the explosion of Wolsey's wrath over the bishopric had elicited, de'Medici pleaded again for his relative; but Gigli quietly suggested that the pope would not object to de Rossi's resignation of his claim, if Wolsey could see to some other suitable provision for him. Wolsey, not even deigning to reply directly to the pope's letters of nomination, was awaiting only the backing of the Habsburg interest to finish direct proceedings against Abbot du Bois himself. Leo X gently claimed the right to nominate to benefices in Tournai, where the Pragmatic Sanction usurped in France had never been in use; and du Bois himself claimed to be exempt from diocesan authority. De Rossi's hopes were reinforced when he was created cardinal on 6 July 1517. Although he carefully omitted mention of Tournai in offering his services to Henry VIII at the time, the College of Cardinals as a whole begged Wolsey on 10 April 1518 to use his influence with the king to secure the coadjutorship of the abbey for a brother cardinal. By the end of 1518 de Rossi did succeed in obtaining the benefice and with Wolsey's approval, but only after the larger issue of the bishopric had been settled to Wolsey's satisfaction.[28]

[27] LP I, 2294, 2594; LP II, 824f., 1434, 1479, 1766, 1823, 1895, 1897f., 1911f. and app. 16.
[28] LP II, 2243, 2502f., 2572, 2580, 2880, 2890, 3146, 3167, 3202, 3422, 3720, 4067, 4420 and app. 35. Leo X admitted that it was a 'delicate subject' and offered to guarantee that Rossi's proctor would be only someone satisfactory to Wolsey. According to Gigli's report, Leo X had offered to grant the restoration of administration of the bishopric to Wolsey, if Wolsey would relent from opposing Rossi's provision.

Although Wolsey's letter of January 1517 had convinced Leo X that something must be done to satisfy England, the strong feelings of the French made him stop short of a complete reversal of his position, and tension continued to mount. In February he had simply confused matters even more by saying in effect that neither Wolsey nor Guillard had the see. In March, while rumours were abroad that Francis I intended to besiege Tournai and reinstate Bishop-elect Guillard by force, Wolsey made a profuse but reserved apology to Gigli, who was given a special commission as ambassador for the king's subjects in Tournai. On 13 April the cardinal protector, then in Florence, remarked upon the arrival of a new English ambassador from the king and advised the king that the firmer cooperation with the papacy had bettered their hope of success.[29] The result was a flurry of new developments. On condition that after three warnings and forty days Guillard had still refused to do homage to Henry VIII, Leo X reinstated Wolsey to the administration of Tournai, pending the outcome of a suit to be decided by Cardinals de Grassi and Remolines. On 25 April Cardinal Accolti acknowledged the letters of the king and Wolsey, who had thanked him for his past services in the matter of Tournai; and on the same day de Grassi wrote assurances of future support. Wolsey, apparently dissatisfied even with this, treated the pope and de'Medici to three months of official silence as a spur to their cooperation.[30]

Contradictory reports of developments abounded, as the Curia sought to put off a final decision until a new Anglo-French peace involving Tournai would make such a painful decision unnecessary. On 1 June Tommaso Spinelli reported from Ghent that he had seen letters from Cardinal de'Medici to Nicholas Schönberg which said the French had required the pope to revoke Wolsey's administration of Tournai and to restore the French bishop, while Gigli reported from Rome that Wolsey's bull for the administration was ready, and that the pope would send it as soon as he was 'safe from the French shears'. In July Sampson sent word that Guillard, now consecrated, had been reconfirmed in possession by the pope, and accused Gigli of mismanagement of the business in Rome. Gigli himself, however, was still pressing

---

[29] *LP* II, 3033, 3041, 3045 and 3122; it is not clear who the ambassador mentioned was, but it was certainly not Sampson and probably not Richard Pace (*LP* II, 3121f. and 4020).　　[30] *LP* II, 3140, 3169ff. and 3352.

the pope to publish the bull in Wolsey's favour as late as November; and the pope was still begging for time.[31]

For Cardinal de'Medici, as protector both of England and of France, the year 1517 was obviously a particularly challenging one. In March he had withstood French pressure to resign the protectorship of England by explaining to the French, rather ingenuously in the circumstances, that his protectorship was limited solely to simple questions of benefices, that he had never meddled in other affairs of Henry VIII, great or small, and freely admitted that the protectorship of France was the more important one.[32] On 22 June de'Medici redressed the balance in letters to Henry VIII and Wolsey. He was pleased at the king's gratitude to him, 'optimo ac fido servitori', for his constancy even during the heat of the Roman summer in not having deserted the protection of England, although 'some' urged him to give it up altogether. As for the business of Tournai, now that he knew it was a question of ancient custom, he would be more zealous than ever in entreating the pope to satisfy the king's desire.[33] The French, however, still dissatisfied with de'Medici's divided loyalty, renewed the pressure. In a masterfully constructed argument, Cardinal de'Medici outlined for Francis I his reasons for continuing to hold both 'blessed' protectorships. If he gave up the

---

[31] *LP* II, 3331, 3352, 3438 and 3801.

[32] When de'Medici was named vice-chancellor in 1517 at the death of Sisto della Rovere Garo, Leo X sought as well to invest him with the abbey of Chiaravalle near Milan, which had been held by della Rovere. Objection was raised by Francis I, newly reestablished in control of Milan, because the right of nomination was his by virtue of the Concordat of 1516, and because de'Medici, already heavily beneficed by France, was acting as protector of England. Only after difficult negotiations extending from February to May was de'Medici allowed possession by grant of the royal *placet*. On 29 March 1517 de'Medici wrote to the bishop of Bayeux, 'Et sopratucto ci premono le parole che vi ha usato et Re et Madama di non si potere interamente fidare di noi, mentre che terremo la protectione di Inghilterra, con ciò sia che tale protectione solamente si extende in cose benefitiali semplici, né mai in altra faccenda di quel Re ci siamo intromessi né grande né piccola. Noi non vogliamo già renunptiarla, perché non preiudica a persona, et liberamente ci fu data da quel Re sanza la ricercassimo. Conosciamo che quella di Francia è maggiore cosa, et tamen per lo honore nostro, che lo stimiano più che lo utile, non habbiamo voluto lassare questa altra' (Guasti [ed.], 'I manoscritti Torrigiani', *Archivio storico italiano*, 3rd series, xx [1874], 382–3). There are other letters in the correspondence among those on pp. 370–95.

[33] De'Medici to Henry VIII and to Wolsey from Rome, 22 June 1517 (PRO, SP 1/15, fols. 182 and 184; *LP* II, 3389f.).

English one just to maintain the more useful French one, his trustworthiness would always remain suspect to the French, nor would honour permit him to be so utilitarian. He had been offered the protectorship of England without his asking for it, and when there was not yet any question of his becoming protector of France. He insisted that the two were not incompatible. There was no question of his freedom to render faithful service to Francis I, to whom he stood so much in obligation. About the hotly contested issue of Tournai he remained wonderfully silent.[34]

The struggle over Tournai was ended the next year with a treaty which formed part of the general peace negotiated in the treaty of London, 1518. Wolsey had carefully enhanced French offers to buy Tournai outright, by making vague approaches to Charles, prince of the Netherlands and king of Spain, who was interested in consolidating his Burgundian territories. Wolsey's personal reward was an annual pension for life of 12,000 Tours pounds to recompense him for surrender of his episcopal rights to Tournai, and for the revenues he had been prevented from collecting during his tenure. Although Francis I granted the patent for the pension on 31 July 1518, the proposed treaty for the restitution of Tournai to France was signed only on 4 October.[35] On 10 February 1519 the earl of Worcester released the populace of Tournai from their oath of allegiance to Henry VIII, and two days later Bishop Guillard made his long-delayed solemn entry into the city.[36] For all their efforts, neither Bishop Guillard nor Coadjutor-abbot Cardinal de Rossi long enjoyed their success. In 1521 Tournai came under the control of the Emperor Charles V; and Guillard, deposed yet again, eventually became bishop of securely French Chartres in 1525. Cardinal de Rossi died on 20 August 1519. Only Cardinal de'Medici, protector of England and of France, surmounted the changes. Within days of de Rossi's death, de'Medici added the abbey of St Martin, Tournai, to his already impressive collection of benefices.

[34] De'Medici to the papal nuncio in France, 29 September 1517 (Guasti [ed.], 'I manoscritti Torrigiani', *Archivio storico italiano*, 3rd series, xx [1874], 399–400).

[35] *LP* II, 4350 and 4670; there is a copy of the treaty, dated 2 October 1518, in Vienna, HHSA, England, Varia, Karton 1.

[36] A. Hocquet, 'Tournai et l'occupation anglaise, 1513–1519', *Annales de la société historique et archéologique de Tournai*, new series, v (1900), 332–334; a contemporary account of Guillard's entry is printed on pp. 463–4.

This long contest of Henry VIII and Wolsey with Francis I and Bishop-elect Guillard for control of the bishopric of Tournai was a kind of rehearsal for their later contest with Charles V in connexion with Henry VIII's effort to divorce the emperor's aunt. In the case of Tournai, de'Medici as protector had shown his willingness to be driven by the stronger force of the moment, while using circumstances to gain a personal advantage. The temporary restoration of Tournai to the French claimant was a direct result of the meeting between Francis I and Leo X at Bologna during the winter of 1515–16. It is small wonder that the two later meetings between Charles V and Clement VII, also at Bologna, while the marriage case was still undecided, raised apprehensions in the court of Henry VIII.

Scotland after Flodden and the cardinal protector of England

As the controversy over the bishopric of Tournai followed amid the diplomatic aftermath of the battle of Spurs and the Flanders campaign, a parallel controversy over the succession to the Scottish archbishopric of St Andrews followed from that of the battle of Flodden. Among the fallen of the more than decimated Scottish host at Flodden were the twenty-year-old Archbishop-elect Alexander Stewart and his father King James IV. It would be folly to try to discover or to impose any pattern upon the subsequent political development in Scotland, which even in more normal times rested uneasily on the verge of chaos. Both England and France sought to manipulate a regrouping of forces which would give the one or the other a kind of control. The initial advantage rested with Henry VIII, whose elder sister Margaret, then twenty-four, had been queen of Scotland since 1503, since her son, not yet two years old, had succeeded as James V. The French interest was represented by John Stewart, duke of Albany, first cousin of the late James IV; and also by Bishop Andrew Forman of Moray. Albany's father had been exiled to France as a rebel; and Albany himself was half French, married to a Frenchwoman, and spoke French as his native language. Bishop Forman, who had been presented to the modest benefice of Cottingham, Yorkshire, for his part in the marriage treaty which had made Margaret Tudor queen of Scotland, had been given the rich archbishopric of Bourges-en-Berry for his part in the renewed Franco-Scottish alliance which had led to the disaster of Flodden.[37] Whoever succeeded in filling St Andrews reckoned to have a telling advantage.

Perhaps anticipating the scramble of candidates and forces to emerge, Leo X took the unprecedented step of giving the administration of the primatial see of Scotland to his own nephew, the new Cardinal Innocenzo Cibò, then twenty-two, on 13 October 1513 within days after the arrival of the news in Rome that it was vacant.[38] If, other than mere venal nepotism, Leo X's motive had been to save the Scottish church from disorder, or to save it from English or French domination without offending either England or France, he totally misjudged the situation. Although there was utter disagreement among the Scots about who at the moment should have the privilege of nominating to benefices, there was a unanimity in protesting that it was not the pope.

Although the English had not followed up their victory with an invasion of Scotland, Henry VIII wrote to the pope from Tournai on 12 October, asking him to reduce all the bishoprics of Scotland to their pristine condition as suffragans of York, to restore the priory of Coldingham in Scotland to the bishopric of Durham, and to name no successors to the bishops fallen at Flodden until Henry had expressed his own wishes. The enlargement of the province of York was never seriously considered, although Cardinal Bainbridge, archbishop of York, was then resident in the Curia.[39] Coldingham, apparently with English acquiescence, eventually went to David Home, a Scot whose family had controlled it before.[40] But the question of nominating a candidate for St Andrews was less easily resolved.

On 13 November 1513 at a meeting in which the widowed

---

[37] *Cal. of Pat. Rolls, Henry VII*, II, 244; *LP* I, 2276f.

[38] Eubel, *Hierarchia*, III, 121; *LP* I, 2373; and *Ven. Cal.* II, 339.

[39] Although the Scots had steadfastly frustrated the English decision of 1072, supported by Rome, to make the Scottish sees effectively a part of the province of York, St Andrews was made an archbishopric only in 1472, and Glasgow in 1492. The entrenched tradition of parity among the Scottish bishops was aided and abetted by numerous subsequent exemptions of individual bishops from metropolitan jurisdiction. This lay behind the effort to strengthen central ecclesiastical control by granting special powers as legate *a latere* to the archbishop of St Andrews four years before Wolsey succeeded in obtaining them.

[40] *LP* I, 2355, 2443, 2552 and 3119; *LP* II, app. 11; *LP* III, 1642; R. Hannay and D. Hay (eds.), *The Letters of James V* (Edinburgh, 1954), pp. 12–13. The death of Alexander Stewart, who had held it, offered the occasion to raise the issue of its return to English control.

Queen Margaret figured prominently, it was determined to nominate to St Andrews the worthy Bishop William Elphinstone of Aberdeen; but Elphinstone was old, dispirited, in failing health, and disinclined to accept the promotion. On 22 June and again on 5 August 1514 Queen Margaret's party renewed to Rome the nomination of Elphinstone. The assistance of Cardinal Accolti, protector of Scotland, was sought; and Cardinal Cibò was tactfully asked to withdraw.[41] This solution was frustrated when Elphinstone died on 25 October; and Queen Margaret, acting in concert with her brother Henry VIII, was forced at that late date to find another candidate to pit against the two already contesting Cibò's provision.

The one rival candidate, John Hepburn, probably came nearest, after Elphinstone, to representing something like a genuine Scottish interest; but that interest was largely his own. As vicar general of St Andrews, he was already in control of the archdiocese. Although he had been elected archbishop by the chapter in 1513, he withdrew in favour of Elphinstone but then reasserted his claim after Elphinstone's death the next year. Hepburn's local power demonstrated when he forced the flight of Queen Margaret by besieging Edinburgh Castle in November 1514, but he lacked influence with the Roman Curia. However much difficulty might foment at home, there was never any real possibility of Cibò's yielding in his favour.[42]

The other rival was the experienced diplomat Bishop Andrew Forman himself, who was totally displeasing to the English but well known in Rome. The fervent opposition of Cardinal Bainbridge could not stop his provision to Bourges or even prevent a dispensation for him to continue to hold the English benefice of Cottingham.[43] Scarcely had Forman made his formal entry into Bourges in November when he began to arrange to exchange it with Cibò for St Andrews. On 11 April 1514 Leo X sought assent to the plan from Albany, who like Forman was still in France, but

---

[41] Hannay, *Letters of James V*, pp. 4, 6, 12 and 13; *LP* i, 2420, 3119, 3121f. and 3532.

[42] Dacre to the English council, 27 November 1514 (*LP* i, 3481).

[43] *LP* i, 2276f. During the sojourn of Perkin Warbeck in Scotland, Forman, not yet bishop of Moray, was in continual attendance upon him (Conway, *Henry VII's Relations with Scotland and Ireland*, p. 114). Forman had been in Italy during the campaigns of 1511, acting in cooperation with the French.

whom the pope already described as governor and viceroy of Scotland. Forman expanded his object to include the cardinalate and a legateship *a latere*, along with the retention of his numerous Scottish benefices, including the bishopric of Moray. In October Forman, armed with letters from Louis XII of France, arrived in Rome to canvass for himself among his many contacts in the Curia.[44]

Meanwhile Henry VIII's efforts to get tangible support from Rome for his Scottish policy had been gathering momentum. Although he counselled Henry VIII to exult less in victory and turn his mind to thoughts of peace, Leo X gave permission for the body of the fallen, excommunicated Scottish king to be buried in St Paul's, London. One of the first services of Cardinal de'Medici as protector had been to assist Bishop Gigli in obtaining an indulgence for the repair of Norham Castle, which had been destroyed by the Scots on their way to Flodden, although the indulgence was not fully in the form first requested.[45] When the Scots refused outright in spring 1514 to admit Cardinal Cibò's secretary, sent to take possession of St Andrews for Cibò, and admitted the papal nuncio Balthasar Stewart only under degrading conditions, Henry VIII posed before the Curia as defender of their honour. It was the report of Balthasar Stewart which would heavily influence papal action in resolving the dispute over St Andrews. Henry VIII, who must have seen his report, wrote a reply to it to Cardinal de'Medici; and when the nomination of Elphinstone had been renewed by Queen Margaret on 5 August 1514, an appeal was made to papal assurance offered through Stewart.[46] Although Cardinal Bainbridge had died in July, the fact that England's new protector was a cousin of both Leo X and Cardinal Cibò gave ground to hope that Cibò could be induced to yield in favour of a candidate satisfactory to Henry VIII. When Forman arrived in Rome, Bishop Gigli hurried to the pope to rehearse the reasons why the provision of Forman, the chief instigator of Flodden, would be particularly offensive to Henry VIII. The Anglo-French peace had just been sealed by the

[44] Hannay, *Letters of James V*, pp. 8, 28 and 30; *LP* I, 3051, 3358, 3407 and 3563.

[45] *LP* I, 2469, 2636 and 2642. For the bulls themselves, Arch. Vat., Reg. Vat. 1195, fols. 34–35ᵛ; and 1198, fols. 45ᵛ–47.

[46] Arch. Vat., A. A. Arm. I–XVIII, no. 4031 (*LP* I, 2884); and *LP* I, 2343, 2633, 2890, 3119 and 3390f.

marriage of Henry VIII's younger sister Mary with Louis XII; and the decaying but love-struck bridegroom promised, apparently insincerely, that neither Albany nor Forman would be sent to Scotland.[47] It was at this crucial juncture that Elphinstone had died.

In August 1514, just two months before, the widowed Queen Margaret had married the young earl of Angus; and it was his uncle, the poet Gavin Douglas, who was put forward as the candidate of the newly regrouped pro-English party. On 23 November the queen informed her brother of England that she had given St Andrews to Douglas and asked him to write to the pope in his favour. But it was already too late. Unaccountably, Henry VIII seems to have done this only on 28 January 1515, when he apparently knew that Forman had already been provided.[48] On 8 December 1514 Leo X announced to Queen Margaret and the Scottish council that Cibò's provision to St Andrews had been withdrawn as they wished, and that Andrew Forman had, by the advice of the cardinals, been named instead and had been given the powers of legate *a latere*. The pope expressed regret that their particular nomination had not reached him before Forman had been provided, but a third change would be quite beneath the dignity of the Apostolic See. In fact, the face-saving exchange between Forman and Cibò of Bourges and St Andrews had already been approved in Consistory on 13 November, apparently even before the news of Elphinstone's death had reached Rome.[49] Although Henry VIII had sought to deprive Forman of Cottingham, Yorkshire, by granting it on 28 June 1514 to the papal kinsman, Leonardo Spinelli, who had brought him the cap and sword of maintenance, Spinelli returned to Rome in the winter to find that Forman had been permitted to retain it as well.[50]

The still absent Forman had infuriated many in Scotland by

[47] *LP* i, 3407 and 3485.
[48] *LP* i, 3468; Theiner, *Monumenta*, p. 513 (Arch. Vat., A. A. Arm. i–xviii, no. 4034). The letter must be dated 1515, as in *LP* ii, 67, which merely raises difficulties, rather than in 1514, which is impossible.
[49] Hannay, *Letters of James V*, pp. 15–16; *LP* i, 3532; and Eubel, *Hierarchia*, iii, 121 and 149. Cibò resigned from Bourges with a pension on the same day in favour of Antoine Bouchier de Prat, osb, who was created cardinal on 1 April 1517.
[50] *LP* i, 3049 (xxx); *LP* ii, 7; and *Ven. Cal.* ii, 433 and 445. For the follow-up, see Chambers, *Cardinal Bainbridge*, pp. 75–6.

accumulating Scottish benefices for himself and his friends, and there was talk of declaring him a traitor. Henry VIII and Wolsey were thrown a sop when Cardinal de'Medici, who had failed of the main object, obtained satisfaction for their wish to have the bulls for the Norham Castle indulgence reissued in the terms requested.[51] The English party soon abandoned any plan of pressing for a resignation of Forman in favour of Douglas and adopted the more realistic strategy of working to obtain for Douglas the vacant but contested bishopric of Dunkeld on the one hand, and to curtail Forman's position as primate on the other. Even before Forman left Rome Leo X wrote to Queen Margaret on 19 February 1515, offering to provide Douglas to Dunkeld as she had requested on 17 January, but not until Forman had been admitted as archbishop and to his various benefices. The reaction of the queen's party was to accuse Forman of being a *parvenu* and rebel whom they were determined never to admit to Scotland; and Cardinal Accolti, protector of Scotland, was advised 'nam etsi Romae causa nostra vincatur, domi tamen victores stabimus'.[52] Gilbert Strachan was sent off to Rome to explain, and Douglas engaged Alexander Trumble as his personal procurator in Rome. While Queen Margaret was compounding with the Homes to thwart Forman's gaining control of his benefices, Cardinal de'Medici, protector of England, referred the provision of Gavin Douglas to Dunkeld on 25 May. There was a rumour that Forman had agreed to it even before he left for France in March, but Gigli wrote to Douglas to claim that the vote in Consistory was favourable because Gigli had given the pope to understand that Henry VIII was as interested as Margaret in his provision.[53]

The strongly worded requests from England to de'Medici to obtain the revocation of Forman's legatine commission carried a special weight in early 1515, since Wolsey's effort to obtain a similar legateship and even his bid for the cardinalate were then being stalled off by the pope and the cardinal protector. At first Leo X attempted to compel Forman to stop in England under safe conduct on his way to Scotland to make his peace with Henry VIII; and Bishop Fox of Winchester was given secret

[51] *LP* ii, 108ff.; Lunt, *Financial Relations of the Papacy with England*, ii, 504.
[52] Hannay, *Letters of James V*, pp. 17–19; *LP* ii, 28, 217f. and 220.
[53] Hannay, *Letters of James V*, p. 23; *LP* ii, 261, 574 and app. 11: and Eubel, *Hierarchia*, iii, 205.

power to recall Forman's legatine commission, if it should be used against the king's interest. In reply to the explosion this offer set off in England, Leo X manfully sent word in April to the nuncio in France to recall the commission before Forman departed for Scotland and advised Gigli to beg Wolsey to urge the king to send milder letters.[54] Forman left Paris, evidently without having come to a full understanding with Albany there, and arrived secretly in Bruges on 18 May, chastened and inclined to peace with England, but before notice of the revocation of his legatine commission could be served on him. Now that it was clear that Albany also had reservations about Forman's pretensions, Cardinal de'Medici and Gigli arranged a special surprise. Gavin Douglas, on being informed by Gigli on 6 June that he was the elect of Dunkeld, was also informed that he had been selected to intimate personally to Forman on the latter's arrival in Scotland that his legateship had been recalled, or, failing that, to fix notice of it on the church doors. The guardianship of the royal family, which was Forman's as archbishop of St Andrews both by tradition and by the will of James IV, was given by the pope to Douglas instead. Leo X swore that he would not have revoked the commission for any other prince for 100,000 ducats, and Gigli reported to the king on 12 June all that he obtained for Douglas, 'though [Henry] and Margaret had desired for him the archbishopric of St Andrews'. On 28 June 1515 Cardinal de'Medici acknowledged the thanks of both the king and Wolsey for having obtained the revocation of the legateship and declared himself most ready to do whatever else might be required in the case.[55]

What had been settled in Consistory was not yet settled in Scotland. When Forman arrived in Scotland in June 1515, Albany had already announced his own arrival as governor and viceroy by writing to Leo X and the cardinal protector of Scotland in protest against the attack on established royal privileges in nominating to benefices and asked to have all controversial provisions suspended until matters were sorted out. He claimed to have become governor with the assent of Queen Margaret and objected to Henry VIII's rumoured intention to assume the title protector of Scotland and to his use of de'Medici and Gigli in

[54] *LP* II, 210, 213, 365 and 374; Hannay, *Letters of James V*, p. 21; Arch. Vat., A. A. Arm. I–XVIII, no. 2836.
[55] Hannay, *Letters of James V*, pp. 23–4; *LP* II, 493, 574 and 634f.

getting benefices for those whom he favoured. Albany seized the bull revoking Forman's legateship before Douglas could serve it, and Douglas himself was imprisoned.[56] Forman was kept in virtual confinement until January 1516 at his monastery of Pittenweem, Fife, where he had landed, while John Hepburn, vicar general of St Andrews, impeded him from possessing his see. By May Forman had got himself accepted as archbishop of St Andrews and commendatory of Dunfermline, but at the price of shedding most of his other benefices, which he coolly claimed to have accumulated to keep them from falling into the hands of the Curia. In the new climate of understanding Forman arranged for Abbot Paniter, as king's secretary, and Alexander Home, as lord chamberlain, to be reconciled with Albany. In his turn Albany, doubtless provoking groans in the Curia, asked that Forman be created cardinal as both Julius II and Leo X had promised, and that his commission as legate *a latere* be left intact.[57] The pope sent regrets; and when on 16 September 1516 Gavin Douglas gained access to the temporalities of Dunkeld, a kind of equilibrium had, for the moment, been reached at last.[58]

The Anglo-Scottish struggle over the archbishopric of St Andrews had ended in a compromise, in part because of mistakes and misfortune on the part of Queen Margaret's party. Again, as in the case of Tournai, there was evidence that it was pressure, not logic, that got results in the Curia. But again it was clear that once an issue became involved in interests outside England and Ireland, Henry VIII's power to influence the Curia was severely limited. De'Medici's position was less delicate than in the conflict between England and France, but even the contrast between the parts he played in the two contests said much. Cardinal Accolti, the protector of Scotland, had shown himself flexible and ready to cooperate when offered sufficient inducement. All these things provided lessons for the future.

[56] Hannay, *Letters of James V*, pp. 25ff.; *LP* II, 561, 604 and 654.

[57] *LP* II, 771, 776, 1869 and 1938; Hannay, *Letters of James V*, pp. 28 and 30; J. Herkless and R. Hannay, *The Archbishops of St Andrews* (Edinburgh, 1909), II, 165–6.

[58] Leo X to Albany, 5 September 1516 (PRO 31/9/1, fols. 263–4); and Albany to Leo X, 28 September 1516 (Hannay, *Letters of James V*, p. 32; *LP* II, 2397).

4

THE EMERGENCE OF
LORENZO CAMPEGGIO, 1518–24

Campeggio's first legation in England

In 1518 began an association of Cardinal Wolsey and Cardinal Lorenzo Campeggio which would endure for the remainder of Wolsey's days as lord chancellor. In the tradition of his father and grandfather before him Lorenzo, the eldest of five sons, had followed the law through which his native Bologna had become famous.[1] After taking the doctorate *utriusque iuris* in the University, he lectured from 1499 to 1508 on the Roman law and from 1508 to 1511 on the canon law.[2] When his wife Francesca died in 1509 Lorenzo was in his mid-thirties and had three sons; his two daughters may have been illegitimate.[3] The support of the

---

[1] Carlo Sigonio, *De vita Laurentii Campegii Cardinalis liber* (Bologna, 1581), lists the brothers in order of birth as Lorenzo (1474–1539); Marcantonio (d. 1553), bishop of Grosseto; Antoniomaria (d. 1558); Tommaso (1483–1564), Lorenzo's successor as bishop of Feltre; and Bartolomeo (1488–1553). He omits mention of the three sisters, Aurelia, Caterina and Lucia. There is a short biography of Lorenzo in the introduction of G. Müller (ed.), *Legation Lorenzo Campeggios 1530–1532 und Nuntiatur Girolamo Aleanders 1531, Nuntiaturberichte aus Deutschland nebst ergänzenden Aktenstücken*, sup. vol. I (Tübingen, 1963), pp. xlvii–lxxiii.

[2] U. Dallari (ed.), *I rotuli dei lettori legisti e artisti dello studio bolognese dal 1384 al 1799* (Bologna, 1888–1924), I, 172, 177, 180, 184, 187, 190, 194, 197, 200, 203 and 206. The Giovanni Campeggio, also in the Faculty of Law, was possibly his father; the Tommaso Campeggio, who lectured on the canon law from 1512 to 1515, was probably his brother.

[3] Alessandro (1504–54), his father's successor as bishop of Bologna and later himself a cardinal; Rodolfo (1507–45), knighted by Henry VIII at Greenwich in 1529; Gianbattista (d. 1583), bishop of Mallorca. The two daughters Lodovica and Eleonora were supposed to have been born in 1510 and 1525 (Müller, *Legation Lorenzo Campeggios*, I, xlvii, follows E. Cardinal, *Cardinal Lorenzo Campeggio* [Boston, 1935], p. 17); but the genealogy prepared by Baldassare Carrati suggests that a daughter Laudomia was the eldest of Campeggio's five children and another daughter Leonora was the youngest (Bologna, Biblioteca Comunale, Misc. Genealogica MSS, Carteggi II. 58. a and B. 699). Since Sigonio stresses Lorenzo's brothers and makes no mention of his sisters, there is no room for insinuation in his omission of Lorenzo's two daughters.

Campeggi for Julius II during the war in Bologna disposed the pope to take Lorenzo and his kin into the papal service. In December 1510 Lorenzo, already a cleric and just named an auditor of the Rota, was given a papal dispensation for priestly ordination and moved to Rome the next year.[4] During the next seven years he was almost continuously absent from Rome as papal nuncio, first from 1511 to 1512 to the Emperor Maximilian, who gave him the bishopric of Feltre; then in 1512–13 to Massimiliano Maria Sforza, restored duke of Milan; and then again, now in the service of Leo X, to the emperor, at whose request he was created cardinal in 1517 while still in Germany.[5] When Campeggio arrived back in Rome in December, he was well established both in the service of the Emperor Maximilian, who named him cardinal protector of Germany, and in the friendship of Giulio de'Medici, several years his junior, cardinal protector of England and of France.

When Leo X named legates to the Empire, France, Spain and England in Consistory on 3 March 1518 to arrange a five years' truce among the powers and an expedition against the Turks, Campeggio was chosen for England.[6] His new association with England, which with those with Cardinal de'Medici and the Empire would dominate the rest of his life, was from the beginning the most difficult of the three. Even before the legates had taken their formal leave of Rome on 12 April, Wolsey was busy at work exploiting Campeggio's coming as a lever to force from the unwilling pope two major concessions long agitated, the granting of a parallel legatine commission to himself and the final deprivation of the unfortunate Cardinal Castellesi.

Although Leo X had during four years steadfastly refused to

---

[4] Bologna, AS, AMC, 2nd series, 55/292.

[5] Leo X to Lorenzo Campeggio, 1 July 1517, indicating that he was yielding 'presertim intercessione et precibus carissimi in Christo filii nostri Maximiliani electi Romanorum Imperatoris semper augusti, qui super hoc nobis per suas litteras instanter et sepe supplicavit' (Bologna, AS, AMC, 2nd series, 55/292). Leo X had renewed Campeggio's commission as nuncio to Duke Massimiliano on 14 March 1513, five days after his election as pope (*ibid.*). There are numerous other items from 1511–17 in this same carton as well as in cartons 26/263 and 56/293.

[6] PRO 31/10/15, fols. 53–4 (Arch. Vat., Arch. Cons., Acta Cancel. 1, fols. 49 and 52). Campeggio was also originally commissioned as legate to Scotland; Campeggio's three letters of introduction of 10 and 11 April 1518 from Leo X to King James V, to the Scottish council and to the archbishop of St Andrews are in Bologna, AS, AMC, 2nd series, 26/263.

create Wolsey legate *a latere* alone, the association of Wolsey with Campeggio as legate was rather easily won. Arguments suspiciously similar to those used in Wolsey's letter of 11 April 1518 to Gigli were used by Cardinal Lang of Germany in insisting that he be associated with Cardinal Cajetan, legate to the Empire. Wolsey and Lang were created legates in the same consistory on 17 May.[7] A papal courier bearing the bulls was rushed from Rome in pursuit of Campeggio, never a rapid voyager, who was then at Lyons. Overtaken on 28 May at La Palice in the Bourbonnais, Campeggio sent the news on to both the king and Wolsey and promised to bring the bulls to England. Although Wolsey professed beforehand to hold the legatine commission 'in small account' because it was to last only during Campeggio's stay, Gigli had already sent instructions from Rome, advising Wolsey that he was mentioned first in the commission as the senior cardinal of the two, and therefore only one cross, Wolsey's, was to be carried before them in procession. Gigli claimed the commission granted more than either Francis I could obtain for Cardinal de Boissy, or the Emperor Maximilian I for Cardinal Lang. Several months later Wolsey, the arranger of the peace, wrote to de'Medici in recommendation of Lang; when Cardinal Protector de'Medici replied that he was already favourably disposed toward Lang, he failed to remember to address Wolsey as legate.[8]

The deprivation of Cardinal Castellesi was largely motivated by the personal vindictiveness of Wolsey, supported by the king, and perhaps for this reason was the more difficult to obtain. By 1518 it was an issue of several years standing. In the late summer of 1514 an attempt had been made to deprive Castellesi of the lucrative office of apostolic collector for England, which he had held *in absentia* with royal approval for more than twenty years after his leaving England. The attempt came just as the long-standing feud between Gigli and Castellesi was intensified by Castellesi's serenely allowing Gigli to suffer under accusation of poisoning Cardinal Bainbridge. While Gigli from Rome accused Castellesi of infidelity to the king and of coldness toward the Anglo-French peace, Polydore Vergil, Castellesi's subcollector in England and his archdeacon of Wells, was reporting Wolsey's

---

[7] Martène and Durand, *Amplissima collectio*, III, cols. 1282–5 (*LP* II, 4073); PRO 31/9/15, fol. 54 (Arch. Vat., Arch. Cons., Acta Cancel. 1, fol. 57).
[8] PRO, SP 1/17, fol. 141 (*LP* II, 4507); *LP* II, 4176, 4179 and 4193f.

faults to his patron in Rome.[9] On 29 September 1514 Leo X assured the king, who had written three times about it, that the change was completed, and that Andrea Ammonio, the king's Latin secretary and nominee as Castellesi's replacement, was free to assume the office. Despite this and the fact that Cardinal de'Medici wrote how pleased the pope was at the choice of Ammonio as collector, Leo X, suspecting that Wolsey had engineered the dismissal for private reasons, asked Fox a month later to tell him the whole truth and even suggested to the king, apparently on the word of Castellesi and Polydore Vergil, that the king's letters had not been spontaneous, a charge emphatically denied by return courier. With characteristic unwisdom Castellesi blandly told the king that three letters had been forged in the king's name, while at the same time asking Wolsey for his favour for himself and Vergil. Recommendations of Castellesi to England from Cardinals Grimani and Riario, and even from the whole College of Cardinals, into which Wolsey was then importunately seeking promotion, sought to offset the firm combination of Wolsey, Gigli and Ammonio against him.[10]

A compromise solution left Castellesi with the collectorship and an annual pension, and replaced Vergil with Ammonio as subcollector in England. Cardinal de'Medici attempted to reconcile Gigli and Castellesi, and, like Leo X and Castellesi, strongly and repeatedly interceded to England on behalf of Vergil, whom Wolsey had imprisoned. In October 1515 Wolsey, who had just been created cardinal with suspiciously elaborate protestations of support from Castellesi, allowed to Castellesi that, while he personally was prepared to forgive Vergil as requested, it was otherwise with the king, whom he would do his best to appease. At Christmas Wolsey sent word to Castellesi that Vergil had been liberated, and that Castellesi's house and property had been restored. In May 1516 Castellesi was pleased to learn that Wolsey's attitude toward him was friendly, but the reconciliation was in no way real.[11]

When Cardinal de'Medici succeeded to the vice-chancellorship in March 1517, Castellesi was one of the five cardinals invited to a

[9] *LP* I, 3302, 3489, 3496 and 3511.
[10] *LP* I, 3311, 3322, 3401f., 3489, 3508ff., 3514ff. and 3562; *LP* II, 215.
[11] Arch. Vat., Reg. Vat. 1196, fols. 85–6; and *LP* II, 30, 215, 269, 272, 546f., 558, 574, 635, 865, 877, 893, 993, 1123, 1216 and 1228f.

dinner in celebration, yet within a few months de'Medici was being driven by Gigli and Wolsey to become, other than Castellesi himself, the chief instrument in Castellesi's destruction. Gigli and Ammonio had continued their personal attack, and Castellesi complained in unanswered letters to Wolsey of his maligners in England and in Rome. In the summer of 1517 Castellesi was somehow implicated in an alleged plot of Cardinals Sauli and Petrucci to poison Leo X. With characteristic ingenuousness he gave colour of truth to the suspicions by again fleeing in disguise to Venice as he had done ten years before. From there he appealed to Wolsey and the king to assist in procuring his pardon from the pope.[12] When news of Ammonio's death reached Rome at the end of August, Gigli got himself named to the collectorship, which his own uncle Giovanni had held before Castellesi, and sent Silvestro Dario off to England as his subcollector, in the happy presumption that these arrangements would be agreeable to the king. Gigli was instructed to assert the king's ownership of the Palazzo Inglese, which Castellesi had again abandoned; and Wolsey piously sought to end the scandal of Castellesi's 'desertion' of the bishopric of Bath and Wells by asking to take it over *in commendam* in addition to York. In fact Wolsey had already taken over the actual administration of the see from Bishop Fox, to whom Castellesi had originally committed it, and was raging at the support being offered Castellesi by the Emperor Maximilian and the Venetians.[13]

Although Leo X wanted to let Castellesi off with a fine, and Castellesi himself even offered to resign Bath and Wells to Wolsey in return for an annual pension of 3000 ducats and a guarantee to stop the deprivation proceedings, Wolsey, firmly supported by the king, relentlessly pressed on. Leo X promised on 15 February 1518 to proceed against Castellesi but insisted that it must be done consistently with the honour of the Holy See. Gigli sent assurance that he himself was working at it as if his life depended

---

[12] Brady, *Episcopal Succession*, ii, 259–60; *LP* ii, 1794, 2194, 3040, 3110, 3165, 3277, 3493 and 3545. In his letter of 31 March 1517 to Henry VIII, Castellesi again tried, more subtly this time, to appeal to the king against Wolsey (*LP* ii, 3085).

[13] Wolsey to Gigli, 27 February 1518 (Martène and Durand, *Amplissima collectio*, iii, cols. 1281–2; *LP* ii, 3973); *LP* ii, 3657, 3688f. and 3781. But see also *LP* ii, 3160 and 4068. The project was already formulated in August 1517 (*LP* ii, 3644).

on it. To both the king and Wolsey de'Medici calmly protested his willingness to fulfil the king's fervent desire but warned of delay, since all the forms of law must be strictly observed to avoid scandal. Richard Pace, secretary to the king and de'Medici's friend, urged the matter; and de'Medici, replying in Italian on 20 March, told Pace that as soon as the pope received the king's letters, signed by his own hand, he determined by all means to fulfil his promise within a very few days.[14]

Although in the end the emperor seems to have made no effort, and perhaps saw no reason, to offer Castellesi effective assistance, and even the motions of Francis I seemed a reflex action aimed chiefly at annoying England, the consistorial machinery turned slowly. Meanwhile Cardinal Campeggio had set out for England as legate *a latere* in the company of his brother Marcantonio and of Bishop Thomas Halsey, who in Rome had served first Cardinal Bainbridge and then Cardinal Castellesi, and who had finally overcome the hostility of Bishop Gigli in his search for a new patron and was now on his way to England to serve Wolsey. When Campeggio's party had reached Lyons, and Wolsey had just gained a share in the legatine commission, Gigli indicated from Rome, on 20 May, that nothing remained in the deprivation of Castellesi except for the pope to pronounce the decree in Consistory, but that despite his promises the pope hesitated out of fear of displeasing the cardinals. Gigli advised Wolsey not to allow Campeggio to cross the Channel or at least not to reach Canterbury until word came that the deprivation had actually taken place. On 29 June Campeggio, who had arrived at Calais only several days before, wrote to Wolsey that he had received through his secretary, whom he had sent ahead from Lyons, the order to stop at Calais. Campeggio protested that there was no just ground for it, since he had now three times informed the pope of the king's wish and was sure he would comply at once. The deprivation did in fact take place just six days later in the consistory of 5 July. Although the services of Cardinal Colonna had been enlisted as well, it was Cardinal de'Medici who sent off the news to the king on the very day.[15] On 23 July Campeggio crossed the Channel to Deal and arrived in London in great state

[14] *LP* II, 3828, 3953, 3961, 3963 and 4020; *Ven. Cal.* II, 971.
[15] *LP* II, 2895, 3876, 3973, 4176, 4179, 4240, 4271, 4289 and 4394f.; *LP* III, 982.

on the 29th. Wolsey was given the bishopric of Bath and Wells only in the consistory of 30 July, but his existing control of it included possession of the bishop of Bath's London house. It was in it that Campeggio was installed during the more than a year he remained in England.[16]

Although Wolsey had adequately demonstrated his power in Rome both in having been created co-legate with Campeggio, and in having succeeded in undoing Cardinal Castellesi, he made a tactless, almost childish effort to upstage and overawe Campeggio in England and seriously sought to assume the role of 'chief legate'. When the two were first formally received by the king at Greenwich on 5 August 1518, Wolsey claimed the right to walk on the king's right, and his gilt chair was somewhat larger than Campeggio's. At a mass in St Paul's, London, on 3 October, offered by Wolsey and designed to celebrate the Anglo-French marriage treaty, Wolsey's throne, the one nearer the altar, had six steps, while Campeggio's had only three. Although Wolsey maintained the standard Roman legal fiction of 'arriving' at court as papal legate when the two legates first presented their credentials and again in March 1519 when they were sent fresh commissions, he took relish in flaunting his importance as lord chancellor before Campeggio. Although he permitted Campeggio to offer the mass celebrated in state at Greenwich on 20 March 1519 at the signing of the treaty, Wolsey could, if occupied with affairs of state, refuse to receive Campeggio for as long as four days.[17]

Even the papally sponsored five years' truce, which Wolsey as papal legate was bound to arrange, was made into a triumph for Wolsey, lord chancellor of England, by his transforming it into the treaty of London. A papal commission of 20 August 1518 empowered Wolsey and Campeggio to treat with the Emperor Maximilian and with the kings of England, France and Spain, for a league defensive and offensive for five years against the Turks.[18]

---

[16] *Hist. MSS Commission, Tenth Report* (1885), IV, 448; *LP* II, 4333, 4348 and 4350; *Ven. Cal.* II, 1042, 1051ff. and 1355.

[17] *Ven. Cal.* II, 1053, 1088 and 1178; *LP* II, 4362; and *LP* III, 133, 217 and 235. Cardinal de Boissy, who was in Paris with three other French cardinals at the time, made no effort even to present himself as co-legate with Cardinal Bibiena, legate to France (*Ven. Cal.* II, 1128 and 1130; *LP* II, 4661).

[18] Rymer, *Foedera*, XIII, 621–2 (*LP* II, 4393) is from an original in the Public Record Office; Arch. Vat., Arm. XLIV, cod. 5, fols. 152^v and 194 (PRO 31/9/1, fols. 278–80). Campeggio's own copy of this bull and a letter of

With the Anglo-French treaties as a foundation, Wolsey built a general treaty of peace of which England, not the papacy, was the mainspring. Suspicious of Campeggio's friendship with Cardinal Bibiena, legate to France, Wolsey did not hesitate to negotiate behind Campeggio's back or simply to assume his role as lord chancellor and omit Campeggio from discussions altogether. Campeggio objected that the treaties made no real provision for the principal object, war against the Turks. Although de'Medici complained bitterly to Campeggio of Wolsey's expressed wish to take from the pope the role of peacemaker, the pope specially empowered Wolsey and Campeggio to confirm in his name what Wolsey had wrought in his own. To mollify the pope, Henry VIII agreed to sign the pope's five years' truce at the urging of Wolsey and Campeggio despite the appearance of seeming to derogate 'the perpetual alliance he had with all Christian princes'.[19] When Campeggio returned ten years later to spend a second year in England, he knew Wolsey and his methods very well indeed.

Both Henry VIII and Wolsey, however, while wishing to impress Campeggio, wished also to win his lasting friendship. There were lavish entertainments and pleasure trips on the Thames and at Hampton Court, Windsor and Greenwich. Wolsey wrote a long letter to Gigli which described the splendid reception for Campeggio in England, and which was intended to be circulated in Rome to redress the bad impression made by his having detained Campeggio at Calais; but Campeggio's own enthusiastic reports to Rome made such propaganda unnecessary. Although it was usual for the pope to pay the expenses of maintaining his legates abroad, the king assumed the cost. In addition to a promise of the bishopric of Salisbury whenever the aged Edmund Audley should die, Campeggio, who was by ordinary standards in the Curia one of the poorer cardinals, was given gifts of up to £7000 in money, much valuable plate, and the still in-

Leo X addressed to Wolsey and Campeggio, 21 September 1518, asking credence also for the letters of Giulio de'Medici and even if addressed to Campeggio alone (Bologna, AS, AMC, 2nd series, 55/292).
[19] Henry VIII to Leo X, 18 August and 8 December 1519 (Br. Mus., Add. MS 15387, fols. 79–81 and 82; Theiner, *Monumenta*, p. 523; *LP* iii, 427 and 538); de'Medici to Campeggio, 6 October 1518 (Guasti [ed.], 'I manoscritti Torrigiani', *Archivio storico italiano*, 3rd series, xxiv [1876], 21); and *LP* ii, 4545; *LP* iii, 96; and *Ven. Cal.* ii, 1075, 1090, 1106, 1131, 1136, 1178 and 1180.

complete Palazzo Inglese built by Cardinal Castellesi, with whose deprivation Campeggio was so familiar.[20] Although Campeggio's formal recall by Leo X was dated 4 June, he took his leave of the king at Greenwish only on 15 August, the feast of the Assumption, in a glow of mutual affection. The bounteous recommendations sent to Rome by Henry VIII and Wolsey were reciprocated by Campeggio's letters of thanks, written to them from Dover on 22 August before he crossed to Calais on the 24th.[21]

Both during his leisurely return trip of three months through Flanders and France, and upon his arrival at Rome, Campeggio proved true to his promise to be Henry VIII's 'observator et buccinator perpetuus'. He wrote, as he would until his return to England a second time as co-legate with Wolsey nine years later, regular letters to Wolsey.[22] At Bruges he took supper with Erasmus. At Brussels he sang the praises of Henry VIII and Wolsey to the Archduchess Margaret and Prince Ferdinand, and at Blois on 20 September did the same to Francis I. Although the French king offered him, with great delicacy, an annual pension of 8000 francs, Campeggio assured Wolsey he had refused it because of his commitment to England. He sent greetings from Cardinal Bibiena, who was still at Blois; but did not mention his pleasant encounter there with Sir Thomas Boleyn, father of Henry VIII's future queen. Although he arrived in Rome on 27 November, Campeggio made his official entry next day and was escorted from Santa Maria del Popolo to Consistory, where he was received by the smiling pope. Afterwards, in accordance with the custom, he was escorted by cardinals on horseback to his

---

[20] *Ven. Cal.* II, 1051, 1057, 1085, 1141, 1198, 1279 and 1355; *LP* II, 4565; *LP* III, 119, 137, 183, 298, 331, 437, 505, 614 and p. 1537. Arch. Vat., A. A. Arm. I–XVIII, no. 2863, describes Bishop Audley as of advanced age and failing health in 1518, but he could hardly have been eighty as Campeggio was told, even though he had been a bishop since 1480; he died only on 23 August 1524. There is an autograph letter of Campeggio to his brother Antoniomaria of 8 May 1519 from London, much of which is concerned with his household (Bologna, AS, AMC, 3rd series, 22/545).

[21] Henry VIII to Leo X, 18 August 1519 (Theiner, *Monumenta*, p. 532, from Arch. Vat., A. A. Arm. I–XVIII, no. 4038; *LP* III, 427); *LP* III, 284, 431 and 433f.; and *Ven. Cal.* II, 1279. Campeggio's return gifts to the king were a hand-made confessional book with special papal indulgences, and a horse (*LP* III, 533, 647, 675f., 1123 and 1159).

[22] PRO, SP 1/19, fol. 2 (*LP* III, 433); see Campeggio's letters from Calais, 26 August; from Blois, 21 September; from Lyons, 3 October; and from Rome, 4 December (*LP* III, 439, 452, 461 and 533).

new palazzo, which Gigli had prepared for his occupancy. Later Campeggio and Gigli returned for a private audience with the pope to discuss the treaties, the truce and Henry VIII's promise of the bishopric of Salisbury. Then Campeggio broached the subject of the extension of the legatine commission for Wolsey.[23]

During Campeggio's stay in England Wolsey had made careful preparation for his canonical separation from his Siamese twin in the legateship. He had obtained bulls permitting him and Campeggio to grant indulgences and to visit exempt monasteries, and evidently they did conduct such a sample visitation of Westminster Abbey on 31 December 1518. In the spring of 1519, while Leo X was seeking assurance that Wolsey intended to collect for the Turkish war as he had promised, Wolsey was piously angling for an extension and amplification of the legatine commission after Campeggio's departure 'not for the sake of extorting money, but to work some good in the Lord's vineyard and among the clergy'.[24] On 25 June 1519 Campeggio wrote to Wolsey, 'Angliae Primati ac Apostolicae Sedis Legato de Latere', from Windsor, where he was a captive of the king's voracious hospitality, promising to follow Wolsey's advice about the legateship. Before Campeggio's departure, apparently the best Wolsey could obtain was a temporary bull, dated 10 June, permitting him to visit exempt monasteries. Wolsey's agitated letters to Rome preceded Campeggio out of England. In September Leo X sent word urging Wolsey to continue in his holy work of reform but demurred at granting a permanent legatine commission, since he had granted the one for France for a year only. Wolsey could only summon a convocation of abbots and priors at Westminster to prove his proper intentions and await Campeggio's arrival in Rome to plead the sincerity of Wolsey's cause.

Although de'Medici kept himself informed of Wolsey's legatine plans, it was Campeggio, not de'Medici, who on this occasion convinced the pope that it would be proper and profitable to extend Wolsey's commission. Campeggio's first report of his efforts

---

23 Arch. Vat., Arch. Cons., Acta Cancel. 1, fols. 112ᵛ–113 (PRO 31/10/15, fol. 61); Paris de Grassi, *Diarium* (PRO 31/9/15, fols. 310–11, from Rome, Bib. Minerva, MS xx. iii. 3); *Ven. Cal.* ii, 1297; and *LP* iii, 533.

24 Wolsey to Gigli, 29 March 1519 (Martène and Durand, *Amplissima collectio*, iii, col. 1289; *LP* iii, 137); *Hist. MSS Commission, Fourth Report* (1874), p. 184; *LP* ii, 4343 and 4399; *LP* iii, 149 and 298.

on 4 December, addressed to Wolsey as primate and legate *de latere*, was followed by a promise on 19 December to send on to England the bulls for proroguing the commission and for granting indulgences. Wolsey, dissatisfied with an extension so limited in scope and of only three years duration, set Campeggio to obtaining wider powers for direct reform of the clergy. Among the subsequent bulls sent on by Campeggio was one of January 1521, which extended the legatine commission still two more years.[25] Thereafter, though Wolsey's haggling for extensions continued, it was never really in doubt that the commission would be continued. When taken singly, the powers eventually granted to Wolsey as legate were not impressive, but with the sufferance of both the king and the pope Wolsey was able to use it to justify his preponderant influence over the English church and his claims over the Irish church as well.[26] In Campeggio Wolsey could hope to have in the Curia an influential cardinal friend who would be more tractable than Bainbridge and more dependable than Castellesi. From the joint legateship of 1518–19 Wolsey had drawn every advantage his fertile mind could conceive.

The alliance of England and the papacy with Charles V
Although de'Medici remained protector of England until his election to the papacy in 1523, Campeggio returned from England as an active supporter of the English interest. If bulk of correspondence were a reliable measure of deeds accomplished as well as of zeal, Campeggio's record left the official protector virtually displaced.[27] Within a year of his return, Campeggio had been given the Signatura Justitiae and been named papal secretary. He

[25] *LP* III, 331, 406, 431, 444, 475, 510, 533, 557, 647, 649, 744, 811, 844f., 853, 980, 1123f., 1216 and 2771. On 20 January 1520 Henry VIII wrote to Leo X thanking him for having prolonged Wolsey's commission for three years, 'although he would have preferred it for an indefinite period' (Martène and Durand, *Amplissima collectio*, III, col. 1304; *LP* III, 600).

[26] Kelly, 'Canterbury jurisdiction', pp. 148–207, is particularly valuable for the discussion of Wolsey's exercise of legatine power in matters of dispensations and judicial appeals.

[27] In the just slightly less than four years between Campeggio's arrival in Rome from England and de'Medici's election as pope, there survive nine letters from de'Medici to Henry VIII, of which six are from Rome and three from Florence; and fifteen to Wolsey, of which four are from Rome and eleven from Florence. From Campeggio there are twelve letters to Henry VIII and sixty-five to Wolsey, all seventy-seven of which are from Rome.

was, however, the newest arrival into the inner circle of power among the curial cardinals, and so long as Leo X lived, his own influence was subordinated to and dependent on that of Cardinal de'Medici. Clearly, the relationship between Campeggio and Wolsey was franker and heartier than that between de'Medici and Wolsey, but Wolsey never lost sight of the basic fact that Campeggio personally had far less to offer and far more to gain from Wolsey than de'Medici had. Campeggio was useful for errands, but the great issues affecting papal policy were shaped by de'Medici's influence. When Wolsey and de'Medici finally reached a new meeting of minds in 1521, it was the richly over-beneficed de'Medici, not the needy Campeggio, who was given the vacant bishopric of Worcester.

The election of Charles V as emperor had radically altered the diplomatic equilibrium embodied in Wolsey's treaty of London almost before the negotiations for the treaty were complete. Although both de'Medici and Wolsey, along with Leo X and Henry VIII, had professed opposition to the election of Charles, they made neither common nor effective cause against it and were soon in the process of responding to the new emperor's diplomatic overtures. Wolsey's having turned the earlier negotiations of 1518–19 to his own private advantage made de'Medici suspicious of Wolsey's motives and chary of frank cooperation with him. The rumours of the planned meetings of Henry VIII with Charles V and with Francis I intensified his caution. In the spring of 1520 Charles V gave Wolsey a Spanish bishopric and pension; and de'Medici, protector of England and of France, entertained at Florence Juan Manuel, the imperial ambassador to Rome, who recommended to the youthful emperor that he nominate de'Medici protector of his realms as soon as possible.[28] Yet neither Wolsey for Henry VIII, nor de'Medici for Leo X, wished to commit himself to the other as favouring the cause of the emperor against France until the other had done so.

The diplomatic fencing lasted for well over a year. In the absence of the personal meeting with Wolsey which de'Medici wanted, Bishop Ghinucci in de'Medici's service was sent off to England as papal nuncio in May 1520, entrusted with the hopeless task of discovering Wolsey's intentions without actually revealing those of de'Medici. On the one hand, de'Medici complained to

[28] *LP* III, 603 and 709; and *Sp. Cal.* II, 279 (p. 302), 302 and 312.

Ghinucci that he could not learn Wolsey's meaning, and that both the emperor and the French king pretended to have England on his side, while on the other hand complaints were sent to Wolsey of Wolsey's statements to Ghinucci about de'Medici's many practices with the emperor. In July Archbishop Stephen Poncher of Sens asked Wolsey, who with Henry VIII had already written to the pope in his favour, to write also to Cardinal de'Medici. With utter tact de'Medici instructed Ghinucci to refuse Wolsey's kind request for a mandate and instruction for negotiating with the emperor in the pope's interest, because the pope and the emperor were already on friendly terms, and there was no need for a treaty 'unless something should emerge in the future to require it'.[29] In December de'Medici was apparently busy accepting guarantees of benefices from both the French and the emperor. By spring 1521, although Henry VIII was still posing as the friendly arbiter between Charles V and Francis I, de'Medici instructed Ghinucci that Henry VIII's neutrality would only encourage Francis I, who ought to be restrained as a recidivist disturber of the peace of Christendom. De'Medici's warm response to the king's and Wolsey's current enthusiasm for heresy hunting gave them the final clue required. He commended Wolsey's design of burning Lutheran books and even sent him one of Luther's latest, with the comment that not only the book but its author as well should be consigned to the flames. The wider legatine powers Wolsey requested for the purpose were declared unnecessary, but more important the king was urged to send an ambassador to the emperor to urge him *viva voce* to the suppression of Lutheranism. The road to joint cooperation of Henry VIII and Leo X with Charles V was now open.[30]

One victim of this diplomatic bout between de'Medici and Wolsey was Bishop Gigli. Unfairly attacked from England for remissness, first in supporting Wolsey's claims to Tournai, and then in bringing about the deprivation of Cardinal Castellesi, Gigli had hitherto received poor recompense for his years of industrious and unprincipled servility to Wolsey's interests in Rome. In 1520 Henry VIII and Wolsey at last went through the motions of supporting Gigli's effort of several years standing to

[29] PRO, SP 1/21, fol. 92 (*LP* iii, 1006); and *LP* iii, 792, 853, 897, 912 and 926.
[30] *Sp. Cal.* ii, 312, 314, 317, 319, 324, 337 and 344; *LP* iii, 1209f.

have himself created cardinal; but in serving Wolsey so well
Gigli had lost the very confidence of the pope and cardinal protector by which he had undone Bainbridge in 1514. In an instruction of May 1520 to Ghinucci, de'Medici requested Wolsey to
send a person of credit to the pope to inform him of England's
diplomatic intentions, and to put no confidence in Gigli, whom
the pope regarded as a faithless negotiator. Although the pope
was anxious to oblige the king, de'Medici explained, Gigli did not
possess the qualities requisite for so high a promotion as the
cardinalate; and the pope was determined against it. Ghinucci
was further instructed that the pope had hitherto dissembled his
intentions and might find it necessary to do so still. Therefore,
Wolsey was not to be startled if he should receive commendations
of Gigli from the pope. In the same private instruction to
Ghinucci, de'Medici made it clear that Ghinucci was also his
personal representative to Wolsey, but he dismissed England in
general as a nation of which he possessed no great knowledge,
and which he thought would not have required so much experience 'as France and other countries'.[31]

Some months later de'Medici reiterated these instructions to
Ghinucci. Wolsey was again urged to send a 'well informed
agent' and was to be advised that questions touching the prorogation of Wolsey's legacy would be best decided whenever this
agent arrived. The pope would rather not have received Wolsey's
latest letters in recommendation of Gigli's promotion to the
cardinalate. De'Medici complained of being constantly pestered
by Gigli, who must take the hint; otherwise the pope must tell
him the plain truth, since he was unwilling 'to incur this infamy'.
To Gigli's chagrin the official reason intimated in the Curia for
his failure to be created cardinal was his part in stripping
Castellesi of the same honour. When de'Medici finally could
thank Ghinucci for having got Wolsey to get the king to desist
from pushing Gigli's promotion, the diplomatic smokescreen was
about to be lifted by a new ambassador from England already en
route for Rome.[32]

[31] Br. Mus., Vitell. B. ɪv, fol. 87ʳ·ᵛ (*LP* ɪɪɪ, 853); the presence of the instruction among these state papers suggests that it had come into Wolsey's
hands. See also *LP* ɪɪ, 4348, 4395 and 4442; *LP* ɪɪɪ, 600, 651, 762 and 847;
for Wolsey's grudging permission for Gigli to visit his native Lucca, in a
letter of 1 August 1519 (*LP* ɪɪɪ, 406).

[32] Br. Mus., Vitell. B. ɪv, fols. 91ʳ–92ʳ (*LP* ɪɪɪ, 1080; *LP* ɪɪɪ, 994 and 1209).

Meanwhile Campeggio was also caught up in the uncertainties of the current diplomatic situation. His own position in 1520 was much different from that of de'Medici. If England had to choose between Charles V and Francis I, Campeggio personally had every reason to want England to join with the Empire. He was wise enough to discern that he dare not seem to wish to influence the opinion of either de'Medici or Wolsey and must wait on their eventual agreement. His regular reporting to Wolsey was as devoid of personal opinion as it was of real information. In December of 1519 he saw an agreement between the emperor and the pope as imminent; but according to his subsequent letters the negotiations, not yet concluded in the following March, were totally interrupted by the appointment and arrival of Juan Manuel as the new imperial ambassador to Rome. In December a year later he saw the diplomatic quiet as the silence in which coming disturbances are awaited. The object of a French messenger was studiously buried in mystery, while the pope was still being pressurised by the imperial ambassador to declare himself for Charles V. Just before Christmas intensely secret negotiations were conducted between the pope and the French with none except de'Medici present, who did not choose to confide in Campeggio. Campeggio thought that Leo X would do no more than urge the preservation of peace; and indeed a month later Leo X and de'Medici, still waiting for signs of a clear commitment from England, instructed Campeggio and Gigli to urge Henry VIII to make himself arbiter between Charles V and Francis I, so that the pope might follow his counsel. In general, Campeggio's letters gave great emphasis to the safe themes, first of universal peace and then that sturdy perennial one, the mounting of a crusade against the Turks.[33]

However cautiously, Campeggio had nevertheless undertaken a private diplomacy. In March 1519, while still in England, he used a letter to Charles in sympathy at the death of Maximilian I to beg him as Maximilian's heir for continued patronage in return for continued service.[34] Even before the nuncio Ghinucci set out from Rome on 30 April 1520 to look in on developments at the meeting of Henry VIII and Francis I and go on to England,

[33] *LP* III, 557, 649, 676, 744, 784, 790, 844, 858, 1054, 1089, 1101, 1123 and 1132. At Christmas-time 1520 Campeggio had not heard from England since January.   [34] Vienna, HHSA, Belgien, PA–101, fol. 366.

Campeggio, who had wished to go himself, sent off his own secretary, Floriano Montini, as a kind of personal ambassador to Henry VIII and Wolsey. Through Floriano, Wolsey and Campeggio began a kind of cooperative approach to the emperor, although the extent of Wolsey's cooperation was far from clear. Wolsey, who owed Campeggio a debt of gratitude for having arranged the prorogation of the legatine commission, was now called upon to support Campeggio's drive to have Charles V confirm him in the protectorship of Germany, which had been given him by Maximilian I after the final collapse of Castellesi's position in the Curia. Charles V had offered Wolsey a generous income from Spanish bishoprics, presumably to hedge any possible loss of Wolsey's French pension; and Campeggio undertook to obtain consistorial approval for it. Wolsey not only spoke personally to Charles V about the protectorship for Campeggio but also wrote Gerard de Pleine, lord de la Roche, from Calais, asking him to present Wolsey's enclosed petition on Campeggio's behalf. Charles V, already advised to name de'Medici protector, was slow to confirm Campeggio in the title; and in August the transfer of the protectorship was still under consideration. Campeggio, in thanking Wolsey for his previous efforts, asked him to intercede yet again. He further wished to be sent as papal legate to Charles V's coronation at Aachen in October and asked Wolsey also to suggest to Charles V that the pope be asked to send him. Although Campeggio was not sent to the imperial coronation, in the end he did retain the protectorship; and his two later legations in Germany were as famous as his two in England.[35] Wolsey would later have reason to regret his having helped Campeggio to cement this tie with Charles V.

In this context it is not surprising, then, that Campeggio should have been exemplary in his cooperation with the English ambassador in Rome, Bishop Gigli. Although Gigli was at first annoyed at Campeggio's serving as Wolsey's special messenger to

[35] *LP* III, 756, 784, 892, 921, 958 and 1016. Part of Floriano's mission may have been to arrange the loan of £1000 requested by Campeggio to repair and complete the palazzo which Henry VIII had given him (*LP* III, 646). See the letter of Juan Manuel to Charles V, 13 July 1521, in which he reported that de'Medici, who had pretended not to care about the emperor's favours, had accepted with greatest gratitude and 'with both hands' *the protectorship*, a Spanish bishopric, and a Spanish pension of 10,000 ducats (*Sp. Cal.* II, 346).

Leo X, there is no evidence that Campeggio had any part in the collapse of Gigli's influence with Leo X and de'Medici. One of his tasks in England had been to request the king and Wolsey to translate Gigli to a richer bishopric.[36] From the moment of his return to Rome in 1519 he seems to have cooperated honestly with Gigli in such endeavours as the extending of Wolsey's legatine commission and in a fruitless effort to obtain a jubilee indulgence for the 350th anniversary of the martyrdom of St Thomas of Canterbury. Both complained of Wolsey's remissness in answering their letters. Even Campeggio's support of Gigli's ill-starred campaign for the cardinalate seemed convincing. Campeggio's chronicle in letters to Wolsey of Gigli's final illness and demise might even be taken as evidence of personal friendship had not his purpose been to beg for Gigli's bishopric of Worcester.[37]

Gigli's death on 18 April 1521, like that of Bainbridge almost seven years before, marked a sharp shift in diplomatic policy by England along lines first drawn by the pope. In 1514 Gigli had undone Bainbridge by making himself the instrument of Wolsey and de'Medici in forwarding an Anglo-French treaty. Now Gigli was undone by the special ambassador so emphatically requested by de'Medici to discuss England's attitude toward Charles V. The ambassador commissioned was John Clerk, dean of the Chapel Royal, who as former secretary to Bainbridge in Rome could only arouse misgivings in Gigli. His hopes of the cardinalate shattered, it is hardly surprising that Gigli's final illness should have coincided with Clerk's approach toward Rome. On 5 March Clerk crossed from Dover to Calais. On 29 March Gigli assured Richard Pace, in an anxious postscript in his own hand, of his determination to seek a harmonious relationship with Clerk but begged Pace to write Clerk to urge him to reciprocate. When in early April Clerk arrived in Florence, where Cardinal de'Medici welcomed him, Gigli was already dying. There is no evidence to

---

[36] Leo X's formal letter to Campeggio, 26 August 1518, requesting him to approach the king and Wolsey about it (Bologna, AS, AMC, 2nd series, 55/292).

[37] *LP* III, 137, 533, 614, 647, 695, 720, 744f., 756, 791, 844ff. and 993; *Hist. MSS Commission, Fifth Report* (1876), p. 446; Lunt, *Financial Relations of the Papacy with England*, II, 513–20; see also the letters of John Grig of the English Hospice in Rome to Warham, whom he was serving as proctor (J. Brigstocke Sheppard [ed.], *Literae Cantuarienses, Rolls Series*, 85 [London, 1887–9], III, 340–7).

indicate clearly that Clerk by intention either slowed or hastened his arrival in Rome, but Gigli died on 18 April and was buried next day in the church of the English Hospice. On 20 April the new ambassador, apparently having just arrived, made his formal entry into Rome, accompanied by servants of both de'Medici and Campeggio.[38]

The progression of events during the following months was the direct result of the new understanding between de'Medici and Wolsey which Clerk's arrival in Rome was intended to implement. It was signalled by de'Medici's ecstatic, if vague autograph letter of 15 April from Florence, in reply to the autograph letter from Wolsey which evidently had been brought by Clerk. There is no way of knowing the extent to which Clerk exchanged confidences with his host at Florence. The menace of a pro-French revolt in Florence at the hands of the Soderini faction required de'Medici's constant presence there until he went in October to the papal army in Lombardy to assist at the expulsion of the French from Milan. It was Campeggio, de'Medici's staff in Rome, and Leo X himself with whom Clerk carried out English business; but de'Medici kept in contact with both Clerk in Rome and Ghinucci in London.[39] The measure of what England expected from de'Medici was indicated not only by his nomination to the late Bishop Gigli's see of Worcester on 21 May 1521,

---

[38] Gigli to Pace, 29 March 1521 (Br. Mus., Vitell. B. iv, fol. 84*; *LP* i, p. xx, which clarifies the misleading summary of *LP* iii, 1204); *LP* iii, 1189, 1222, 1228 and 1247. 'Die 19 Aprilis Reverendissimus Dominus Gilientis natione Lucanus et regis Angliae orator obiit. Magistri caeremoniarum interfuerunt in funeralibus. Sepultus in Hospitali Angliae. Die 20 Aprilis introitus novi oratoris Angliae' (PRO 31/9/62, fol. 16, from Rome, Chigi Library, L. ii. 22). On 11 May 1521 Leo X granted permission to the heirs of Silvestro Gigli to transfer the body from the Hospice church to a 'capella sita in Ecclesia Sancti Michaelis in foro Lucano' (PRO 31/9/1, fols. 289–91). It is not clear that the transfer was ever made, but there was provision for excommunication *latae sententiae* and a fine of 1000 ducats for the governors of the Hospice or anyone else impeding the transfer. There is an impressive tomb in St Michael's church, Lucca; and nothing remains of any monument in the church of the Venerable English College.

[39] Clerk to Wolsey, 9 July 1521, 'The Cardynall de Medicis kepith still Florence. [T]her is on heer: whom he wyllid me to reasort unto: when I had any thyng to do with hym for the kyngs matters. I have spokyn with this man in all matters att large and the Cardinall de Medicis shall have knowledge of your pleasure; in every poynt' (Br. Mus., Vitell. B. iv, fol. 132ᵛ; *LP* iii, 1402); *LP* iii, 1228, 1247, 1264f., 1325, 1333 and 1402.

but also by the granting of the collectorship for England, which Gigli had held, to Felice Trufino, one of de'Medici's secretaries. Both these facts were studiously noted by Charles V's ambassador in Rome.[40]

Upon or shortly after Henry VIII's announcement to Leo X that he was preparing a book against Luther, Clerk as instructed intimated to Leo X, de'Medici and Campeggio, among others, that the granting of a papal title to Henry VIII should be completed. From Bainbridge's earlier effort to get Henry VIII the French king's title of 'Christianissimus', Gigli had gone on actually to get approval for a title finally decided upon as 'Defensor Fidei'; but even this was irritating to Francis I, whose mighty presence in Italy led Leo X to shelve the project in the spring of 1516. On 10 and 14 June 1521 the question was discussed at length in Consistory and after numerous suggestions Leo X expressed himself in favour of 'Defensor Fidei'. Although Campeggio wrote on 27 June to seek Wolsey's opinion about a choice of title, de'Medici had already sent his own list on to England. As Wolsey was preparing to cross over to Bruges to negotiate with Charles V, Ghinucci wrote from London on 12 July to remind Wolsey before leaving, to have the king's book completed and sent to the pope, and to resolve with the king on one of the titles proposed by de'Medici.[41]

At Bruges Wolsey's policies meshed. On 25 August he drafted a long letter to Clerk with detailed instructions for presenting the king's book in Consistory and for having the bulls for the king's title prepared. After despatching the matters with Leo X, Clerk was to tell the pope in secrecy that Henry VIII had agreed to join the pope and the emperor against France as requested, but to gain time for preparation he was sending Wolsey to Calais in the guise of mediator between Charles V and Francis I. In a postscript in his own hand Wolsey thanked Clerk for expediting his bulls of legation with such ample faculties and asked him to thank Leo X and de'Medici. On the very same day Wolsey and the Archduchess Margaret signed articles for a treaty, the seventh

[40] Silvestro Dario continued to act as the collector's agent in England; Trufino received his faculties as collector the day after Gigli's death (Arch. Vat., A. A. Arm. I–XVIII, no. 4046); *Sp. Cal.* II, 340; *LP* III, 1876.
[41] PRO 31/10/15, fols. 68–70 (Arch. Vat., Arch. Cons., Acta Cancel. 1, fols. 168–9), and PRO 31/9/62, fols. 87–8; *LP* II, 887, 967, 1418, 1456 and 1928; *LP* III, 1297, 1332f., 1336, 1369 and 1411.

of which pledged the emperor and England to be protectors of the pope and of Cardinal de'Medici; the articles as a whole were subject to papal approval before ratification.[42]

In a sense it was a return to the holy alliance of the days of Julius II but much more grandly conceived. The liberty of the Holy See, and coincidentally of the de'Medici in Florence, was again at stake; and the culprit was still France. To it were added new elements of a reforming legate in England and his warrior-theologian king, battling against heresy at home and abroad. England had joined hands with pope and emperor to rescue a Christendom still threatened from without by the advance of the Turks but now threatened from within by the Lutheran revolt as well as the perennial treachery of the French. A righteous cause can support as well as merely disguise self-seeking. It would be unwise to dismiss either Wolsey or Henry VIII as insincere in their conception of righteousness. Wolsey the peace-maker of 1518 had now become Wolsey the saviour of Christendom.[43]

Even before Wolsey's design had been fully promulgated it was in need of adjustment. Of the carefully circulated advance copies of the king's *Defense of the Seven Sacraments*, one went to Campeggio, who professed himself overcome with joy at the 'aureus libellus' of the royal 'Lutheromastica'. The book was officially presented to the pope in private consistory on 2 October, but Clerk's request to present it again in public consistory was refused. On 11 October Leo X proposed in Consistory that Henry VIII be granted the title 'Defensor Fidei', and the issue of the

[42] *LP* III, 1325, 1468, 1508, 1510, 1522 and 1714. Campeggio, who like the rest did not know whether Wolsey intended to arbitrate between France and the Empire, or make an alliance with Charles V, wrote to Wolsey on 9 July asking him to arrange through Clerk for Campeggio to be sent to Calais as papal legate (PRO, SP 1/22, fol. 236; *LP* III, 1404 and 1400). Clerk also wrote to Wolsey on 9 July, mentioning that de'Medici could not leave Florence to go to Calais as legate, and that if one were sent it would most likely be Campeggio (*LP* III, 1402). In 1527 in instructions to Cardinal Farnese, who was being sent as legate *a latere* to Charles V, de'Medici, then Pope Clement VII, claimed personal credit for having won a disinclined Leo X over to the idea of an alliance with the Empire (*Sp. Cal.* III, ii, 280).

[43] R. B. Wernham, *Before the Armada, the Growth of English Foreign Policy, 1485–1588* (London, 1966), pp. 98ff., argues strongly that the Anglo-imperial alliance was chiefly the doing of Henry VIII, who wished to assure the English succession through the family marriage of his daughter Mary and his nephew, Charles V.

covering bull and brief were definitively approved on 25 October 1521.[44] On 15 September, or immediately after the draft of the treaty of Bruges and the copies of Henry's book would have arrived in Rome, Ghinucci was commissioned by Leo X to treat with England and the Empire for the suppression of Lutheranism. Wolsey, Ghinucci and the imperial envoys signed the preliminary treaty at Calais on 25 November, five days after the expulsion of the French from Milan; but it was not Leo X who ratified it. On the morning of 2 December Campeggio informed Clerk that Leo X had died the previous night.[45]

Cardinal de'Medici suddenly saw his own future in Florence and in Rome completely dependent on English and imperial support. The successful but unfinished war against the French in Italy had driven the French to join with Cardinals Colonna and Soderini in eager pursuit of de'Medici's ruin. On 24 December, two days before entering the conclave, de'Medici, apologising for not having written sooner, unfolded his vast grief to Henry VIII. Although fortune had substantially reduced his power to serve him, there had been no diminution of love or regard for Henry, whom he now proposed to serve as protector with renewed diligence. The title 'Christianae Fidei Defensoris', which Leo X had bestowed on Henry VIII, and for which he now sent the bull, was Henry's most durable monument and the last witness of Leo X's esteem for him.

In another grief-laden letter of the same day de'Medici informed Wolsey that he was sending on some papal letters to the king to which Leo X had intended to add something in his own hand had not death prevented him, and he expressed appreciation for Clerk's special efforts to console him. This could hardly have touched Wolsey to tears, since by Wolsey's own instruction of 24 August to Clerk Leo X was to prepare, in addition to the bull with the title, a brief of most cordial thanks to the king 'with

---

[44] PRO 31/10/15, fols. 72, 74 and 74–5 (Arch. Vat., Arch. Cons., Acta Cancel. 1, fols. 178ᵛ, 180ʳ and 181ᵛ); *LP* III, 1592, 1607, 1618, 1642, 1654ff., 1767 and 1802. Campeggio's congratulatory letter to the king, which Campeggio feared had been intercepted in Italy by the French, is missing.

[45] Clerk to Wolsey, 2 December 1521, 'This is to advyse your Grace. . .that this morning the Cardynall Campegius ded send me word that the Popes Holynes war departyd owt of thys present lyff, God rest his sowll' (Ellis, *Original Letters*, 3rd series, I, 280; *LP* III, 1825); and Campeggio to Wolsey, 26 November 1521 (*LP* III, 1809).

certain words to be inserted therein by the Pope's own hand'.[46]
Clerk had been further instructed then to obtain multiple copies
of a special papal bull of approbation to be sent out with specially
bound copies of Henry's book, which Wolsey had sent on to Rome
for forwarding to a select list of princes and universities. Although
before his death Leo X had assured Clerk that these were ready
save for some verses the pope was having written in the king's
honour, Clerk and de'Medici, who had them in his possession,
decided to delay sending them out until after the election against
the chance that de'Medici might be elected pope. During this
same interview Clerk showed de'Medici final copies of the Anglo-
imperial treaties.[47] Perhaps this had been what Leo X had been
waiting to see before expediting the bulls, which could readily
have been sent off in October. As it was, Leo X's unexpected
death made them anticlimactic. Neither de'Medici nor Wolsey,
supposedly also a candidate in the impending papal election, had
had proper time to prepare for the contest.

Pope Adrian VI: de'Medici in eclipse

The election of Charles V's viceroy in Spain and former tutor as
Adrian VI was made possible because Cardinal Colonna was able
to prevent the election of de'Medici. Facing that fact, de'Medici
eventually threw his support to the absentee Cardinal Adrian of
Tortosa, whose personal virtue and zeal for reform made him the
most generally acceptable among the imperialist cardinals.
Colonna's support assured his election. Both de'Medici and
Campeggio had created the impression that if de'Medici's own
candidacy were unsuccessful they would favour Wolsey, who had
already been assured the support of Charles V at Bruges whenever a vacancy should arise. Wolsey, knowing that only
de'Medici's support could win him election, professed support for
de'Medici. It is possible that Wolsey may really have considered
himself a serious candidate. However different in character from
Adrian of Utrecht he may have been, his position as an absentee
and an imperialist was not unlike that of the winner. However,
there is also a certain service to vanity and even policy in being

---

[46] PRO, SP 1/23, fol. 162^{r-v} (*LP* III, 1894); *LP* III, 1510 and 1893. Clerk
had tried to get possession of the bull on the day after Leo X's death, but
the cardinals would not give it to him (*LP* III, 1825).

[47] *LP* III. 1895 (p. 804) and 1960.

seriously considered for the papacy, even if there is no practical desire to be elected.[48]

Before the opening of the conclave John Clerk, while supporting Wolsey's candidacy, seems to have been more impressed with that of de'Medici. At de'Medici's request Clerk called upon Cardinal Colonna in an effort to plumb his opposition to de'Medici, and he consulted with Campeggio about it. Juan Manuel, the emperor's ambassador, openly asked Colonna to vote for de'Medici and promised him that Charles V would reward him; de'Medici in turn promised to support whomever Juan Manuel would designate, if his own candidacy failed. In the absence of any immediate instructions from Wolsey, Clerk did the best he could. Richard Pace, instructed to cooperate with Juan Manuel in pressing for Wolsey's election, while seeming to give priority to that of de'Medici, sought letters from Charles V at Ghent on 27 December and then hurried on toward Rome. Thomas Clerk, a servant of Pace's evidently sent out later from London, overtook Pace at Speyer and hurried on to Rome with letters from Wolsey and the king for de'Medici and Campeggio. On 9 January 1523, before Pace had even got to Florence, Campeggio sent the English ambassador John Clerk a cryptic note from the still closed conclave saying that a man 'nother known nor spoken of' had been elected. If the courier Clerk had instructed the ambassador Clerk to pursue the election of Wolsey, he gave scant indication of it afterwards to de'Medici. On 12 January de'Medici wrote thanks to the king and Wolsey for their letters as explained by John Clerk, from which he understood Richard Pace had been sent to Rome to secure de'Medici's election to the papacy.[49]

Although de'Medici and Campeggio had every reason after the election to play up their championing of Wolsey's candidacy in the conclave, they apparently did make at least some effort on his behalf. Stressing his not having received Wolsey's instructions until after the opening of the conclave, Campeggio noted his considerable consultation with Clerk beforehand and claimed to

[48] D. S. Chambers, 'Cardinal Wolsey and the papal tiara', *Bulletin of the Institute of Historical Research*, xxxviii (May 1965), 20–30, maintains that Wolsey was not so eager to be elected pope as A. F. Pollard, *Wolsey* (London, 1929), pp. 25, 121 and 164, asserts.

[49] *LP* iii, 1884, 1895, 1904ff., 1918, 1944, 1952, 1956f., 1981 and 1985; *Sp. Cal.* ii, 369f. On 31 December Pace arrived at Speyer (*LP* iii, 1918).

have acted in concert with de'Medici in the conclave to forward the interests of absent cardinals. Campeggio often proposed Wolsey's name; and Wolsey received some votes at every scrutiny, sometimes eight or nine. For those cardinals who objected to Wolsey's youth, Campeggio urged, without being able to satisfy them, that Wolsey was over fifty and nearly sixty years old; and he likewise defended Wolsey against those who objected that Wolsey would be too aloof as pope. Clerk, although crediting de'Medici and Schiner as well as Campeggio with answering objections to Wolsey raised in the conclave, repeated substantially the version of Campeggio, his probable source.[50] At Florence, Cardinal de'Medici personally gave Pace an even better report, claiming that he had voted for Wolsey in every scrutiny and had got seventeen or eighteen of his friends to vote for him. On his way from Florence to Rome Pace was fetched from his hotel in Siena to stay the night with the archbishop, Cardinal Giovanni Piccolomini, who credited de'Medici with having collected numerous votes for Wolsey, and claimed himself to have voted for Wolsey at de'Medici's request. On 28 January, the day after his arrival in Rome, Pace had already seen Campeggio, who volunteered praise for Clerk's diligence in furthering Wolsey's candidacy. Although Pace could visit Cardinals Schiner and Pucci only the day after he wrote, Schiner had already testified on Clerk's behalf.[51]

The enthusiasm for Wolsey voiced by de'Medici and so heartily seconded by Piccolomini had a ready explanation. The war in Italy against the French and their allies, interrupted by the papal election and the depleted papal treasury, was about to resume. Siena and Florence were being threatened with French encourage-ment by Francesco Maria della Rovere, duke of Urbino, whom Leo X had sought to replace with his own nephew, Lorenzo de'Medici. Cardinal de'Medici, and possibly Cardinal Piccolomini

---

[50] *LP* iii, 1945, 1952 and 1960. It had been agreed by the cardinals that no one under fifty years of age would be elected; according to the best estimates Wolsey was almost exactly fifty at this time, about the same age as Campeggio himself.

[51] *LP* iii, 1932, 1967, 1981, 1990, 1995 and 2024. Cardinal Giovanni Piccolomini was the nephew of Francesco Todeschini Piccolomini (Pius III), the first cardinal protector of England and his immediate successor as archbishop of Siena. Juan Manuel wrote to Charles V on 11 January 1522, crediting chiefly de'Medici but also della Valle and Campeggio with having obtained Adrian VI's election (*Sp. Cal.* ii, 376).

with him, left Rome quickly on 12 January by ship for Pisa, since the direct route by road was blocked. When de'Medici arrived in Florence on the night of 22 January, he immediately sent a secretary, Friar Nicholas Schönberg, to welcome Pace to Florence and request his presence the following morning. Although the duke had made friendly gestures toward Pace, whom he knew from the days when Pace was secretary to Cardinal Bainbridge, Pace had already put himself firmly on record by exhorting the turbulent elements in Florence to loyalty to Cardinal de'Medici, whose arrival they were awaiting.[52]

Without making any careful distinction between his position as ruler of Florence and that as the most influential curial cardinal, de'Medici sent off Gianmatteo Giberti to cement the alliance of the de'Medici with Henry VIII and Charles V. While de'Medici informed Pace in confidence of his stout rejection of impressive offers recently made by Francis I, Giberti showed Pace letters from Lyons saying that Francis I would shortly attempt to recover Milan. Both de'Medici and Pace issued Giberti with introductions to Wolsey from Florence, and Campeggio added his own from Rome.[53] Before Giberti's arrival in England de'Medici's need had stiffened. His secretary Felice Trufino, apostolic collector for England, had been captured at sea by the French, while he was on his way to Adrian VI in Spain in de'Medici's name; on 22 March de'Medici begged Wolsey's intercession to obtain his release from prison in Lyons. As French pressure on Milan was increasing, de'Medici despatched appeals to Charles V and Henry VIII with Richmond herald, who had come into Italy with Pace. When Giberti crossed over to England at the end of April, the emperor had already added his recommendation.[54] At the end of May the emperor himself would cross to England for the signing of the treaty of Windsor in June.

[52] *LP* III, 1980f. and 2114. The duke of Urbino, the nephew of Julius II, had been adopted as heir by Duke Guidobaldo of Urbino, Julius II's captain general, in 1504, the same year Henry VII had created Guidobaldo a knight of the Garter.

[53] De'Medici indicated that Giberti was coming on 'business that was to have been transacted with the late pope' (Br. Mus., Vitell. B. v, fol. 25°; *LP* III, 1985); *LP* III, 1981, 1986 and 2004.

[54] Charles V to Wolsey, 'le cardinal d'York, legat, primat et lieutenant general d'Angleterre', 12 April 1522 (*LP* III, 2171); *Sp. Cal.*, sup. 2 to vols. I–II, pp. 118, 129, 134 and 138; *LP* III, 2076, 2105, 2123, 2148, 2157, 2179, 2205f. and 2224.

Pope Adrian VI provided the major surprise. It was so thoroughly assumed that he would be an imperial puppet that Pace and Juan Manuel presumed even in January, and with no knowledge of the new pope or his opinions, to propose to Wolsey and Charles V that Adrian VI go to Rome by way of England, where he could meet with Charles V and Henry VIII, and then make his progress to Italy through the Empire, possibly in the company of the emperor.[55] Even before he presumed to call himself pope, Adrian wrote to Henry VIII from Vitoria on 2 February 1522 to ask him to join the emperor in preserving the peace and sent similar instructions to de Mesa, the imperial ambassador in London. Wolsey energetically proposed to the emperor the wisdom of having the Cardinal de'Medici at the pope's side 'to further your Majesty's affairs, and those of the King, and of the Church'.[56] Charles V agreed to take his advice, but the pope insisted on heading the Church himself. Bishop Ghinucci and Thomas Hannibal, sent to Spain from England to further the interest of de'Medici and Wolsey, won personal favour from the pope for themselves but little for the causes they represented. From Zaragoza the pope advised Wolsey that he desired peace, and that on reaching Rome he would send bulls, which Wolsey had wanted forthwith, renewing Wolsey's legateship for five years, and permitting him to hold St Albans abbey *in commendam*. Just when Charles V arrived in Spain from England at the end of July, the pope made his excuses for not seeing him and sailed for Rome.[57]

Cardinal de'Medici's first personal meeting with the man who was Adrian VI apprised him of what would surely follow. On 23 August 1522 the pope's ships put in at Leghorn, where de'Medici and four other Tuscan cardinals were on hand to welcome him. In place of praise for their strenuous efforts in the war against the French in Italy, they received from the pope a sharp rebuke for their worldly demeanour and the wearing of

---

[55] Juan Manuel to Charles V, 29 January 1522 (*Sp. Cal.* ii, 383); and Pace to Wolsey, 29 January 1522 (*LP* iii, 1996). Pace attributed the idea to Juan Manuel, who himself attributed it to Pace. There is a draft of a bull of 1522 from Adrian VI naming de'Medici his legate *a latere* for Italy in Vienna, HHSA, Rom, Varia.

[56] *Sp. Cal.* sup. 2 to vols. i–ii, pp. 134 and 138; *LP* iii, 2018.

[57] *LP* iii, 2138, 2202, 2242, 2279, 2298, 2313, 2521 and 2713; *Sp. Cal.* ii, 457.

arms. In Rome Adrian VI focused the real issue for de'Medici, who was protector of the Knights of St John, by asking him to arm two ships with a thousand men each and send them to the aid of Rhodes. De'Medici, 'the bulwark of Italy against the French' and scion of Leo X's brilliant humanistic worldliness, found what he held in esteem was contemned by the man he had made pope. Ghinucci, now bishop of Worcester and fast friend of Hannibal, was now more in favour with the pope than his patron de'Medici was. Hannibal remarked upon de'Medici's kindnesses to him and spoke of de'Medici's promise to assist in obtaining additions to Wolsey's legatine faculties, but in fact de'Medici's supremacy in the Curia was temporarily at an end. He left Rome on 13 October during an outbreak of the plague and retired in dismay to a troubled Florence.[58]

On the other hand, Campeggio seemed charged with new zeal. At the insistence of the other curial cardinals he had given up an impetuous plan to go to the pope in Spain and sat like them, idle amid the welter of rumours running loose in Rome. Like Cardinal Schiner, however, he made an initial good impression by sending on to Spain a plan of curial reform with his brother Tommaso.[59] With a view to maintaining his ties with Wolsey, Campeggio sent his chamberlain to him when John Clerk returned to England during the summer of 1522. The arrival of Hannibal in the pope's entourage gave Campeggio a double opportunity to assure his usefulness in the Curia. He received Hannibal and his household in his own palace, until Hannibal's own house should be ready. Campeggio was confirmed in the presidency of the Signatura Justitiae; and already on 8 September Hannibal was able to report that Campeggio was in great favour with the pope and zealous for the interests of Wolsey. Campeggio solicitously insisted to his guest that the provost of Wolsey's titular church of St Cecilia in Rome had improperly taken over some of its revenues for himself. Surprisingly Wolsey, who habitually caused others to expend so

[58] Hannibal to Wolsey, 12 September 1522, 'Also my Lorde de medicis hath shewyde me grette humanite in every thynge: the both [Campeggio and de'Medici] be yours to the best of theyr power' (Br. Mus., Vitell. B. v, fol. 95ʳ; *LP* III, 2539); *Sp. Cal.* II, 438; *Ven. Cal.* III, 545; *LP* III, 2423, 2713f., 2791 and 2891. The bulls confirming Wolsey's legacy and the briefs continuing it for five years were sent off to England by Hannibal in January 1523 with a Florentine in de'Medici's service; any amplification was refused by the pope (*LP* III, 2771).

[59] Müller, *Legation Lorenzo Campeggios*, I, liv.

much effort in obtaining reductions in consistorial taxes for his provision to benefices, apparently took no interest in this loss of personal income.[60] Campeggio was willing to support openly Wolsey's persistent effort to obtain increased legatine powers, but in the matter of foreign policy he deftly managed to seem to favour both the pope's policy of peace as well as Wolsey's and de'Medici's policy of war. His reputation as a good imperialist remained intact.[61]

During the winter of 1522–3 de'Medici remained withdrawn at Florence, while his dismay with Adrian VI ripened into chagrin. When Giberti had returned from his English mission at the end of summer, de'Medici expressed enthusiastic regret that the king's and Wolsey's kindness toward him was such that his own dedicated service in their behalf could never merit it. Evidently he meant their policy of war against France and the treaty guarantees to Medicean control of Florence. By January 1523 Cardinal de'Medici was so preoccupied with England's role as his protector in Florence that his own role as England's protector in the Curia was overshadowed. Still remarking the kindness of the king and Wolsey to Giberti, he sent off to England Gabrile Cesano, who collected en route the recommendations of the duke of Ferrara and the marquis of Mantua.[62] De'Medici's mortal enemy, Cardinal Soderini, was profiting from de'Medici's absence from Rome to cultivate the pope and to plot with Cardinal François de Clermont, leader of the French party in the Curia. Adrian VI attempted to compose the differences between Soderini and de'Medici as a basic step toward peace in the Curia and in Tuscany, but de'Medici saw his own place in Rome and in Florence as dependent on Soderini's destruction. So long as Adrian VI persisted in his policy of peace with France, de'Medici was deaf to the pope's requests that he come to Rome.[63]

Meanwhile in Rome Campeggio became in effect the cardinal protector of England. He seems to have avoided exalting himself at de'Medici's expense and willingly shared credit with de'Medici

[60] *LP* III, 1979, 2037, 2506, 2521, 2539 and 2771.
[61] Campeggio to Henry VIII, 26 December 1522, in which he intimated vaguely that if there were peace, it would be Henry's doing; but if there were war, it would be the work of Francis (PRO, SP 1/26, fol. 208; *LP* III, 2726); *LP* III, 2771; *Sp. Cal.* II, 395.
[62] *LP* III, 2504f., 2759f., 2779f. and 2789f.
[63] *LP* III, 2771, 2891 and 2903.

for the successful expedition of English business, even though de'Medici had resigned the bishopric of Worcester in favour of Ghinucci rather than of him. In the same letter in which Hannibal complained of de'Medici's continued absence from Rome, he praised Campeggio to Wolsey as 'a faithfull servant of the Kyngs highness and a sure friende of your grace' and declared himself 'moche bounde to hym and not only I but all that comyth oute of England'.[64] Yet there is little evidence that Wolsey showed Campeggio much gratitude. Even Adrian VI, who allowed Campeggio alone among the cardinals to live in the papal palace, gave him a pension of 500 ducats but no bishopric.[65]

De'Medici's triumphant arrival back in Rome on 23 April 1523 was a kind of promulgation of the triumph of his foreign policy formulated under Leo X. Among the more than 1000 horse who escorted him from Santa Maria del Popolo to his palace was Hannibal, rejoicing at the return to 'good favor' of 'a faythfull servant to the kyng'.[66] Proof of Cardinal Soderini's involvement in pro-French machinations for the invasion of Naples had been obtained at last in letters of Soderini's which had come into de'Medici's hands at the end of March. They were sent to the duke of Sessa, Charles V's new ambassador in Rome, who laid the evidence before the pope. This time de'Medici responded to the pope's summons to Rome. Soderini was received by the pope in the presence of de'Medici and Sessa and summarily imprisoned in the Castel Sant'Angelo to await trial. As auditor of the Chamber, Bishop Ghinucci was to be one of his examiners. De'Medici, in reporting to England the circumstances of his return, made a renewed pledge of service. The king and Wolsey happily complied with his request for letters to the pope urging instant justice for Soderini, 'the chief cause of the present disturbance in Italy'; but Adrian VI was not quite ready for full surrender to the importunities of de'Medici and his Anglo-imperial allies for a clean break with France.[67]

[64] Br. Mus., Vitell. B. v, fol. 167ʳ (*LP* III, 2891).
[65] *LP* III, 2891. Upon his arrival in Rome Adrian VI dislodged all the 'eight or nine' cardinal friends of Leo X from the papal palace with the exception of Cardinal Schiner, possibly because of his illness (*LP* III, 2611); Schiner died about a month later. On 11 June 1523 John Clerk remarked on the fact that Campeggio 'solus ex omnibus Cardinalibus habitat in Palacio' (*State Papers of Henry VIII*, VI, 125; *LP* III, 3093).
[66] Br. Mus., Vitell. B. v, fol. 180ʳ (*LP* III, 2999).
[67] This despite the optimism of Hannibal to Wolsey, 15 May 1523, 'I dar

To bring the pope round and to obtain for Wolsey the grant of his legatine powers for life, John Clerk, now bishop-elect of Bath and Wells, was again sent to Rome in late spring 1523 as resident ambassador.[68] Campeggio and de'Medici outdid themselves in repeating their cordial reception of Clerk during his first mission more than two years previous. Clerk wrote at great length to Wolsey on 11 June.

> My Lord Cardinal de Medicis and Campegius shewed me great humanitie. They, beying here in Rome, caused me to be honorabley receyved and feasted in Bononye [Bologna], and also in Florence, where I was lodged in the Cardinallis awn palais, and solemply feasted and accompanyed thorough oute the dominion of the Florentynes. It was please your Grace to cause theym to be remembered for their kyndenes, when occasion shal fal, that they may thinke it wel bestowed.[69]

The enthusiastic and familiar ease with which de'Medici and Campeggio took the initiative in cooperating with Clerk was scarcely surprising, for it meant a happy resumption of the state of affairs prevailing at the death of Leo X a year and a half before. Clerk's primary purpose was to present his commission to treat with Adrian VI with a view to an alliance with England, the Empire and, it was hoped, also Venice and Milan against France. Both de'Medici and Campeggio had strong personal reasons for wanting Clerk's mission to succeed. As before, Campeggio was the first off the mark in offering his service; but it was still de'Medici, now back in favour, who held the real power to serve.

nat woritte to your grace by every curar that departyth hens: for many of them goth by france and specialy they that marchaunt men despachythe. Shortly I shall despache a curar to your grace: for the Car[dinal] de Medicis: the duk of Cesa: and I be all most at a gude conclusion with the pope' (Br. Mus., Vitell. B. v, fol. 186ʳ; *LP* III, 3025); *Sp. Cal.* II, 544ff. and sup. 2 to vols. I–II, p. 235; *LP* III, 3000 and 3002.

68 Clerk to Wolsey, [2 December?] 1523, from Rome, 'I intend by the grace of God this next weke to be consecrated. I pray God send me grace to behave myself hensforth accordingly in this high and holy ordre, wherunto most unworthyly I have ben callyd only by your grace' (Br. Mus., Vitell. B. v, fol. 234ᵛ; *LP* III, 3594). Hannibal seemed not to have it clear that Clerk was to remain in Rome, nor did he himself wish to be recalled.

69 *State Papers of Henry VIII*, VI, 123 (*LP* III, 3093). In April 1521 de'Medici, then out of favour, had received Clerk in Florence. Bologna was Campeggio's native city, of which he was later made bishop; de'Medici had long served as papal legate to Bologna.

The very night of Clerk's arrival Campeggio called on him informally and inquired earnestly about the king and Wolsey. The next evening Clerk, at the invitation of Giberti, privately called on de'Medici, who made very much of him. De'Medici made evident the extent to which Florentine and imperialist hopes in Italy were indebted to Henry VIII and Wolsey 'and loked for no more favour of the Poope, then they wolde have done, if he had been borne within the citie of Paris'.[70]

There is just a shadow of suspicion that de'Medici's eagerness to assist in transacting this English business with the pope was partly grounded in the wish to know that Wolsey was being completely frank with him. Clerk delayed presenting the letters of the king and Wolsey to de'Medici until he had seen the pope; and de'Medici asked Clerk if he might accompany the ambassador on his first audience with the pope, 'saying that he thought it belongyng to his dutie because he was Protector, that he shulde so do, and the Courte shulde see therby that he had dependenciam a tanto principe, which thing shulde be greately to his estimacion and honour'.[71] Clerk assured de'Medici that he was under instructions to pursue de'Medici's honour as much as that of the king, and that there was nothing so secret that the king should not as soon disclose it to de'Medici as to any other mortal man living. Three days later Clerk and Hannibal on their way to the first papal audience called at de'Medici's palace to find him eagerly awaiting them. They rode on either side of him in a great procession to the Vatican, where they were met by Campeggio, who alone of all the cardinals lived there. 'And so thies two Cardinallis brought us through the Palais to the Popis presence, with all the honour they coude, wher the Popis Holynes sate at ease upon a lowe stole, underneth a cloth of astate.'[72] When Clerk and Hannibal returned next day for a second audience with the pope, de'Medici was again on hand, this time in company with the emperor's ambassador Sessa.

About two weeks later Bishop Clerk had still another audience with the pope. This time the discussion turned about Wolsey's desire for a lifetime grant of his legatine commission with enlarged faculties. Clerk stressed Wolsey's usefulness as a legate in England to gain support for action against the Turks and in his

[70] *State Papers of Henry VIII*, VI, 123.
[71] *Ibid.* VI, 124.   [72] *Ibid.* VI, 125; *LP* III, 3090.

loyal support of the pope's pleas for peace in western Europe. Although de'Medici was not present, Campeggio was and actively pressed Wolsey's suit. Out of deference for Campeggio Clerk tactfully suggested that if the pope were to send a legate to England, none could be more acceptable to the king and Wolsey than Campeggio, who indicated he should be happy to go 'no somoche to have don the popis holynes service: but also for his particuler dutie and bondage towards the kings higness and also your grace'.[73] After detailing Wolsey's dedication as legate to the service of the pope and thanking him for the previous confirmation of his legatine powers, Clerk raised the sensitive question of the enlarged powers and the grant for life. Cardinal Campeggio 'helpyd herin right well' and heartily seconded Clerk's praises of Wolsey; but after expressing gratitude for Wolsey's good will and commending his diligence, the pope turned the discussion to the problems with the Venetians. Immediately afterwards Clerk and Hannibal went to Ghinucci, the auditor of the Chamber, with the formula for the bull as Wolsey desired it. Ghinucci promised to do his best and gave encouragement; but in fact Adrian VI never complied with Wolsey's request.

The very detailed letters of Clerk and Hannibal provide evidence that the formal letters of the cardinal protectors to England imply more than they state about the extent and nature of their cooperation with the English ambassadors in the furthering of English business. From de'Medici's single letter of 10 June to the king, or from Campeggio's four, one to the king and three to Wolsey, it would be impossible to reconstruct what had actually occurred. Both de'Medici and Campeggio acknowledged the receipt of letters from England and the request made through Clerk for assistance. Campeggio did note that he and de'Medici had been present at Clerk's first audience with the pope; later he reported to Wolsey that he alone had gone with Clerk to urge Wolsey's personal business, but without specifying the nature or object of the discussion. It was the proper business of an ambassador to send home detailed reports. DeMedici and even an insistently regular correspondent like Campeggio were willing to leave that task to Clerk.[74]

Although Adrian VI at first gave the anti-French movement

---

[73] Br. Mus., Vitell. B. vi, fols. 98ʳ–99ᵛ (*LP* iv, 446, where the letter is mistakenly dated 1524); *LP* iii, 3090.   [74] *LP* iii, 3088f., 3091f. and 3125.

scant encouragement, the French insistence on the restoration of Milan as a condition to truce and their menace of still another invasion of Italy dissolved the pope's resistance to a partisan foreign policy. The Venetians had been under great pressure from England to settle their differences with the Empire. In January 1523 Richard Pace, who had been in Venice as English envoy since the preceding summer, was joined by Bishop Tommaso Campeggio, the cardinal's brother, sent as papal nuncio to work toward the same object.[75] As his letters to Wolsey reflect, Cardinal Campeggio followed these negotiations with the interest proper to the cardinal protector of Germany. The Venetians, who had earlier criticised de'Medici in England, came round. In early July when Henry VIII, Charles V and de'Medici were chafing to take the offensive against France, Adrian VI went only so far as to appeal to Henry VIII for assistance in the event of an attack upon Italy by the French. On Wednesday, 5 August, Adrian VI and the cardinals attended a solemn mass offered by Cardinal Colonna in Santa Maria Maggiore, at which was published the defensive treaty made two days before between the pope, the emperor, the king of England, the duke of Milan, the Venetians, the Florentines, the Sienese and the Luccans 'against the infidels, for the defense of christian religion, against invaders of Italy, leaving room for all princes wishing to join'.[76] After a year and a half as pope, Adrian VI had taken the purely imperialist position he was assumed already to have when elected. De'Medici once more wielded the dominance in the Curia by which he had made Adrian VI pope. The following month the pope was dead.

De'Medici in triumph

As Adrian VI lay dying he relied increasingly on Cardinals de'Medici and Pucci. He gave 'veray sildom audience except it were onys or twise [to the Cardinal] of Medicis and to the Emperours Orator, for the importance [of the] affayres of Lom-

---

[75] Adrian VI, 24 March 1523, and Clement VII, 29 January 1524, both to the doge of Venice (Bologna, AS, AMC, 2nd series, 26/263); *Sp. Cal.* II, 519, 537 and sup. 2 to vols. I–II, pp. 252 and 257; *Ven. Cal.* III, 615, 627, 697, 708, 714, 724 and 734.

[76] A. Mercati (ed.), 'Diarii di consistori del pontificato di Adriano VI', *Studi e testi*, CLVII (1951), 97; *Sp. Cal.* II, 562, 565 and 604; *Ven. Cal.* III, 464 and 468; *LP* III, 2847, 2865, 2904, 3022 and 3089.

bardy'.[77] On 14 September Clerk and Hannibal, already busy canvassing for Wolsey's election, reported that 'our hed cardynalls here in Rome of authorities creditt and estymacion been the Cardinalls Medicis, Sanctorum Quatuor [Pucci] and Campegius', who seemed to constitute a triumvirate in the College of Cardinals, and who were having many secret meetings together. The ambassadors seemed satisfied that all three of them and those who would follow their lead were friendly to Wolsey, and that their influence was sufficient to make either de'Medici himself, Farnese or Wolsey pope. A postscript announced that the pope had died that day.[78]

In many respects the conclave was simply a reenactment of the previous one. De'Medici was the leading candidate, again opposed by the French, whose protector he once was, and by Cardinal Colonna. Again any hope Wolsey might have of election depended on militant support from de'Medici and upon the impossibility of de'Medici's own election. To arouse passionate Roman patriotism Colonna 'noysed throughout Rome, that by the said Cardinall [de Medicis] meanys, at the last tyme, Cardinales eligerunt barbar[um Fle] mingum in Pontificem, et quod nunc idem conabatur eligere Ang[licum]'[79] Clerk, Pace and Hannibal, all three in Rome, knew even before receiving Wolsey's instructions of October what tactics to pursue, but both they and Wolsey would doubtless have been as startled had he been elected as they would have been offended had his candidacy been taken lightly.[80]

Between the conclaves of 1521 and 1523, there was one telling difference. This time de'Medici, realising it was now or never, and much wiser about the difficulty of remaining the power behind the papal throne, was determined never to yield however long the conclave might last. His party was adamantly loyal, and he was certain of the imperial support which Charles V only

[77] Clerk and Hannibal to Wolsey, 14 September 1523 (*State Papers of Henry VIII*, vi, 175; *LP* iii, 3331).

[78] *State Papers of Henry VIII*, vi, 176. Cardinal Farnese succeeded Clement VII in 1534 as Paul III.

[79] *State Papers of Henry VIII*, vi, 181–2 (*LP* iii, 3464); *LP* iii, 3463 and 3514; *Sp. Cal.* ii, 597.

[80] Wolsey had sent two sets of letters, one favouring de'Medici and one favouring himself, with instructions that the latter be used only if the circumstances made it clear that de'Medici could not be elected. Wolsey had presumed to compose those for the king and sent them to him only for approval and his signature (*LP* iii, 3377 and 3389).

wished to seem to be giving Wolsey's candidacy.[81] From 1 October in the face of mounting, and what would have been thought unbearable pressures from within and without the conclave, de'Medici remained fixed in his purpose but amenable nonetheless. Of his two arch enemies among the cardinals the first, Soderini, was released from prison and allowed to participate in the conclave. De'Medici even made a reconciliation with him, and he was eventually granted full pardon. The second arch enemy, Colonna, who had prevented de'Medici's election in 1521, eventually succumbed to the offer of the vice-chancellorship which would be vacated by de'Medici's election as pope and opposition collapsed. There is evidence that the rigours of the fifty-day-long conclave had softened de'Medici as well as the opposition, but nonetheless he emerged from it on 19 November as Pope Clement VII.[82]

The new pope was too prudent ever directly to refer in writing to his having served as cardinal protector of England, but he gave early assurances that he would not forget what had gone before. In addition to the supremely objective bull notifying Wolsey of de'Medici's election, there were personal letters from Giberti to Wolsey and to Henry VIII. Clerk, Pace and Hannibal followed their original report of the election of Wolsey's 'singuler and especial lover and fry[nde],...the Cardinall de medices', with an account of their later audience with him.[83]

> His Holyness shewed unto us veray lovyngly that the kings meritts have ben so great unto hym: that he now beyng pope wull never declyne from the same good mynde that he had towards his grace: beyng Cardinall de medicis: and that though he wer bounde to no liegge to yeve any ayde or succursse to

---

[81] Already in July 1523 Charles V had instructed his ambassador in Rome to support de'Medici's candidacy 'should. . .a new election become necessary'. On 2 October, unaware that the pope had died, indeed thinking his health improved, he renewed his instructions. Mendoza on 5 October wrote to the emperor that de'Medici's election was not probable (*Sp. Cal.* II, 562, 604f. and sup. 2 to vols. I–II, p. 295).

[82] *LP* III, 3547. Pompeo Colonna was made vice-chancellor on 11 January 1524 but deprived on 21 November 1526; he died on 3 August 1527. Soderini died in the Roman Curia on 17 May 1524 (Eubel, *Hierarchia*, III, 17). The occasion for Colonna's fall was his rebel opposition to Clement VII's abandoning of the pro-imperial policy.

[83] *State Papers of Henry VIII*, VI, 195 (*LP* III, 3592); *LP* III, 3549, 3560 and 3562.

his highnes yet he wolde entre som newe liegge and bynde hymself so to do, remembrying how lovingly his highnes toke hyme to his protection being in minoribus.[84]

They held out high hopes to Wolsey for the confirmation and broadening of his legatine powers. Clerk was confident that he would be able to write good tidings to Wolsey by the next.[85]

Immediately upon receiving the first news of de'Medici's election, Wolsey wrote it on 6 December from Westminster to the king, claiming that in the end it had been a choice only between him and de'Medici. He remarked upon Clement as the king's 'perfect and faithful friend', whose election was in large part due to Henry. Wolsey professed himself more joyous than if he had himself been elected.[86] Indeed Wolsey may have been more satisfied at having his king thus impressed and the pope beholden than at being pope himself. Three days later Charles V's ambassador in London, Louis de Praet, made an identical interpretation of Wolsey's reaction as one both of personal satisfaction and of triumph for the Anglo-imperial alliance.[87]

The official letters of congratulation to Clement VII from Henry VIII and Wolsey, written just before Christmas, reflected a special exuberance.[88] Again Wolsey claimed to be more overjoyed than if he had been elected himself and gave Clerk, Pace and Hannibal detailed instructions for presenting them. The king's letter and their words of commendation from the king were to be carefully separated from the presentation of Wolsey's own letter and their words on his behalf.

After the redyng whereof, ye shal with chereful and gladd countenance shewe and declare unto His Holynes at length, what rejoise comforte and gladnes it is bothe to the Kinges Highnes and me to perceyve and understonde, that oons in our lif it hathe pleased Almyghtty God of his infynite goodnes to provyde and send suche a pastour hed and governour unto his

---

84 Letter of 2 December 1523 (Br. Mus., Vitell. B. v, fol. 234ᵛ; *LP* III, 3594).
85 Clerk to Wolsey, also on 2 December 1523 (Br. Mus., Vitell. B. v, fol. 234ᵛ; *LP* III, 3594).
86 The full text is in G. Burnet, *History of the Reformation of the Church of England*, rev. N. Pocock (Oxford, 1865), VI, 15–16 (*LP* III, 3609).
87 *Sp. Cal.* II, 610ff. and 619, and sup. 2 to vols. I–II, p. 293.
88 *LP* III, 3655 and 3658; the original of Henry VIII's letter of 20 December 1523 is in Arch. Vat., A. A. Arm. I–XVIII, no. 2383.

Churche, as His Grace and I have longe and inwardely desired.[89]

Almost like a voice out of the past came congratulations from Bishop Fox at Winchester as well.[90] With a cardinal protector of more than nine years standing just elected pope, and Cardinal Campeggio in high favour in the Curia and thoroughly prepared and eager after an association of five and a half years to succeed to the English protectorship, England seemed in this respect never before to have had it so good.

The election of Giulio de'Medici as Pope Clement VII promised a golden era in Anglo-papal relations. Henry VIII, awarded the first Golden Rose of the new pontificate and confirmed in his title of Defensor Fidei, could safely regard himself as holding first place among the rulers of Europe in the pope's affection. Wolsey was at last commissioned as papal legate for life.[91] The very name chosen by the new pope was an oblique assertion of his Anglo-imperial views. Had he wished to curry the favour of the French, it is unlikely that he would have raised a direct challenge to the claims of the Avignon line of popes of the Great Schism by styling himself Clement VII.[92] Those close to de'Medici as cardinal, Friar Nicholas Schönberg and Gianmatteo Giberti, were now his chief councillors as pope and long cultivated as friends both by England and by the emperor. In addition England possessed a special bond with the pope through Bishop Geronimo Ghinucci

[89] *State Papers of Henry VIII*, vi, 221–2 (*LP* iii, 3659).

[90] Richard Fox to Clement VII from Winchester, 22 April 1524, 'Sed ne diutius meis ineptis a gravioribus negotiis vestram Sanctitatem remover, commendo me totum tum omni subjectione, obedientia et reverentia vestro imperio, regimini et protectione ei in omnibus pariturus semper; commendo et vestrae Sanctitati meum Collegiolum quod in Academia Oxoniensi ad Dei honorem et bonarum literarum utruiusque linguae incrementum e solo erexi ac pro opibus, quas mihi Deus commiserit, unde vivant condonavi, dotavi et locupletavi' (Arch. Vat., A. A. Arm. i–xviii, no. 6521, fol. 50; modern copy in Cambridge Univ. Lib., Add. MS 4883, fol. 94).

[91] *LP* iv, 45, 148, 723 and 758; the Golden Rose was brought by Hannibal, who was recalled from Rome and left on 3 June (*LP* iv, 23 and 408).

[92] Rodrigo Borgia in taking the name of Alexander VI (1492–1503) had implied suspended judgment on the claims of the Pisan pope Alexander V (1409–10). Giulio de'Medici's challenge to the claims of Robert of Geneva (Clement VII, 1378–94) as a genuine pope was the first such. The name of the other pope of the Avignon line, Benedict XIII, was not so challenged until 1724; the other of the Pisan line, John XXIII, was challenged only in 1958.

of Worcester. But above all it was Cardinal Lorenzo Campeggio whose long attachments to the de'Medici as well as to the Empire and England made him a kind of embodiment of their common policy. He was not only one of the cardinals closest to Clement VII, but was cardinal protector of Germany and would soon be cardinal protector of England as well.[93]

Campeggio, protector at last

Now assured of an even greater importance in the Curia, Campeggio allowed his subservience to Wolsey to take a somewhat loftier tone. Although in 1522 Wolsey had acknowledged neither his efforts on behalf of Wolsey's candidacy nor his accounts of the conclave itself, the persistent Campeggio sent him a hurried note on 19 November 1523 even before leaving the conclave. He decided, however, against the promised fuller account of this latest conclave and suggested instead that Wolsey might obtain the details from Campeggio's factor in England, Giacomo, to whom he had directed his secretary to write more fully. Campeggio exuberantly presumed even to congratulate Henry VIII on de'Medici's election and merely noted to the king in passing that, had that not been possible, they would have concentrated on electing Wolsey. With a strained pun Campeggio remarked to Wolsey that, because both he and Wolsey now had a more clement pope and devoted friend, Campeggio could make more vigorous suit to him for Wolsey's affairs than was previously possible. Of Wolsey's own candidacy he made no mention whatever.[94]

The evidences of Campeggio's special relationship with Clement VII quickly became clear. Not only was he confirmed in the Signatura Justitiae but was made bishop of his native Bologna when Cardinal Achilles de Grassi conveniently died on 22 November. Although originally named to the pope's special committee on the Turks rather than that on Luther, it was decided in Consistory on 9 January 1524 to send Campeggio as papal legate to the Imperial Diet at Nuremberg to treat with the rise of Lutheranism.[95] Campeggio, perennially eager to serve as a papal

---

[93] Lannoy to Charles V, 20 December 1523, 'Vous avez le Cardinal de la Val et Campegere qui vous sont bons serviteurs' (Brussels, Archives National, Papiers d'Etat et de l'Audience, no. 75, fol. 201ᵛ).

[94] PRO, SP 1/29, fol. 87 (*LP* III, 3588); *LP* III, 2210 and 3587.

[95] Many letters and documents relating to the legatine mission of 1524 to

legate, accepted this difficult assignment with enthusiasm and as a mark of favour.[96] The laconic report of his nomination made to England by the English ambassadors gave little indication of a major difficulty it would raise. Henry VIII and Wolsey were currently zealous in support of the emperor's efforts against the spread of Lutheranism, but they had little desire to engage a protector who would begin his career with a long absence from Rome. Should Clement VII create Gianmatteo Giberti or even Geronimo Ghinucci cardinal, a logical expectation, either might be preferable as a cardinal protector who would be both present and not already committed to any other nation.[97]

One purpose of the pope's and Campeggio's writing to England was surely to muster English support for Campeggio's mission; but another, however discreetly broached, was to explain away any objections to Campeggio's absence in Germany. Clement VII advised Henry VIII that Campeggio was instructed to make common cause with the English envoys at Nuremberg. The pope, acting at Campeggio's request, assured both the king and Wolsey that English interests at Rome would not suffer and ever so subtly even seemed to suggest the naming of Campeggio as protector, or at least to suggest that this occasion should not be taken to ignore him. Several days later Campeggio made his own announcement to the king of his appointment as legate and offered to serve him in Germany in whatever way possible. To his promise to see to Wolsey's interests while in Germany, he added notice several days later that the English ambassador would doubtless inform him of progress made in obtaining confirmation and increase of

Germany are in Bologna, AS AMC, 2nd series, 55/292. In carton 26/263 in the same series there is an original of Clement VII's letter of 3 April 1524 to Erasmus, which Campeggio evidently carried with him to Germany; it has been edited from copies by P. S. Allen (ed.), *Opus Epistolarum Des. Erasmi Roterodami* (Oxford, 1924), v, 438ff., no. 1438.

[96] *Ven. Cal.* III, 781, 794 and 796. According to the Venetian Hieronimo Lippomano, Campeggio accepted only on condition that he be given 2000 ducats before leaving 'et che morendo lui in ditta legation, el Papa dagi lo Episcopato di Bologna a suo fiol, et maritar una sua fiola, tutti do naturali' (*Ven. Cal.* III, 795). Campeggio's son Alessandro, actually made bishop-elect of Bologna in 1526, was beyond question legitimate; it has never been established that any of Campeggio's children were illegitimate.

[97] *LP* IV, 14, 40 and 568. Ghinucci was created cardinal only in 1535 and by Paul III (Farnese); Giberti was never created cardinal. Clement VII himself created no cardinals until 3 May 1527, when he was attempting to raise money.

Wolsey's legatine powers, although, however much Campeggio might obtain for Wolsey, it could never equal the gratitude Campeggio owed him.[98]

The purpose was served. On 22 February, that is, shortly after these letters would normally have arrived in England, the king, writing from Greenwich, chose Campeggio as protector of himself and his kingdom. The king professed himself overjoyed at news of Campeggio's daily growth in prestige as befitted his virtues. The king's good will toward him was further increased upon hearing that the pope wholly concurred in his high estimation of Campeggio; and he asked the pope to give Campeggio a kindly hearing, assistance and encouragement in all matters of English interest.[99]

These letters, which arrived in Rome just about the time Campeggio arrived in Nuremberg on 16 March, were evidently accompanied by a parallel set, now lost, which were forwarded to Germany. Campeggio's reply, dated at Nuremberg, 2 April 1524, was profuse in gratitude for the king's appointment and for his commendation of Campeggio to the pope. Carefully remarking that he had just received the king's letter, Campeggio indicated that he regarded the protectorship as a great and indissoluble bond and regretted more than ever his necessary absence from Rome which prevented him from fulfilling his duties.[100] That Henry VIII's letter to Clement VII nominating Campeggio protector should be dated the same day as another thanking the pope for having made Wolsey legate for life is more than coincidental. To ensure that Campeggio should succeed with Clement VII

---

[98] *LP* IV, 35, 41, 46 and 77. Clement VII's letter of 17 January 1524 to Wolsey (PRO 31/9/2, fols. 6–8) is not calendared in *LP*.

[99] Theimer, *Monumenta*, p. 534, who erroneously gives it as addressed to Adrian VI; the original in Arch Vat., A. A. Arm. I–XVIII, no. 1437, is printed in part by Wodka, *Protektorate der Kardinäle*, p. 13, who worries because the letter is dated 1523 rather than 1524. The king's letter of 22 February is both by date and content a logical reply to the pope's letter of 17 January 1524, as Campeggio's letter, clearly dated 2 April 1524, is a logical reply to the king's letter. The general circumstances require such an adjustment of date. De'Medici was clearly referred to as still being protector by John Clerk in his letter to Wolsey of 11 June 1523, several months after the supposed transfer would have taken place *LP* III, 3093). Campeggio's letter of 27 January 1537 to his brother Marcantonio states that he succeeded to the protectorship only upon de'Medici's election as pope (*LP* XII, i, 255).

[100] *LP* IV, 170 and 222; *Ven. Cal.* III, 813.

where he had failed with Leo X and Adrian VI, the king and Wolsey seem to have resorted to the tactic used so successfully with Campeggio in 1518 and conditioned his being named protector upon the pope's commissioning Wolsey as legate for life.[101]

The king and Wolsey waited only four months before giving Campeggio the English protectorship; but they tantalised him for six years before eventually giving him the bishopric of Salisbury, which they had promised him in 1518. When Campeggio had arrived back in Rome in November 1519, he gave maximum publicity to the promise, made in writing, by reporting it to Leo X in Consistory in the presence of the English ambassador. Although Bishop Edmund Audley had been described to Campeggio, perhaps wrongly, as already eighty and in failing health, his grip on life proved a firm one. Meanwhile Campeggio was indelicately importunate but unsuccessful in begging an interim bishopric from Wolsey's bounty, most notably that of Worcester. Audley died at last, most conveniently, on 23 August 1524, just a few months after Campeggio had been made English protector. Almost as soon as the news could have reached Rome, and almost as if by some previously agreed plan, Clement VII abruptly sought to thwart any other nomination by reminding both the king and Wolsey of their previous promise. Campeggio, now in Vienna, again reduced himself to the role of an abject petitioner to Wolsey. Writing on 1 October, without actually saying that the one would be proper recompense for the other, and protesting that it was not really necessary to refresh Wolsey's memory, Campeggio sought Wolsey, whom he credited with getting the protectorship for him, now also to obtain him the long-awaited bishopric. He sent an accompanying, shorter letter to the king, which Wolsey was to present if he thought it fit. Twice Campeggio asked Giberti in Rome to pursue the matter.[102]

Rumours, perhaps purposefully cultivated by Wolsey, and the

---

[101] All five of the letters printed in Theiner, *Monumenta*, pp. 534–6, and listed as sent from Henry VIII and Wolsey to Adrian VI in February 1523, must in fact have been addressed to Clement VII in February 1524. Wolsey was still seeking the grant of the legatine commission for life from Adrian VI in the summer of 1523. Both the enthusiastic tone and the contents of the letters place them logically at the beginning of Clement VII's pontificate.

[102] Campeggio to Giberti from Vienna, 23 September and 17 November 1524 (Arch. Vat., Lettere di Principi I, fols. 36–7 and 41–2); Clement VII to Henry VIII, 21 September 1524 (printed by C. W. Boase in the

appearance of delay aroused suspicion in Rome that Wolsey intended to hedge the gift of Salisbury with crippling reservations or even go back on his promise altogether. On 19 November 1524 Clerk wrote to Wolsey at the pope's request to forestall difficulty and to testify on Campeggio's behalf that there was 'no strangier lyving, battar mynded, ne more affectionatt to our nation, ne gladder to do the Kinges Highnes and your Grace pleasour and service, then he hath been, to the best of his power; and I do not doubt butt your Grace hath this good opynion of hym, and wyll remember hym accordyngly'.[103]

The worst fears in the Curia were unjustified, for letters of nomination from the king and others from Wolsey were already being rushed on their way to the pope in Rome and to Campeggio in Vienna. The king praised the nominee's many virtues, which had been evident from the very beginning of their friendship. He recalled the pope's recent concurrence in his high estimation of Campeggio, when the king had chosen him as cardinal protector, and declared himself overjoyed at this occasion of satisfying the promise made. Wolsey, with a small-minded bluntness which Piero Vannes' deft phrasing could not completely cushion, put the pope in the position of having taken the initiative in seeking the bishopric for Campeggio. Against the king's readiness to give it to a so worthy and zealous friend, Wolsey set what he presented as the concerted and open opposition of the whole diocese of Salisbury and of almost every cleric in England to giving the bishopric to a cardinal both a foreigner and an absentee. Moved by his sincere friendship for Campeggio, Wolsey credited himself with having exerted himself to the full. His solitary intercession was enough to counter the opposition's urgent request and maintain the king in his original purpose.[104]

Campeggio's letters of thanks, written from Vienna on 29 November, offer a sufficient clue to the tone and contents of

English Historical Review, III [1888], 321–3); *LP* IV, 679, 696 and 721; *Ven. Cal.* III, 875.

[103] *State Papers of Henry VIII*, VI, 363 (*LP* IV, 837).

[104] Henry VIII to Clement VII, 1 November 1524 (Theiner, *Monumenta*, p. 545, from Arch. Vat., A. A. Arm. I–XVIII, no. 2377; modern copies in Br. Mus., Add. MS 15387, fols. 140–2, and in PRO 31/9/3, fol. 19; *LP* IV, 191); Wolsey to Clement VII, 11 November 1524 (Theiner, *Monumenta*, pp. 545–6, from Arch. Vat., Lettere di Principi II, fol. 328; a modern copy in Br. Mus., Add. MS 15387, fol. 143; *LP* IV, 820); and *LP* IV, 820, 884ff. and 910.

those he had received from England. To the king he only hinted at the numerous difficulties supposedly encountered in so greatly increasing Campeggio's fortunes and dignity, and he promised that his constant zeal in the king's service would be the proper expression of his gratitude. To Wolsey he made the appropriately submissive reply to insistence that the nomination was contrary to the customs, laws and usages of the realm, and that it was the result solely of Wolsey's own influence and the king's generosity. Happy at gaining a see whose net revenues were perhaps five times those of his see of Bologna, Campeggio was content to surrender administrative control to Wolsey in the established pattern and to instruct his London agent, Giacomo, to follow Wolsey's instruction.[105] Campeggio also wrote, this time in his own hand, to thank Clement VII as well.[106] Clement VII's own message of thanks to Wolsey was written on the very same day as Campeggio's, and the pope himself referred the provision in Consistory on 2 December. Both the pope and Campeggio strove to gratify Wolsey by giving wide publicity to the promotion among the *curiales*. On 5 December Bishop Clerk reported to Wolsey their universally favourable reaction and Campeggio's devotion to the king, Wolsey and all England. Although Clerk had even gone so far as to draft explanations to the Curia why the bishopric could not be given to Campeggio as promised, he declared himself relieved at not having had to use them. The College of Cardinals, probably at Campeggio's suggestion, expressed their pleasure at the promotion in separate letters of 2 January 1525 to the king and to their brother cardinal, Wolsey.[107]

Possibly Wolsey was really registering a protest to the Curia against the difficulties he was experiencing in collecting the pensions from Spanish bishoprics given him by Charles V. If in fact there had been open opposition of the clergy to the Salisbury nomination, it was probably as much directed against Wolsey himself as Campeggio. Even the dullest cleric might have fore-

---

[105] *LP* iv, 885f.; Eubel, *Hierarchia* iii, 151 and 311, lists the official income of Bologna at 2000 florins yearly and that of Salisbury as 10,000 florins. What the incomes were in fact, and what portion of the Salisbury income Campeggio actually received, is open to question.

[106] Arch. Vat., Lettere di Principi ii, fol. 349.

[107] PRO 31/10/15, fol. 90 (Arch. Vat., Arch. Cons., Acta Cancel. 2, fol. 47ᵛ); *LP* iv, 884, 902, 910 and 986f.

seen that in reality it would be Wolsey who would control
Salisbury as he already controlled Worcester for Ghinucci, perhaps Llandaff for de Athequa, and possibly even Bath and Wells
for the absent Clerk, as well as his own sees of York and Durham.[108] This prospect would have intensified the opposition in
Salisbury itself where the bishop exercised civil powers over the
city as well. On 10 January 1525, the day before the restitution of
the temporalities to the new bishop, and acting through the
powers of a commission from Campeggio, Wolsey constituted his
chaplain, Thomas Benet, as vicar general of Salisbury. Although
it was Bishop Tunstall of London whom Wolsey named as
Campeggio's proxy in making the prior oath of allegiance to the
king, it was Benet, acting expressly in Wolsey's name, who was
proxy for the installation at Salisbury on 25 January. From
Leaden Hall within the cathedral close at Salisbury, Benet continued to administer the see in Wolsey's interest.[109] From 1529
until 1533 Benet was temporarily replaced by Richard Hilley but
then restored by direct action of the king himself. Campeggio
carefully deferred to Wolsey in the rare instances when he took
an active interest in the internal affairs of his diocese.[110]

[108] *LP* III, 2439; and A. F. Pollard, *Wolsey* (London, 1929), pp. 173 and 318.
Pollard says that de Athequa was a non-resident; in his *Henry VIII*,
2nd ed. (London, 1951), p. 255, he says that he could not speak a word
of English. His reference to P. S. Allen (ed.), *Erasmi Epistolae*, III, 547–8,
hardly supports this contention. Clerk not only made Wolsey's son,
Thomas Winter, dean of Wells by accepting the resignation of the
incumbent, but he also took Winter to Paris with him in 1526 (*LP* IV,
1790 and 2868).

[109] Benet wrote to Wolsey from Salisbury on 4 March 1525 that the office
of vicar general had now been vacant six weeks (*LP* IV, 1150), but
Campeggio's register shows him regularly instituting to benefices from
the first occasion on 4 February 1525 onward (Salisbury, Diocesan
Registry, Register Campegii, fols. 1ff., 18ʳ, 39ᵛ and 40ʳ). On 26 January
1526 Benet was described in a papal dispensation to hold multiple
benefices as 'devotus S. V. orator Thomas Benet, legum doctor ac dilecti
filii vestri Laurentii tituli Sanctae Anastasiae presbiteri Cardinalis, qui
ecclesiae Sarum ex concessione apostolica praeesse dignoscitur, in civitate
et dicta diocesi Sarum vicarius in spiritualibus generalis' (PRO 31/10/17,
fols. 181–2, from Arch. Vat., Reg. Suppl. 1873, fol. 228). Hilley was
constituted vicar general for Campeggio 'apostolicae sedis de latere
legatus Sarumque episcopi in remotis extra Anglia agentis' some time
between 23 August and 20 October 1529; after Hilley's death on
1 September 1533, Benet resumed the office. See also *LP* IV, 1011, 1067f.,
1291, 1345, 3743, 3886 and 5560.

[110] Campeggio to Wolsey from Bologna, 21 July 1525, reminding him of his
request that of the two houses occupied by Francesco Bombarderio in

When Campeggio returned a second time to England as legate, in 1528, Wolsey, wishing to emphasise Campeggio's obligation to the king whose matrimonial suit was pending, suggested that it would afford Campeggio the opportunity of visiting his bishopric.[111] In the months immediately before Campeggio's arrival, Benet and Wolsey seem to have settled a delicate controversy over the election of an abbess of Wilton in Campeggio's diocese, without referring to the bishop; but Wolsey's refusal to permit the intrusion of the unsuitable sister of Anne Boleyn's brother-in-law and his conferring the position on the prioress instead, subject to royal confirmation, may have been as much a calculated effort to avoid bringing the Boleyns unfavourably to his co-legate's attention as to protect his influence in the conferring of benefices from the intrusion of the Boleyns.[112] Although there is no evidence that Campeggio ever went personally to Salisbury, he did send his brother Marcantonio there as his proctor at least on occasion.[113] Before departing England Campeggio confirmed Wolsey's delegated control of Salisbury.[114]

If Campeggio did not totally ignore the affairs of his diocese, his interest in it was never a pastoral one. He regarded his episcopal oath of fidelity to the king seriously and saw it as strengthening the obligation of service to the king which he already had as protector. In this he was probably considerably more conscientious than the great number of *curiales* and other ecclesiastics who held foreign benefices; but from the first it was the prospective income from the see which occupied the centre of his consciousness, and which most spurred his sense of obligation to the king.

the cathedral close of Salisbury, the smaller might be taken from him and the keys sent to him (PRO, SP 1/35, fol. 161; *LP* IV, 1507).

[111] *LP* IV, 3693.

[112] *LP* IV, 4197, 4488 and 4528; M. D. Knowles, 'The "matter of Wilton" in 1528', *Bulletin of the Institute of Historical Research*, XXX (1958), 92–6.

[113] On 10 December 1528 Marcantonio as the bishop's proctor received the oath of Edmond Fox, under bailiff of Sarum, that he would do no unlawful act, but would administer justice impartially to all, succour widows, orphans and the poor against all that would do them wrong, defend the liberty of the bishop, etc. (*Hist. MSS Commission, Various Collections* [1907], IV, 214, from the MSS of the Corporation of Salisbury, Leger B. II, fol. 266). Leger B. II is now being edited for the Wiltshire Record Society.

[114] Br. Mus., Add. MS 5847, fol. 159^{r-v} (*LP* IV, 5951); dated 22 September 1529, it gives Wolsey fullest powers over the diocese whether exercised directly or indirectly.

His expression of gratitude from Vienna in November 1524 was echoed a month later from Budapest. On 26 April 1525, still in Budapest, he begged Wolsey's assistance, as his creditors were demanding repayment, thinking him enriched through the king's liberality.[115] Although Wolsey wrote by return courier on 31 May to describe the arrangements made to pay the revenues of Salisbury to Giacomo, Campeggio's agent in England, this and Giacomo's own letter, forwarded to Campeggio from Budapest, reached him only two months later in Bologna.

Campeggio, never a rapid traveller even in the context of the early sixteenth century, claimed that despite his personal wish to remain in Bologna to rest and to escape the Roman August, he would return to Rome at the pope's request as soon as the settlement of family matters in Bologna would permit. The knowledge that Wolsey and the king would employ him in Rome eased his vexation. Nevertheless, it was only on 18 October 1525 that Campeggio arrived in Rome. He assured the king that nothing during his legation in Germany was a greater hardship than his absence from the City, and his consequent inability to serve the king, on whose liberality both by desire and by duty he depended.[116] After an absence from Rome of more than twenty difficult months, the cardinal protector could at last begin his work.

[115] *LP* iv, 946, 1069 and 1286.   [116] *LP* iv, 1506, 1575 and 1716f.

5

THE ROUTINE WORK OF CARDINAL PROTECTORS GIULIO DE'MEDICI (1514–23) AND CAMPEGGIO (1524–8)

De'Medici and papal provisions to English bishoprics

The services of Cardinal de'Medici in seeing to the consistorial provision of royal nominees to bishoprics began on 15 September 1514 with the provision of Wolsey to York, vacant by the death of Cardinal Bainbridge, and lasted, with numerous exceptions, until his election as pope in 1523. Among the documents preserved from the old Archivio di Castel Sant'Angelo are eight original nomination letters of Henry VIII to de'Medici as cardinal protector, all in similar, punctiliously correct form,[1] and presumably part of an unbroken series covering the whole period of his protectorship.[2] For these eight and for the provision of four suffragan bishops *in partibus infidelium* for England,[3] there are, in the same archive, numerous related documents, including some parallel nomination letters to Leo X, testimony to establish the authenticity of vacancies and the suitability of nominees, and consistorial *cedulae* of provisions.[4] Of these, the provision to Hereford in

[1] Bainbridge and Gigli to Henry VIII, 17 September 1513, 'There cometh no letters from any other prince unto his Holiness to be exhibited in Consistory that be judged more elegantly written than they be' (*LP* i, 2276).
[2] Four are for English and Welsh sees: Hereford (1516), Llandaff (1517), St Asaph (1518) and Worcester (1521); four are for Irish sees: Clogher (1515), Clonmacnois (1516), Ross (1517) and Ardagh (1517) (Arch. Vat., A. A. Arm. i–xviii, nos. 2866, 2856, 2870, 2874, 2880, 4042, 4043 and 4044). Four of these are cited by Wodka, *Protektorate der Kardinäle*, p. 13; and two, Worcester and Clonmacnois, are printed in Theiner, *Monumenta*, pp. 514 and 533. Parallel letters from Henry VIII to Leo X exist for all except Worcester (Arch. Vat., A. A. Arm. i–xviii, nos. 2852, 2855, 2865, 2869, 2873, 2876, 2878 and 4040).
[3] For Lincoln (1516), Exeter (1516), York (1516) and Salisbury (1518).
[4] Arch. Vat., A. A. Arm. i–xviii, nos. 2782, 2783, 2784, 2793, 2840, 2842, 2851, 2853, 2854, 2857, 2858, 2859, 2860, 2861, 2862, 2863, 2864, 2867, 2871, 2875, 2877, 2881, 2954, 3020, 4041, 4043, 4544 (p. 7). Six additional items, nos. 2841, 2850, 2868, 2872, 2879 and 2955, in the same archive are printed in Theiner, *Monumenta*.

1516, for which the documents preserved are the most complete, might serve as an example.

Charles Booth, archdeacon of Buckingham, Doctor of Laws, chancellor of Wales when Henry VIII was prince of Wales, and afterwards royal councillor and commissioner for Wales, was first nominated to Hereford by the king on 22 April 1516, four days after the death of the incumbent, Richard Mayew, and was granted custody of the temporalities by the king on 17 May. Unaccountably, two identical nomination letters were sent to Leo X, one from Eltham on 26 April and a second from Greenwich on 28 May.[5] A parallel letter was also sent on 28 May to Cardinal de'Medici, 'Protector of Us and Our Kingdom in the Roman Curia', along with a commission drawn up in London on 21 May by Robert Cressy with William Hulle of Worcester and John West of Exeter as witnesses, arranging for Aloisio de Gibraleon and Andrea Gentile to act as agents in expediting the bulls. In Rome, Gianmatteo Giberti, de'Medici's youthful secretary, was commissioned by de'Medici to take testimony of witnesses to establish the location and description of the city and cathedral of Hereford, the income of the see, the fact of the vacancy and Booth's fitness to fill it. On 5 July Giberti recognised Federico Baranitio and Aloisio de Gibraleon as Booth's proctors; written record was made of the reading of the king's letters and of the formal interrogation of John Blythe, archdeacon of Coventry and prebendary of Hereford, and of Elias Bodley, priest of London, both associated with the English Hospice in Rome. Additional testimony was taken on 16 July from a priest Ralph Sneyd, and a layman, both of Coventry. A formalised summary of this evidence was then prepared for de'Medici's use in Consistory, and the provision was made on 21 July.[6] The same day, a consistorial *cedula* was drawn up by the papal chancery authorising the expedition of the bulls; and de'Medici wrote to the king. The bishop-elect was consecrated on 31 November and enthroned in January 1517.[7]

[5] LeNeve, II, 3; Theiner, *Monumenta*, pp. 517–18, from Arch. Vat., A. A. Arm. I–XVIII, nos. 2873 and 2876.

[6] Arch. Vat., A. A. Arm. I–XVIII, nos. 2874 (the letter), 2877 (the commission) and 2872 (the *processus*). There is a copy of the letter in Cambridge Univ. Lib., Add. MS 4878, fol. 4; part of the *processus* is printed in Theiner, *Monumenta*, pp. 514–15.

[7] LeNeve, II, 3; Arch. Vat., A. A. Arm. I–XVIII, no. 2875; and PRO, SP 1/13,

A similar set of documents illustrating a provision referred by de'Medici as protector of France, that of Guillaume du Prat to Clermont on 3 June 1517, follows the same pattern. The letter of Francis I to de'Medici was, however, written in French and, in the brusque style characteristic of sixteenth-century France, addressed de'Medici simply as 'Mon Cousin'. However strong the royal influence in naming bishops may have been previously, Francis I carefully cited the privilege of royal nomination granted by the Concordat of the preceding year. In many cases capitular election would still count for something in France until 1531.[8]

By de'Medici's own account, the obtaining of provisions to benefices was his dominant concern as English protector; but his frequent and long absences on business as legate to Bologna and to all Italy, and in overseeing the affairs of Florence, made it impossible for him always to fulfil this function in person. As his substitute he turned to his fellow Florentine, Cardinal Lorenzo Pucci, papal datary, who seems to have assumed at this time a virtual monopoly in referring all provisions of whatever country.[9] With the exception of the provision to Ardagh in Ireland on 14 December 1517, for which de'Medici had made the *processus*, Pucci's services are limited to the period from May 1519 until October 1521. In early 1523, while Cardinal de'Medici was withdrawn at Florence in pique with Pope Adrian VI, Campeggio was called upon as his substitute; but after his return to Rome in

---

fol. 251 (*LP* II, 2199). The use of 'ad meam relationem' in the chancery document suggests that de'Medici had already taken over the functions of the incapacitated Sisto della Rovere Garo, although he would not become vice-chancellor himself until the latter's death the next spring.

[8] Arch. Vat., A. A. Arm. I–XVIII, no. 2785 (inquiry into the state of the diocese of Clermont, 15 January 1517); no. 2786 (summary of evidence for use in Consistory); no. 2787 (nomination letter of Francis I to Leo X, 12 January 1517); no. 2788 (nomination letter of Francis I to 'mon cousin, Le cardinal de Medicis, mon protecteur en court de Romme', 12 January 1517); and no. 2789 (consistorial *cedula* of provision made on 3 June 1517). Cited in M. Boulet, 'Les élections épiscopales en France au lendemain du Concordat de Bologne, 1516–1531', *Mélanges d'archéologie et d'histoire* (*Ecole française de Rome*), LVII (1940), 205f. In the case of Bourges in 1519, after long controversy the king was obliged by the pope to withdraw his candidate in favour of the one elected by the chapter; the chapter of Bourges again succeeded in electing a successor in 1525.

[9] Wodka, *Protektorate der Kardinäle*, pp. 17f., 98f. and 118. Wodka, p. 62, lists de'Medici also as protector of Hungary; he was bishop of Eger (Erlau) in Hungary from 1520 until 1523 (Eubel, *Hierarchia*, III, 110).

April de'Medici resumed his role. In all only about half the nominations were referred by de'Medici himself.[10]

Wolsey's demands in connexion with his own bishoprics alone required considerable attention. Although Cardinal Bainbridge had actually referred the nomination of Wolsey to Lincoln on 6 February 1514, de'Medici, who protested that he would have been willing to do it, had been requested to aid in obtaining a reduction of the consistorial taxes. The best Wolsey could get was the remission of the taxes for the dispensation to retain the deanery of St Stephen's, Westminster. When Wolsey was promoted to York on 15 September, he demanded the remission of the consistorial tax paid for Lincoln, not for the benefit of his successor in Lincoln, William Atwater, but for himself. De'Medici, in reporting the completion of these promotions to the king, expressed regret that the pope could not give Wolsey full satisfaction. Leo X had remitted 1000 ducats from his half of the taxes, and the College of Cardinals then agreed also to remit 1000 ducats from their half. Wolsey's proctors obtained a delay for paying the taxes and pressed for the remission of still more. The cardinals refused, but Leo X apparently remitted another 500 ducats of his portion. Belatedly, de'Medici sent word that half the taxes, or 2500 ducats worth, had been remitted, as Wolsey's proctors had explained that the see had been twice vacant in one year.[11]

When Wolsey began collecting bishoprics, reductions became more difficult. Since Castellesi, *quondam* Cardinal of Bath, had been deprived chiefly to satisfy Wolsey, and since he was shattering English precedent by taking over a second English see, Wolsey evidently paid 6000 ducats in curial fees for Bath and Wells without objection. When he sought to exchange Bath and Wells in 1523 for the wealthier second see of Durham, which

---

[10] Arch. Vat., A. A. Arm. I–XVIII, nos. 2880 and 2879; and PRO 31/9/5, fol. 145 (Bib. Vat., MS Reg. 387, fol. 22). Excluding suffragan bishops, of which records are incomplete, the tally for the eighteen provisions to English and Welsh bishoprics from 1514 to 1523 were: de'Medici, 9; Pucci, 3; Campeggio, 3; Leo X, 1; Bainbridge, 1; uncertain, 1. Of the fifteen for Ireland: de'Medici, 5; Pucci, 4; Campeggio, 3; Bainbridge, 1; uncertain, 2.

[11] PRO 31/9/52c, fol. 433 (Arch. Vat., Acta Cons., Cam. Div. 63, fol. 182ᵛ); *LP* I, 2629, 2642, 2653, 3301f., 3494, 3496f. and 3560; *LP* II, 20. Wolsey had sent Gigli 7000 ducats to cover the total expenses, which Gigli said amounted to only 6821 ducats, a figure Gigli considered low (*LP* I, 2644).

bordered York, there was a long tradition of hard-won but consistently granted consistorial tax reductions; but it was also a question of getting consistorial approval to continue to hold St Albans abbey, which Henry VIII had given him the preceding year. Campeggio, to whom it fell to see the matter through Consistory, and de'Medici, who was absent in Florence, both wrote congratulations to Wolsey even before the provision had been made.[12] The question was not whether Wolsey would be permitted to possess three so important English benefices, but only at what cost in consistorial taxes. De'Medici, posing as the defender of Wolsey's and all the cardinals' interests against Pope Adrian VI, said he had written to all his cardinal friends in Rome and felt confident that Adrian VI would not depart from the footsteps of Leo X in the matter. Wolsey himself had already taken the initiative in that by contacting Ghinucci and Giberti. On 30 March, four days after it had been settled in Consistory, Campeggio wrote to Henry VIII and Wolsey that the favourable result was due to the splendour of the king's name, Wolsey's merits, and the powerful aid of the absent de'Medici. While praising the efforts of Campeggio, de'Medici regretted his own inability to obtain all that Wolsey had wanted; but he felt that he and his friends had, in view of the difficult times, obtained surprisingly much. The tax settled on in Consistory for Durham and St Albans together was 9000 ducats, the full tax for Durham alone. Although in the end somewhat less than that was paid, Wolsey had been prepared to pay more. He had sent 10,000 ducats to Rome to cover the expected costs.[13]

In terms of service repaid and of income from his own foreign sees and ecclesiastical pensions, Wolsey perhaps gained almost as much as was lost by the holding of English sees by foreigners. Although George de Athequa, whose provision to the relatively poor see of Llandaff was referred by de'Medici on 11 February 1517, was a Spanish Dominican, he had long been resident in England as confessor to Queen Catherine of Aragon and remained in England until her death, when he lost the see.[14] On the other

---

[12] Ellis, *Original Letters*, 3rd series, ɪ, 277 and 282–6; *LP* ɪɪ, 4068; *LP* ɪɪɪ, 2903ff. Probably Wolsey paid nothing for the revoked bulls for the administration of Tournai.

[13] *LP* ɪɪɪ, 2905, 2910, 2918f., 2928f., 2933, 2999 and 3025.

[14] Henry VIII's nomination letter of de Athequa to de'Medici, 'Bononiae Legato, nostroque ac Regni nostri in Romana Curia Protectori et Amico

hand, Wolsey first gained a generous annual pension from Francis I in 1518 for surrendering his tenuous claims to the see of Tournai and then, on the occasion of Charles V's first visit to England, was given in 1520 the Spanish bishopric of Badajoz and an annual pension of 2000 ducats from that of Palencia, although the emperor probably meant to hedge Wolsey against the loss of his income from France. By the emperor's wish the nomination was referred in Consistory by Cardinal Pucci on 4 July; but Campeggio, who saw to the expedition of the bulls, claimed for himself and for Gigli their share of the credit for having obtained remission of the 15,000 or 16,000 ducats in consistorial taxes ordinarily due for so profitable a pluralistic combination. Even before Wolsey received the bulls, however, he was invited from Spain to resign the see in return for an annual pension, eventually set at 2500 ducats or one half the revenues from Badajoz, to supplement the pension of 2000 ducats from Palencia.[15] Campeggio, whose poverty had already driven him to ask Wolsey for the loan of £1000 to repair and complete the palazzo given him by the king, made an urgent bid for Wolsey's aid in getting Badajoz for himself, in return for the promise to manage it according to Wolsey's wishes and to grant Wolsey an additional future pension from the bishopric of Salisbury which he had been promised. Not only did Wolsey proceed with his original plan of resigning it in favour of Bishop Bernardo de Mesa, OP, the Spanish ambassador in London; but he asked Campeggio to see it through Consistory.[16]

Campeggio's extreme poverty and the bishop of Salisbury's amazing longevity kept Campeggio begging for an interim bishopric from Wolsey's bounty. As Bishop Gigli of Worcester lay on his deathbed in Rome, Campeggio, with surprising indelicacy, began

Carissimo', from Greenwich, 18 January 1517, is in Arch. Vat., A. A. Arm. I–xviii, no. 2866 (modern copy in Cambridge Univ. Lib., Add. MS 4878, fol. 5); and nos. 2865 (Theiner, *Monumenta*, p. 519) and 2864, for the king's letter to the pope and the *processus*.

[15] *LP* iii, 709, 866, 880, 882, 892, 899, 900, 921, 958, 1012, 1016, 2361 and 3244. The pension from Badajoz was later assigned to other sees in Spain, and Wolsey experienced considerable difficulty in collecting it.

[16] *LP* iii, 646, 1094 and 1187. When Campeggio was created cardinal in 1517, Leo X had in that one consistory doubled the number of cardinals; accordingly each curial cardinal's portion of the cardinals' half of consistorial taxes on provisions to benefices was reduced by half. Actually, Campeggio had resigned the see of Feltre on 1 June 1520 in favour of his brother Tommaso.

an intense campaign to become his sucessor. On 10 April 1521 he reported to Wolsey that Gigli was dying and urgently pressed his own candidacy, although lightly suggesting Geronimo Ghinucci, then papal nuncio in England, as a possible second choice. Five days later Campeggio wrote separate letters to the king, to Wolsey and to the king's Latin secretary, Piero Vannes, to announce that Gigli's life had been despaired of, and that all was in readiness for the funeral; he repeated his request for the bishopric and took the trouble to enclose a copy of his previous letter. After Gigli's death on 18 April, Campeggio took occasion still three more times during the following month to renew his request for Worcester, urging that as a curial cardinal he would be dispensed from consistorial taxes both for a provision to Worcester and for his later translation to Salisbury.[17]

The see of Worcester by Wolsey's wish was to remain in Italian hands; but it was given instead to the Cardinal Protector de'Medici, who may have appreciated the friendly gesture but was hardly in dire need of an increased income.[18] On 21 May notice of the decision was rushed from England to both the cardinal protector and Cardinal Campeggio. On 8 June a notarial instrument was drawn up in de'Medici's name, constituting Wolsey his proxy in procuring his provision to the see and in administering its affairs through the vicar general, John Bell, a former associate of Silvestro Gigli, the previous bishop. In fact Leo X himself had already referred the provision in Consistory on the preceding day and sent off thanks to Wolsey. Campeggio acknowledged what had been done, and de'Medici himself sent fulsome thanks for a favour he had 'neither expected nor asked for'.[19] Within a month Ghinucci appealed to Wolsey to ask the

---

[17] *LP* III, 1222, 1229ff., 1247, 1265 and 1282. The report even went back to Bologna that Campeggio, not yet bishop of Bologna, might be given Worcester (Bologna, AS, Archivio del Reggimento, Lettere dell'ambasciatore bolognese in Roma al Senato).

[18] According to a schedule dated 13 February 1522, Cardinal de'Medici's total income during the preceding year was 19,790 ducats, including 6000 ducats from the French chancery, evidently the income from his French benefices (Florence, AS, Carte Strozziani, 1st series, x, c. 299).

[19] Henry VIII's nomination letter to de'Medici, 'Vicecancellario, nostroque ac Regni nostri in Romana Curia Protectori et Amico carissimo', 21 May 1521, is in Arch. Vat., A. A. Arm. I–XVIII, no. 4043 (Theiner, *Monumenta*, p. 533; *LP* III, 1298; modern copy in Br. Mus., Add. MS 15387, fols 90–1); *LP* III, 1332, 1334f., 1348f. and 2178. Possibly it was Wolsey's intention to recompense de'Medici for the loss of revenue from his French benefices

king to allow de'Medici to resign the see to him. On 12 January 1522, three days after the election of Adrian VI, de'Medici, thanking both the king and Wolsey for their efforts to secure his election to the papacy, again asked to resign Worcester in favour of Ghinucci, who under Leo X had become a personal bond between England and the de'Medici. When Ghinucci's provision was referred by de'Medici himself in the consistory of 26 September 1522 after the long-delayed arrival of the new pope in Rome from Spain, de'Medici explicitly reserved a pension of 2000 ducats to himself, with the right of transferring it to one or more persons. Ghinucci was given control of the temporalities of the see only on 20 February 1523, because Wolsey was provoked by Ghinucci's supposed remissness in expediting his bulls for St Albans. De'Medici, who had granted Ghinucci not only the income of the see beginning with 25 March 1522 but also the unpaid arrears, pointedly asked Wolsey to stop making difficulties in their collection.[20] When Wolsey exchanged Bath and Wells for Durham the next year, Wolsey assured Campeggio that he had been thought of for the vacancy thus created before it was given to John Clerk, Gigli's successor as resident English ambassador in Rome.[21] Only on 2 December 1524, when he had succeeded de'Medici as protector of England, could Campeggio at last be provided to Salisbury. Worcester and Salisbury were the only two sees permitted to the Italian *curiales*. Both Ghinucci and Campeggio, and the administration of their sees, were kept under Wolsey's careful surveillance.

In the procedure for filling vacant English bishoprics the *processus* in Rome, for all its pretensions, remained a formalised inquiry which simply rationalised the acceptance of royal nominees. Because royal nomination was not disputed in England, it was not disputed in Rome. Whatever the appearances, Wolsey's influence over nominations to bishoprics was always conditioned by whatever interest the king might or might not choose to show in each particular case. On 4 May 1518, less than two weeks before he received his first papal commission as legate, Wolsey received a commission from the king to grant under the great seal

cut off because of the war with France. The Consistorial Acts made specific mention of de'Medici as 'Protectoris Angliae in Romana Curia'.
[20] *LP* III, 1410f., 1956f., 2791, 2842, 2844 and 2866; *LP* IV, 4589; Brady, *Episcopal Succession*, I, 49–50.
[21] *LP* III, 2904.

of the lord chancellor, *congés d'élire*, royal assents to episcopal and abbatial elections, and patents of the restoration of temporalities, as well as the writs of *dedimus potestatem* 'to suche as ye shall think convenient to take the homagis and feaute' of such ecclesiastical dignitaries.[22] Wolsey was under no illusion about the exercise of this authority being dependent on his serving the king's pleasure, and the king's pleasure was that Wolsey control the English church in the king's interest. Nothing made this so clear as the nominations, by the king, to St Asaph just before, and to Exeter just after the grant of this commission to Wolsey.

Henry Standish, OFMCON, nominated to St Asaph on 29 April 1518, had first really attracted the king's attention to himself in 1515 by publicly defending the ultimate subordination of the ecclesiastical to the civil authority. When he was summoned before the Convocation of the Clergy in November 1515, Standish appealed to the king; and the clergy present at Standish's citation were declared guilty of *praemunire*. Although a face-saving compromise was later found, Wolsey had been required to make on his knees before the king a kind of submission on behalf of the English clergy. For personal as well as ecclesiastical reasons he had grounds for disliking this opportunist friar, who had used such *ad hominem* arguments in his defence as saying that it was also the law that bishops be resident in their sees.[23]

When St Asaph fell vacant in 1518 two years later, Wolsey suggested the nomination of William Bolton, prior of St Bartholomew's, West Smithfield, as a reward for his services as master builder to the king. But Pace informed Wolsey that the king objected to Bolton as lacking in other qualifications and was already minded to give the bishopric to a friar, 'a grete lernyede man and an honestman', who 'must have better knowliege off the cure off sowle than the sayde Prior'.[24] Pace bewailed, 'Hys Grace wolde not name the sayde freer unto me, but itt is suerly

---

[22] Cited in G. R. Elton, *The Tudor Revolution in Government, Administrative Changes in the Reign of Henry VIII* (Cambridge, 1953), p. 53; *LP* II, 4147.

[23] *LP* II, 1313f. The argument had grown out of an Act of Parliament of 1512, denying benefit of clergy to criminals in minor orders, and out of the subsequent wave of anti-clericalism in London which followed on the mysterious death of John Hunne in the Tower (A. F. Pollard, *Wolsey* [London, 1929], pp. 29–52; and G. R. Elton, *England under the Tudors* [London, 1962], p. 107).

[24] Ellis, *Original Letters*, 3rd series, I, 186 (*LP* II, 4083).

Standyche: to my greate discomforte in so muche that I dydde nevyr wryte Lettres in my lyffe more to my displeasor than thiese: parte for your Graces causes, and parte for the sayde Priors, whoo is more wurthy to have greater promotion than thys, than is the other to be in lyffe. Sed Principum voluntatibus arduum est refragari.'[25] Four days later, on 18 April, Pace wrote from Woodstock, 'Thys daye His Grace haith yevyn the bushopryche off S. Assaph to Doctor Standyche and commanundydde me to advertise your Grace thereoff, and to desyre the same in hys name to be goodde lorde unto the sayde doctor.'[26]

On 29 April the nomination was sent off to Rome. To Cardinal Protector de'Medici, who was asked to refer the nomination in Consistory, the king praised only the nominee's learning, probity and holiness of life; but for the pope he itemised many additional virtues including Standish's not inconsiderable renown as a preacher.[27] Although Warham, Fox and even Wolsey had previously thought to refer to Rome the *praemunire* accusation which Standish had brought down on them, no objection whatever was raised to the nomination in Rome. There could not have been time for anything but a most superficial *processus* before Standish was provided in Consistory on 28 May. If either the pope or the cardinal protector knew the true significance of Standish's provision, there was not the slightest indication of it in de'Medici's announcement to the king.[28] Of the next two English sees to fall vacant, the one, Bath and Wells, was given to the legate Wolsey himself as prize for the deprivation of Cardinal Castellesi; and the other, Exeter, was given to John Veysey, who had been only slightly less vocal than Standish in defending the royal prerogative in 1515.[29]

[25] *Ibid.*   [26] *Ibid.* I, 189 (*LP* II, 4089); and *LP* II, 4074.
[27] Arch. Vat., A. A. Arm. I–XVIII, nos. 4040 (Theiner, *Monumenta*, p. 531) and 4042; modern copies in Cambridge Univ. Lib., Add. MS 4878, fol. 13, and Br. Mus., Add. MS 15387, fols. 66–9. Standish was one of those paid for preaching before the king in 1511 and then each year from 1515 till 1520; evidently it was one of the Sundays in Lent in each case (*LP* II, pp. 1450, 1467, 1470, 1474, 1477; *LP* III, pp. 1535 and 1539).
[28] PRO, SP 1/16, fol. 300 (*LP* II, 4220). Curiously and exceptionally, the letter is addressed 'Sacrae Serenissimae Angliae ac Franciae *Christianissimae* Regiae Maiestati' (my italics). In fact Franco-papal, Anglo-papal and Anglo-French relations were all enjoying a strikingly sunny period at the time, and the question of granting Henry VIII the title 'Most Christian' had been dropped.
[29] *LP* II, 1313. Wolsey punished Standish with a *praemunire* action of his

The consistorial provision of suffragan bishops with titles *in partibus infidelium* as auxiliary bishops for English sees was also normally handled by Cardinal de'Medici as protector, or by Cardinal Pucci as his substitute. It included the same preliminary *processus* as in the case of bishops who were diocesan ordinaries. There the similarity ended. The majority of the English bishops were active royal councillors or functionaries who seldom if ever went near their sees. Most such bishops were content to govern their sees through a vicar general, and what provision was made for the administration of the sacraments of confirmation and holy orders was of the individual bishop's own choosing. Whether the bishop ordinary was aged and failing, as in the case of the provision of John Pynnock as suffragan for Salisbury in 1518,[30] or simply an absentee like William Atwater, who petitioned for John Brainfort, OSB, of Bury St Edmunds as his suffragan in 1516, the initiative in making the nomination and the responsibility of finding financial support for the bishop provided rested with the individual bishop ordinary.[31] These suffragans were episcopal lackeys, employed to fulfil those functions the bishop ordinary was unable or uneager to perform himself. Normally there was neither the hope nor even the thought that such a suffragan would ever become a bishop ordinary of an English see. Absentee Irish bishops might seek episcopal piecework as suffragans in England, but the later promotion to an Irish see of an English suffragan bishop originally provided *in partibus* was rare indeed. Richard Wilson, OSA, prior of Drax, made suffragan for York in 1516 and then bishop of Meath in 1523, was the notable exception during de'Medici's protectorship. Further, although Henry VIII as a rule did not himself supplicate the pope to provide suffragans, since no interest of the crown was directly at stake, both the king and Wolsey, the archbishop of York, wrote on Wilson's behalf. On

---

own in Star Chamber; years later Warham was indicted for having consecrated Standish before he had done homage to the king. See Kelly, 'Canterbury jurisdiction', pp. 145 and 247.

30 Arch. Vat., A. A. Arm. I–XVIII, nos. 2863 (Pynnock's own letter to Leo X), 2858 (the *processus*) and 2862 (testimony).

31 Bishop William Atwater of Lincoln to Leo X, 11 November 1516 (Arch. Vat., A. A. Arm. I–XVIII, 2783; modern copy in Cambridge Univ. Lib., Add. MS 4878, fol. 12). Testimony by Bishop Thomas Halsey of Leighlin, then resident in Rome (Arch. Vat., A. A. Arm. I–XVIII, nos. 2782 and 2864). See also for Thomas Vivian, suffragan for Exeter, the notarial instrument appointing proctors and the consistorial *cedula* (*ibid.* nos. 2793 and 3020).

21 July 1516, the very day on which he had referred the provision, Cardinal de'Medici wrote to Wolsey to explain that Wilson could not attend to his duties as suffragan for York.[32]

The Irish church, de'Medici and Campeggio

In Ireland royal control of episcopal nominations was now consistent, and provisions were handled by the cardinal protector in exactly the same way as English ones. Although Irish candidates still frequently went to Rome to see to their own provision, they were dependent on letters from Henry VIII for success. In a continued effort to clear up the earlier chaos of multiple, conflicting provisions to the same see, even the king's nominations could be challenged. In September 1514 de'Medici advised the king that the provisions to York and Lincoln were complete, but that he could not refer the king's nominations to the Irish sees of Achonry and Kilfenora, because it had not been possible to obtain the necessary testimony. In fact each had a bishop still living, and no conflicting provision was made.[33] The man provided to an Irish see might not obtain possession of his see, he might be an English absentee, or he might be an Irishman who later allowed his temporary fervour for royal authority to lapse; but the king, either in his own person or through Wolsey, and the cardinal protector in cooperation were the one avenue for obtaining episcopal provision.

For the only four provisions to Irish bishoprics made between 1515 and 1518, those to Clonmacnois, Clogher, Ross and Ardagh, there are original nomination letters of Henry VIII to Cardinal de'Medici, in exactly the same form as those for English sees; and considerable other parts of the original documents survive. Shortly after the death of Bishop Eoghan MacCathmhail of Clogher, Henry VIII wrote from Windsor on 27 September 1515 to nominate an Irish Augustinian friar, Patrick O Cuilin, to fill the vacancy; but the long history of a disputed title to the see, of which Bishop Edmund Courci of Ross, apostolic nuncio and collector for Ireland, had been a past party, led to delay until satisfactory testimony could be obtained.[34] The long delay in

---

[32] Arch. Vat., A. A. Arm. I–XVIII, nos. 2840 (consistorial supplication), 2842 (consistorial *cedula*) and 2872 (part of the *processus*); and *LP* II, 2200.

[33] Rymer, *Foedera*, XIII, 450 (*LP* I, 3301).

[34] Arch. Vat., A. A. Arm. I–XVIII, no. 2856 (modern copy in Cambridge Univ.

filling Clonmacnois, vacant by the translation of Thomas O
Mulally to the archbishopric of Tuam on 19 June 1514, is more
difficult to understand. The king's letters to Leo X and de'Medici
in nomination of a Franciscan friar, Quintin O h-Uigin, were
dated at Greenwich, 18 June 1515; but consistorial provision was
made almost a year and a half later. On 9 November 1516
de'Medici's secretary, Gianmatteo Giberti, received the testimony
of Nicholas Houran, an Irish priest of the English diocese of
Hereford. O h-Uigin, dispensed from the impediment of illegitimacy, was provided soon afterward.[35] Although no mention was
made of O h-Uigin's presence in Rome, it was he and J. Offlande-
galle, an Augustinian canon of Killala, who testified on 27 January
1517 on behalf of Patrick O Cuilin, who was at last provided to
Clogher on 11 February.[36]

The provision to Ross, the southernmost Irish bishopric, also in
1517, proceeded more smoothly. On 17 July Henry VIII wrote to
de'Medici from Richmond to ask that Edmund Courci, bishop of
Ross since 1494, might be permitted to resign in favour of Sean
O Muirmhuile, Cistercian abbot of Fonte Vivo, and that the abbot
might be permitted to continue holding his abbey and several
small benefices. The instrument of resignation itself, notorised by
Donatus O Morthy, priest of Dublin, was dated 24 March and
gave old age as the reason. Giberti was commissioned by de'Medici
to receive testimony on 29 October and the next day heard
separately as witnesses two priests from the diocese of Ross, one
a Cistercian monk and the other a diocesan. De'Medici referred
the provision on 4 November.[37]

Less than five months elapsed between Henry VIII's nomination letters of 27 July 1517 to Leo X and de'Medici and the provision of Roger O Maoileoin, canon of Clonmacnois, to the
dilapidated see of Ardagh. It was de'Medici who gave the com-

Lib., Add. MS 4878, fol. 3); and Gwynn, *Medieval Province of Armagh*,
pp. 162–81.
[35] Arch. Vat., A. A. Arm. I–XVIII, nos. 2869 and 2870 (Theiner, *Monumenta*,
pp. 514–15 and 518–19).
[36] Arch. Vat., A. A. Arm. I–XVIII, no. 2854 (*processus*); and PRO 31/9/3,
fol. 2 (Arch. Vat., Nunciatura Angliae, Arm. XI, Caps. 4, no. 88).
[37] Arch. Vat., A. A. Arm. I–XVIII, nos. 4043 (the king's letter to de'Medici;
LP II, 3488), 2852 (the king's letter to Leo X; Theiner, *Monumenta*,
p. 520), 2851 (instrument of resignation; Theiner, pp. 519–20) and 2850
(the *processus* and consistorial supplication; Theiner, pp. 528–30). The
consistorial supplication concluded 'Scribit Rex et commendat eundem.'

mission for the taking of the testimony of the three Irish witnesses who came forward. However, O Maoileoin was in Rome himself and eager to have the provision made so that he could set out for home. De'Medici, detained from appearing in Consistory on 14 December, sent the *processus* to Cardinal Pucci the preceding evening and asked him to make the relation. Because the whole revenue of the see was only ten ducats a year, although the official book of the Camera read thirty-three and a third, the new bishop of Ardagh was permitted to retain his canonry in Clonmacnois and dispensed from the consistorial taxes.[38]

Cooperation of the cardinal protector with the king in the filling of Irish bishoprics meant also cooperation with Wolsey, who quickly established personal control over the four bishops of the English Pale. On 28 January 1512 Hugh Inge, former *custos* of the English Hospice in Rome, had through Wolsey's influence been provided to Meath, on the same day that William Rokeby was translated from there to the archbishopric of Dublin. Both Rokeby, who was lord chancellor of Ireland, and Inge were extremely active and docile to Wolsey's leadership. John Kite, archbishop of Armagh and primate, was so forthrightly English and so thoroughly subservient to Wolsey that he was never a success in Ireland. On 12 July 1521 Cardinal Pucci referred the translation of Kite to the relatively humble see of Carlisle in England and, on 2 October, the provision of another Englishman, George Cromer, to Armagh. Archbishop Rokeby died on 29 November 1521; and Inge, who had also administered Armagh during Kite's absence in 1520–1, was Wolsey's obvious choice as successor to Dublin.[39]

The provision of Inge to Dublin was delayed, however, because of a dispute over the consistorial taxes. De'Medici and Pucci were petitioned; and Campeggio on 20 February 1523 explained in Consistory, the third time the matter had come up

[38] Arch. Vat., A. A. Arm. I–XVIII, nos. 2880 (the king to de'Medici; modern copy in Cambridge Univ. Lib., Add. MS 4878, fol. 7), 2878 (the king to Leo X; Theiner, *Monumenta*, pp. 520–1) and 2879 (the *processus*; Theiner, p. 521); and PRO 31/9/52c, fol. 436 (Arch. Vat., Arch. Cons., Cam. Div. 66, fol. 92ᵛ).

[39] *Cal. of State Papers, Ireland*, I, pp. 1 and 2; *LP* I, 2907 and 2977; *LP* II, 899 and 1269; PRO 31/10/15, fols. 73–4 (Arch. Vat., Arch. Cons., Acta Cancel. 1, fol. 178ᵛ); and Gwynn, *Medieval Province of Armagh*, pp. 43–61 and 120–1. Cromer later refused to recognise Wolsey's legatine authority as valid for Ireland (*LP* IV, 5625).

for discussion there, that as lands held by the see had been taken over by Irish lords, the common service tax had been reduced at the last provision in 1512 from the 1600 ducats shown in the official books of the Camera to only 1000; he asked that Inge be provided at an even lower tax. Thomas Hannibal, English ambassador in Rome, appealed directly to Adrian VI, and in a fourth consistory Campeggio referred the provision on 27 February with a tax reduced 'pro hac vice tantum' to 1000 ducats. In the same consistory Campeggio referred the provision to Meath of Wolsey's suffragan for York, Richard Wilson, who had been mentioned before. Although Hannibal complained to Wolsey that de'Medici's absence in Florence had delayed these changes, Campeggio's report to Wolsey made no admission of it.[40] On 19 February, while Inge was technically still bishop of Meath, Wilson subserviently wrote to Wolsey from the priory of Drax, Yorkshire, which he was permitted to retain, that he had already collated someone to the benefice of Trim which Wolsey requested be given to Bishop George Braua of Elphin, but that Wolsey could use his legatine authority to revoke all his proceedings. For all his subservience Wilson was of little value to Wolsey in his effort to control Ireland. Although Wilson had visited his diocese at least briefly, Archbishop Inge complained to Wolsey in 1528 of the spiritual and temporal injury done to Meath by the absence of the bishop, and suggested Wilson's resignation. It was made the next year.[41]

An occasion for Wolsey to extend his own and English influence arose when the bishop of Cork and Cloyne died in 1520. John FitzEdmund FitzGerald had been provided there in 1499 at royal insistence after a long struggle in Consistory, but it had been at best a compromise with the Irish. The earl of Surrey, for the time in Ireland as lord lieutenant during one of Henry VIII's sporadic efforts to take effective control of Ireland, wrote to Wolsey on 27 August 1520:

> Plesith it Your Grace to understonde, the Busshop off Cork is ded; and grete [sute is made] to me to wright for men off this

---

[40] PRO 31/10/15, fols. 77 and 79 (Arch. Vat., Arch. Cons., Acta Cancel. 1, fols. 200^v and 202^v); PRO 31/9/52c, fols. 452–4 (Arch. Vat., Arch. Cons., Cam. Div. 73, fol. 78); and *LP* III, 2872 and 2891.
[41] *LP* III, 2197, 2838 and 2845; and Gwynn, *Medieval Province of Armagh*, pp. 121–3.

contre; some say it is worth 200 markes by yere, some say [more]. My poure advyse shuld be that it shuld be bestowed upon som Inglish man. The Busshop of Leyghlyn [Thomas Halsey], your servaunte, havyng both, my thynk myght do gode service here.[42]

But after consultation with the council of Ireland, Surrey wrote ten days later to recommend, instead of Halsey, Walter Wellesley, prior of Connall and himself soon to be a councillor, 'a man of gravitie and vertuous conversation, and a singular mynde having to Englishe ordre'.[43] Although on 7 April 1521 Richard Pace wrote to Wolsey from Greenwich to say the king intended to take the suggestion, the nomination was never made.[44] On 28 January 1523 Campeggio referred the provision of John Benet from the diocese itself, which had been vacant almost two and a half years.

Just before his last of many times as lord deputy, the Great Earl of Kildare wrote to Wolsey on 8 February 1523 from his seat at Maynooth, asking to name a bishop of Kildare and sent the letter on with his candidate, 'Maister Edward Dillon, Deane of the Cathederall Chirch of Kildare foresaid; which is of vertuous living, and of English name and condicion'.[45] After long delay in Rome, Cardinal Campeggio succeeded in obtaining a remission of consistorial taxes on 8 August 1526 on grounds of poverty and referred the provision on 23 August of a Thomas Dillon, who may or may not have been the same man as Edward Dillon.[46] In 1529 Dillon was succeeded as bishop of Kildare by Walter Wellesley, originally mentioned for Cork. Despite the support of de'Medici as protector and of Pucci and Campeggio as his substitutes, Wolsey neither strengthened nor altered the limited English control over the Irish bishops which the king and the protectors had established before Wolsey's rise to prominence. What lay

---

[42] *State Papers of Henry VIII*, ii, 42 (*LP* iii, 962).
[43] *State Papers of Henry VIII*, ii, 42n. (*LP* iii, 971; *Cal. of State Papers, Ireland*, i, p. 3).
[44] *Cal. of Carew Manuscripts*, i, p. 18, no. 13 (*LP* iii, 1220).
[45] *State Papers of Henry VIII*, ii, 98–9 (*LP* iii, 2824; *Cal. of State Papers, Ireland*, i, p. 4).
[46] '23 Augusti 1526, referente Reverendissimo Domino Campegio, [Sanctissimus Dominus Noster]. . .providit ecclesiam Darensem in Hibernia, quae per XIII annos vacavit per obitum Edmundi extra Romanam Curiam vacante, de persona Thomae cum retentione monasterii Sancti Petri et aliorum benefitiorum et prout in cedula' (PRO 31/10/15, fols. 100–1, from Arch. Vat., Arch. Cons., Acta Cancel. 2, fols. 108–9).

beyond the Pale still lay beyond his grasp. Resurgent Irish culture seemed to threaten even the Pale itself.

After his election as pope, Clement VII, already fully conversant with English control of provisions to the Irish church through his own days as protector, took the lead over Campeggio and Cesi, who regularly acted as Campeggio's substitute, in cooperating with the king and Wolsey in maintaining it. On the death of Archbishop Maurice FitzGerald of Cashel the king and Wolsey after some delay reversed the alliance with the FitzGeralds and nominated Edmund Butler, bastard son of the earl of Ossory, as his successor. Wolsey, eager to make Irish sees financially more attractive to royal supporters, asked the pope to allow Butler to retain the archdeaconry of Ossory and to exercise leniency in expediting the bulls. The provision, referred by Cesi on 21 October 1524, dispensed Butler from defect of birth and allowed three years' grace for payment of taxes. The pope, explicitly acknowledging the king's control of Ireland, wrote the same day to ask royal support for Butler in taking control of his see.[47]

Three Irish provisions referred by Campeggio in 1526 illustrate the tone Butler brought to the Irish church. On 6 June an Augustinian, Demetrius MacCarthy, bastard son of an abbot, was made bishop of Ross. The king's letter of nomination recommended him for his modesty, circumspection, probity and erudition, and suggested that MacCarthy would restore the wild Irish to a more civilised and upright life.[48] On 8 August Campeggio arranged in Consistory for provisions to be made to Killaloe and Kildare free of consistorial taxes. Fifteen days later Killaloe, also a suffragan to Cashel, was provided with James O Currin, who was dispensed from illegitimacy and permitted to retain his other benefices. On the same day, as already mentioned, Thomas Dillon was provided to Kildare in the province of Dublin, but supposedly through the influence of Archbishop Butler and Lord Desmond, with whom the former was now cooperating against Lord Ossory. Complaint was made to Wolsey that they had 'opteyned the

---

47 Arch. Vat., A. A. Arm. I–XVIII, no. 6521, fol. 3; PRO 31/9/3, fol. 18; and *LP* IV, 757. A separate royal letter of nomination had been sent earlier; in 1528 Cesi referred the provision of a FitzGerald as bishop of Ossory.

48 Henry VIII to Clement VII, 28 August 1525, 'Confidimusque illum industria dexteritateque sua non solum huic episcopatui magno usui futurum sed etiam silvestres illos hibernicos ad civiliorem rectioremque cultum redacturum esse' (Bologna, AS, AMC, 2nd series, 26/263).

Bisshoprik of Kildare to a symple Irish preste, a vagabounde, without lernyng, maners, or good qualitye, not worthy to be a hally water clerc. And as I here, the Kinges Highnes wol pay for his bulles out of his awne cofers; whereof others in Irland wold greatly mavaill such as have doon the Kinges Grace good service.'[49] On 23 February 1528 Archbishop Hugh Inge of Dublin and Chief Justice Patrick Bermyngham wrote to Wolsey:

> Your Grace, we doubt nat, hirithe the sorroufull decay of this londe, aswell in good Christianitie, as other laudable maners; whiche hathe growen for lakke of goode prelates and curates in the Chirche. Wherefore your Grace may doe meritoriously, to se such persons promoted to busshoppricks, that ther maner of living may be exemple of goodenes and vertue. The residens of suche shall doe more goode, than we can express.[50]

Although Archbishop Cromer of Armagh denied that Wolsey's legatine authority had ever been extended to Ireland by the Holy See, John Alen was enlisted from 1524 onward as Wolsey's special agent in promulgating and exercising it there.[51] Alen reported personal doubts about the validity in Ireland of Wolsey's bulls for dispensing from the impediment of consanguinity among the much intermarried Englishry there and suggested that Wolsey obtain a bull similar to one supposedly just granted by Clement VII to the apostolic collector for Ireland and used there by Raphael Maruff. He accused Archbishop Inge, lord chancellor of Ireland, of being difficult in granting dispensations in Wolsey's name, and worried that either they would not be sought at all or sought in Rome,

> whereof hath insued the decaie of the Church of Irelonde, for, whan an idill person gooth to the Courte of Rome, the compositions be to Irishmen so small for ther povertie, that by him many other exorbitant matiers be sped. So that, in this

[49] Robert Cowley to Wolsey, September 1528 (*State Papers of Henry VIII*, II, 141).
[50] *Ibid.* II, 126–7 (*LP* IV, 3952).
[51] 'D. Primas cum ejus suffraganeis ac consiliariis tenent expresse et palam, quod non est Legatus in Hibernia, et multum nocent, quia ejus ecclesia Armachana et tota provincia, praeter diocesem Midensem, sunt inter Hibernicos in Ultonia'; marginal note in a letter of John Alen to Wolsey from Dublin, 1 June 1524 (*Cal. of Carew Manuscripts*, I, 24; *State Papers of Henry VIII*, II, 102–4). In *LP* IV, 5625, the letter is dated 1529; in the *State Papers* as 1523.

lande, your Graces dispensations be necessarie to be graunted
with lesse difficultie than elles wheare, for thavoiding of
contempte of holy canons, and thoccasion of the inconvenience
that foloith of the Rome runners.[52]

Clement VII implied his support for Wolsey's position by denying
that he had ever granted the Irish collector any such powers and
asked Wolsey to promulgate that fact by means of all the bishops
both in England and Ireland.[53] To what extent Wolsey succeeded
in cutting off direct recourse to Rome on this lowest level as well
is not clear. In 1528 Alen was made 'Lord Chancellor and Vice-
Legate of Ireland', and the next year was provided as successor
to the late Hugh Inge as archbishop of Dublin. Edward Staples,
another creature of Wolsey's, was provided as bishop of Meath
on the same day; but Wolsey's legatine power collapsed in
England only a few months later while still under attack in
Ireland as invalid.[54]

England, Campeggio and Clement VII

The first and most important item of English business in the new
pontificate after Cardinal Protector de'Medici's election as pope,
had been the renewal of Wolsey's legatine commission. Clement
VII, yielding where Leo X and Adrian VI had resisted, confirmed
Wolsey as legate for life and protested that it was not equal to
Wolsey's merits, a sentiment with which Wolsey cordially agreed.
Although Wolsey's reply to Clement VII was an unruffled stream
of gratitude, Wolsey complained to Pace in Rome that 'I esteme
somewhat more straugnes to be shewed unto me then my merytes
requiere, in that there hath bene difficultie made to amplifie my
faculties.'[55] However, it was not Campeggio, the perennial pleader

---

[52] *State Papers of Henry VIII*, ii, 103–4 (*LP* iv, 5625), addressed to Wolsey
as 'ap. sedis in Angl. et Hibern. de Latere legato'.

[53] *LP* iv, 640f. The clarification of Wolsey's legatine powers in Ireland was
possibly part of the amplification of powers being sought during the
summer of 1524 by Wolsey's agents in Rome.

[54] *LP* iv, 4942 and 5625. The Consistorial Acts refer to Alen as 'cancellarii
serenissimi Regis Angliae'; the provision was referred by Cesi on
3 September 1529 (PRO 31/10/14, fol. 90).

[55] *State Papers of Henry VIII*, vi, 257 (*LP* iv, 126). Pace was instructed to
explain 'how by Popes Leos graunte and by Popes Adryans, who passed
my legation with as large faculties as now I have, ad quinquennium, and
so from 5 yere to 5 yeres, promysing by speciall breves to proroge the
same de quinquennio in quinquennium during my life' (*ibid.*).

for Wolsey's legatine desires, who was directly involved, but
Giberti, now usefully situated as datary, who had cooperated with
Clerk in obtaining the bulls with which Wolsey was still dis-
content.[56]

Campeggio, not yet officially named protector in succession to
de'Medici, had left as legate for Germany in February 1524 before
his aid could be enlisted. When Thomas Hannibal left Rome for
England on 3 June with the Golden Rose for Henry, it was without the anticipated bulls increasing Wolsey's legatine faculties
still further. Clerk felt that the delay might be explained by
Wolsey's remissness in transferring the pension of 2000 ducats
reserved from Worcester to Cardinal de'Medici which the pope
now wished to settle on Giberti and another unnamed; and he
advised Wolsey not to stick at it, as Giberti might be very useful.
By July Nicholas Schönberg, Giberti and even the pope were
cooperative, but Cardinal Pucci was 'untreatable'; and Clerk
asked the pope to entrust the matter to Cardinal Pietro Accolti
instead. In the matter of granting Wolsey control of the collectorship through his secretary, Piero Vannes, and of permitting
Wolsey to suppress monasteries, even Accolti raised difficulty.[57]

It was Giberti who emerged as the effective agent for Wolsey.
Ghinucci dismissed as superfluous his own part in obtaining
additions to Wolsey's legatine powers, since the pope and Giberti
were such firm friends of Wolsey's. When Giberti was made
bishop of Verona on 8 August 1524, he pointedly explained that
he had received it without any conditions and would therefore
not become alienated from England. In December he again
acknowledged Wolsey's thanks for services performed. Within
several weeks of Campeggio's return to Rome on 18 October
1525, Bishop Clerk, then the only English ambassador in Rome,
was recalled to England and was succeeded by the team of Bishop
Ghinucci of Worcester and the layman Gregorio Casale. Although
Campeggio and Clerk were good friends, Clerk's final report of
the despatch of items of business for Wolsey gave credit to
Giberti along with Schönberg and unspecified 'others'; even his

[56] *LP* iv, 6, 15, 49 and 150.
[57] *LP* iv, 49, 252, 344, 376, 408, 511, 568 and 4921. See Clement VII to
Wolsey, refusing to transfer the office of collector to Piero Vannes (*LP* iv,
app. 5), and Wolsey's original letter making the request (Arch. Vat.,
A. A. Arm. i–xviii, nos. 1436 and 2581); Theiner, *Monumenta*, p. 535,
prints the first but erroneously gives it as addressed to Adrian VI.

letter en route from Campeggio's Bologna failed to mention the cardinal protector. Significantly, Clerk carried not only a complimentary letter given him by Campeggio for the king, but another from Giberti, whom Wolsey had sent a cipher for writing secret correspondence.[58]

In the two years that followed, Wolsey's chief item of business in the Curia was the foundation of his colleges at Oxford and Ipswich. On 21 August 1526 Giberti notified Wolsey that he had procured all that had been requested, and he expressed interest in assisting Wolsey in obtaining transcriptions from the Venetian and papal libraries along with a lecturer. The grant of papal bulls of foundation was a simple matter; the gaining of permission to suppress selected small religious houses to endow them was more complicated. On his return from a special mission to England in 1526 Gianbattista Sanga explained Wolsey's wishes to Clement VII and to Giberti; but the bulls were so full of errors in the spelling of place names that Wolsey requested fresh copies from Rome. Giberti promised to see to this and to the renewal of a dispensation to hold incompatible benefices for Wolsey's son, Thomas Winter, of whom Giberti had news from Paris, and for whom he professed great affection. Sir John Russell wrote from Rome in defence of Gregorio Casale, whom Wolsey had severely attacked for negligence, and explained that the errors of which Wolsey complained in his college bulls were in the original minutes sent to Rome by Wolsey. Difficulties in promulgation made still more corrections necessary, and Giberti had the bulls done yet again, removing the phrase 'de fundatorum consensu'.[59]

Curiously, Campeggio does not seem to have been connected with Wolsey's colleges before 1528, or with much other English business, in spite of his faithfulness as a writer of newsletters. Shortly after returning to Rome from Germany he intervened at the king's request to prevent an unpromising suit of Antonio Bonvisio, a merchant in London, from coming to trial before the Rota or the Camera, and arranged for Bonvisio's proctors to

---

[58] *LP* IV, 568, 587, 1742, 1745 and 1771. See Giberti's role in the grant of pilgrimage indulgences for the king and queen at Walsingham, Bury St Edmunds and Canterbury (*LP* IV, 652). Clerk specifically mentioned the obtaining of a two-years restraint on the Greyfriars and of a plenary indulgence for the Lady chapel at Ipswich for three days a year (*LP* IV, 1777).

[59] *LP* IV, 2419, 2444, 2620, 2770, 2868f., 2879 and 3562

obtain a favourable hearing from the pope himself. On 12 June 1528, just before Campeggio left for England as legate, a draft was prepared for him as bishop of Salisbury giving assent to the annexation of the prebend of Blowbery to Wolsey's college in Oxford, as provided in a papal decree of the same date. Shortly before departing from England in 1529, Wolsey was granted licence from Campeggio to take timber from the manor of Sonnynge, Berkshire, for the Oxford college. This was in keeping with other concessions made, and of which Campeggio was presumed to be informed when Jacobo Salviati wrote to him from Rome. Henry VIII was permitted to appropriate monastic property to enrich two colleges founded by his 'grandfather'; and, reluctantly, Wolsey was allowed still three more monasteries for his college. The request to erect certain monasteries into cathedrals was deferred until the cardinals could be consulted in Consistory, and Wolsey was merely empowered to inquire into the expediency of such action. The king's request for an indulgence was granted, but during a few days only in order not to debase still more the sinking prestige of indulgences.[60]

After 1523 the only English business in Rome consistently entrusted to Campeggio was that staple activity of cardinal protectors, the referring of episcopal provisions in Consistory. His first, even before he was officially named protector, was that of the Dominican Maurice Doran to Leighlin, Ireland, on 28 January 1524, as successor to the late Thomas Halsey. That it was made at the supplication of the king and, because of the poverty of the see, without consistorial taxes suggests that Campeggio was specifically chosen by the king. Thereafter, and until 1534 when no further royal nominations were made by Henry VIII, Campeggio obliged whenever he was in Rome, or in his absence enlisted the regular assistance of Cardinal Paolo Cesi. During the eleven years before the first Act of Supremacy, Campeggio was absent from the Curia for a total of more than six of them on his missions as legate to Germany in 1524–5 and 1530–2, and as legate to England in 1528–9. Of the twenty-seven royal nominations made to English and Irish sees or as suffragans to them,

[60] *LP* IV, 1865, 2614, 4364, 4920f., 5607f. and 5951. Salviati does not mention the more important bull also of 12 November 1528, empowering Wolsey to merge monasteries with fewer than twelve monks or nuns with larger ones (Rymer, *Foedera*, XIV, 272; *LP* IV, 4921). Another bull gave him power to suppress outright monasteries with fewer than six religious.

Campeggio referred five English and six Irish ones, while Cesi referred four English and eight, possibly nine, Irish ones. Three English provisions were referred for the absent Campeggio by Clement VII, that of Campeggio himself to Salisbury in 1524 and those of Edward Lee to York and Stephen Gardiner to Winchester in 1531 after Wolsey's death.[61]

By Campeggio's own testimony he regarded the proposing of candidates to bishoprics in Consistory as his by right as protector of England. While he was absent from Rome in 1531 as legate to the Empire, he was unable to refer the provisions made to York and Winchester but complained nevertheless at not receiving his fair share of the taxes paid. In 1530 Thomas Boleyn and John Stokesley had in person prevailed upon Campeggio at Bologna to refer at reduced charge the translation of Tunstall from London to Durham and Stokesley's own provision to the London vacancy thus created without charge. Because none of the other sees which had fallen vacant between 1524 and 1531, most of which were Irish ones, were of any great value, Campeggio claimed that his total income thus far from *propinae* for the English protectorship had not been even a thousand *scuti*, a poor recompense for all his exertions in England's behalf. He objected to the granting of reductions to assuage English feelings as inconsonant with the practice of other great princes. On the other hand, however, the imperial ambassador in Rome had complained to Charles V in 1529 that the system of protectors was a late innovation and that his three protectors, Campeggio for Germany, Colonna for Castile, and Cesarini for Aragon, considering their protectorship as part and portion of their patrimony, were not the least grateful for the fees they got, as they would have been if they were chosen *ad hoc* as before.[62]

While Campeggio was protector of England, but largely apart from his efforts, Wolsey and the king revived attempts of ten years before to control provisions to Scottish benefices. The occasion arose when the duke of Albany sailed from Scotland for France. This time, however, in place of invoking the aid of the absent English protector, Campeggio, to intervene in Scottish affairs, as that of Giulio de'Medici had previously been used, Wolsey appealed directly to Cardinal Pietro Accolti, protector of

[61] Wodka, *Protektorate der Kardinäle*, p. 14, calls Cesi vice-protector.
[62] Arch. Vat., Lettere di Principi xi, fols. 112ᵛ–113ʳ; and *Sp. Cal.* iv, 4.

Scotland. Albany, who accompanied Francis I of France into northern Italy, and Albany's party about James V continued for a time to hold the allegiance of Cardinal Accolti; but Wolsey obtained letters from Henry VIII and, through Henry's sister Queen Mother Margaret of Scotland, from the twelve-year-old James V, informing Clement VII that the two nations were at concord, and that the granting of Scottish benefices to their nominees was calculated to maintain it. Bishop John Clerk not only explained the state of things to the pope but remonstrated with Accolti himself as protector. He threatened to find a means to remove Accolti from the office altogether, if he persisted in favouring Albany's nominees. Pressure from Clement VII and Clerk's combination of flattery and offers in the name of Henry VIII, Wolsey and James V finally brought Accolti round; and he genially proclaimed 'quicunque est rex, ipse erit dominus meus'.[63] During the next three years nominations made in James V's name according to English pleasure were duly referred in Consistory by Accolti.[64] In 1528, after James V, then sixteen years old, took personal charge of his government, he countermanded Henry VIII's nomination of Alexander Douglas to be bishop of Moray by nominating Alexander Stewart, half-brother of Albany. The flexible Accolti adjusted to this new change; after more than a year's delay, he referred the provision of Stewart on 13 September 1529.[65]

[63] *LP* IV, 899, 901, 1002, 1356 and 1451.
[64] For example, Henry VIII to Clement VII, 23 February 1525 (?), nominating Robert Shaw to be bishop of Moray, 'vehementissime' in the name of his sister and nephew (Arch. Vat., A. A. Arm. I–XVIII, no. 2381; modern copy in Br. Mus., Add. MS 15387, fols. 157–9; in Theiner, *Monumenta*, p. 548, under date of 1524; *LP* IV, 1116). At the same time John Hamilton was nominated to be abbot of Paisley; Shaw was provided on 17 May 1525. The other five bishoprics filled during this period of English ascendancy were Robert Montgomery to Argyll (1525); George Crichton to Dunkeld, William Chisholm I to Dunblane, Robert Maxwell to the Orkneys, and Henry Wemyss to Galloway (all in 1526) (Brady, *Episcopal Succession*, I, 130, 136, 140, 150, 151, 158 and 160). Papal provision or confirmation of abbots had been delegated to Wolsey in England but was still handled from Rome for Scotland.
[65] *LP* IV, 4303; and Hannay, *Letters of James V*, pp. 145 and 164. Upon the recommendation of Cardinal Pietro Accolti, James V named the former's nephew, Cardinal Benedetto Accolti, assistant and successor to Pietro with full powers; see James V to Pietro Accolti, 6 April 1530 (Hannay, p. 173, and numerous related letters, pp. 195–7). Pietro Accolti died on 11 December 1532. On 16 December 1538 James V transferred the protectorship to Cardinal Pio Rodolfo de Carpi, faithful substitute for the absent Benedetto

The persistent tradition in Scotland of suffragan bishops ignoring or obtaining outright exemption from metropolitan jurisdiction was very much to the advantage of the English party so long as Archbishop James Betoun of St Andrews remained a staunch opponent of English domination. Betoun, for his part, was eagerly striving to obtain the very kind of legatine powers *a latere* which his predecessor, Archbishop Forman, had been given, but which Wolsey had got Giulio de'Medici to have rescinded in 1515.[66] At first Wolsey attempted to bargain by offering to ask Henry VIII to request legatine powers for Betoun to confirm abbatial elections as Wolsey did in England, if Betoun would cooperate with the English party in Scotland. Although Henry VIII wrote to the pope in commendation of Betoun, and Bishop Ghinucci and Casale assured Wolsey that the pope would do as the king and Wolsey said, Wolsey and the pope were guilty of duplicity of the meanest sort with Betoun. While Ghinucci went through the motions of supporting Betoun's agents in Rome, even to the point of going to the pope with Cardinal Pietro Accolti at their request, he informed Wolsey with relief that efforts had been abandoned to have Betoun created cardinal, and that he had suggested to the pope that the likelihood of the French asking for a similar legatine commission be used as justification for delay in granting one for Scotland. The next year Francis I of France, probably at the request of Albany, came out in support of James V's request to the pope that Albany's half-brother, Alexander Stewart, not yet bishop of Moray, should be made legate to Scotland with the powers conferred upon the late Archbishop Andrew Forman. At

Accolti (Hannay, p. 358; *LP* xiii, ii, 1080). This supplements Wodka's list of protectors of Scotland (*Protektorate der Kardinäle*, pp. 122–3).

[66] James V to Clement VII, and James Betoun to Pietro Accolti, 16 January 1524, asking that the authority of St Andrews be kept intact in the promotion to the archdiocese of Glasgow or to any other vacancy (Hannay, *Letters of James V*, p. 97; *LP* iv, 33 and 34). On 13 January 1525 someone wrote in the name of James V to Clement VII, thanking him for promoting Gavin Dunbar to Glasgow with an exemption from the primacy and legatine authority (*legatus natus*) of St Andrews (Hannay, p. 113; *LP* iv, 1012); but on 1 March 1525 there were letters from James V to Clement VII, asking that exemptions from the metropolitan authority of St Andrews be rescinded, and that Betoun be made legate *a latere* (Hannay, p. 117). Albany, no longer in Scotland, had written Clement VII on 8 December 1524, asking that all requests of the English in Scottish affairs be disregarded, and that Betoun be made legate *a latere* (Hannay, p. 111; *LP* iv, 916).

the end of 1530 Betoun was still pressing his unsuccessful campaign on the strength of a royal signature which James V disowned, and the king of Scotland had a new candidate for legate in Gavin Douglas.[67]

Campeggio's involvement with these Scottish developments came late indeed. In September 1528, when he was passing through Paris on his way to England, the duke of Albany attempted, unsuccessfully, to arrange with Campeggio and the English ambassador in Paris for Henry VIII's permission to return to Scotland. In 1533, after the imprisonment of Betoun, and when Rome was making radical efforts to soften Henry VIII's mounting anger, the case against Betoun was committed by Clement VII to Campeggio. The pope ordered Betoun to be kept in custody pending an investigation by the apostolic nuncio and suspended any order of release given either by Campeggio or by himself.[68] The English break with Rome came before continuing, effective control had been established by England over either the Irish or the Scottish church.

---

[67] *LP* IV, 1028 (ii), 2084, 2158, 2199, 2208ff. and 2221f.; and Hannay, *Letters of James V*, pp. 138f., 164 and 183. On later efforts of Cardinal David Betoun to obtain a legatine commission *a latere* in 1538–9, see Hannay, pp. 349–52 and 358–62; *LP* XIII, ii, 102, 417 and various others between 1079 and 1167.

[68] *LP* IV, 4739, 4760 and app. 8; Hannay, *Letters of James V*, p. 251.

6

THE END OF AN ARRANGEMENT, 1528–34

The divorce: Campeggio under pressure from pope, England and emperor

When the great question of the divorce broke, Campeggio was lionised by the English; this represented an eventual return to favour. During the years 1526–7 Henry VIII and Wolsey made surprisingly little use of the services that Campeggio, long since returned to Rome from the Empire, had always been so eager to perform in the past, and to which as bishop of Salisbury he was more than ever bound. For some reason his relationship with England was under a cloud. When Sir John Russell arrived in Rome on 6 February 1527 as special ambassador, he was not met by Campeggio, who had received John Clerk so cordially in 1521 and again in 1523, but by Giberti, who was more than cordial. Although Russell tactfully declined Giberti's invitation to lodge in the papal palace, he was flattered by Giberti's riding about Rome with him for recreation and by the other special attentions shown him. Russell, as instructed by Wolsey, urged Clement VII to create Giberti as well as Ghinucci and the nuncio Gambara cardinal. Campeggio's indirect efforts to overcome Wolsey's displeasure with him proved unnecessary. In a letter, possibly brought by Russell, Wolsey graciously chose to restore Campeggio to his good graces and claimed credit for having reinstated him with the king as well. Campeggio poured out his obsequious gratitude in a letter of 7 February, insisting that he had crossed the English channel from France in 1518 as an Italian but returned to Italy an Englishman and bondsman to the king. Neither his detractors nor his supposed offences were named.[1]

Possibly Campeggio had been remiss in seeing to Wolsey's personal affairs in the Curia, but the difficulty is better explained

[1] *LP* iv, 2819, 2857 and 2875.

by the current diplomatic situation. The abandonment of the pro-imperial policy, first by the pope and then by England, had thrown affairs out of joint. Again following the signal given by the pope and the wishes of the king, Wolsey, after a period of disengagement, eventually brought England over to the side of France. Henry VIII had been tactfully named protector of the Italian league in August 1526, and Russell's mission in February 1527 was to bring money and to denounce the imperial advance into Italy. Since 1525 Giberti, once a dedicated imperial, had been a passionate advocate of a general alliance against Charles.[2] Ghinucci remained staunchly pro-English, and the German Schönberg an imperial. Only Campeggio attempted to maintain his traditional loyalties intact. He had been retained as protector of Germany after the election of Charles V in 1519 and had spent most of the years 1524–5 in Germany as papal legate. Wolsey, who had earlier even assisted Campeggio to cement these ties with the Empire, now had reason to regret it and perhaps, as was his wont, attempted to bully Campeggio into showing that he could be relied on.[3]

Free from the intense feelings of a zealot like Giberti, Campeggio saw his loyalty to the pope as his primary one; but he could only regret the growing rift between pope and emperor. His brother Tommaso, who as nuncio to Venice had cooperated with Pace in bringing Venice into the general alliance against France in 1523, was now less than eager to see this alliance reversed. While still in Hungary, Campeggio had sent his brother Bartolomeo down into Italy to Charles V before the 'French war' in progress there had been decided in battle, and when the Peasants' war in Germany was in full flood. After arriving back in Bologna himself, Campeggio sent his brother on a return mission to the emperor and offered congratulations on his victory at Pavia. It was hardly the appropriate moment for the legate so recently recalled from Germany to assume a position of neutrality, even if

---

[2] F. Gualterio (ed.), *Corrispondenza segreta di Gian Matteo Giberto datario di Clemente VII col Cardinale Agostino Trivulzio dell'anno MDXXVII, dicifrata e pubblicata* (Turin, 1845); *LP* iv, 1017, 1521, 1624, 1817, 1831, 2398 and 2769f.

[3] Campeggio to Charles V from Rome, 7 March 1522, thanking him for his generosity and offering assurance of services; and 31 March 1523, asking him to make good his promise of a bishopric (Madrid, Real Academia de la Historia, Colección Salazar, A-23, fol. 86, and A-27, fol. 258).

he had been so inclined.[4] In the wake of the Turkish victory at
Mohács on 24 September 1526, there was even talk of Campeggio's returning as legate to the emperor, then in Spain.[5]
Campeggio as well as Giberti wrote to Henry VIII in support of
Ghinucci's mission in search of aid and assured the king that the
whole hope of the Holy See rested in him. There was no direct
mention, however, of the sack of St Peter's and the papal palace
just four days before by the partisans of Cardinal Colonna, or of
the fact that Campeggio's apartments, guarded by some Spanish
soldiers, were alone among those spared. Campeggio's commitment was clear enough so that he could speak of 'our troops'
successfully besieging the imperialists in Cremona, but he still
seemed to hope that Wolsey could arrange a general peace. After
Henry VIII's promise to send the pope funds for defence, Campeggio wrote to Wolsey on 7 November of 'our king', but with
the guarded implication that all was not well between them.[6]

When Russell and Wolsey's forgiveness arrived together in
February 1527, Campeggio responded with the enthusiasm of one
dedicated only to the pope, England and the defence of the Holy
See. In April the German and Spanish troops had already done
much damage to Bologna, Campeggio's bishopric and native city,
and threatened to continue the siege in violation of a truce concluded with the pope unless they were offered a large sum of
money besides. As the war came closer to Rome, Campeggio and
Giberti seemed to draw closer together; and they found themselves together, along with Gregorio Casale, among those with
Clement VII in the Castel Sant'Angelo during and after the sack
of Rome in May. This time Campeggio was plundered of all he
had and was forced to ransom himself with income from his
English bishopric. His was but one among the nine abject letters
written to Wolsey on 6–8 June by the cardinals and others from
their fortress prison; Clement VII himself wrote in his own hand.
When the pope fled to Orvieto in December, however, Giberti,

---

[4] Campeggio to Charles V from Bologna, 25 July 1525 (Madrid, Real
Academia de la Historia, Collección Salazar, A-35, fol. 107); cited by
Müller, *Legation Lorenzo Campeggios*, i, lxiv.
[5] Madrid, Real Academia de la Historia, Collección Salazar, A-39, fol. 108;
in November 1526 Charles V acknowledged the good intentions and wishes
of Cardinals Campeggio, Cesarini, della Valle, Enkevoirt and Piccolomini
(*Sp. Cal.* iii, 611).
[6] *LP* iv, 1937, 2513ff., 2522, 2613f. and 2648.

his policy shattered, was held as hostage and then, as he wrote to Wolsey, went off to his bishopric of Verona 'to serve God'. It was Campeggio who was left behind in the Castel Sant'Angelo as papal legate to Rome to deal with the chaos rampant there. At this most inconvenient of times Henry VIII publicly raised in the Curia the issue of the validity of his marriage to the emperor's aunt.[7]

In so far as Henry permitted him to manage the matter, Wolsey's strategy turned upon the pope's permitting the marriage case to be tried in England by himself and, as seemed unavoidable, a co-legate from among the curial cardinals; and Campeggio was ever the choice he had most in mind. Wolsey was well aware of Campeggio's position as protector of Germany and surely understood that this must have figured in Clement VII's choice of Campeggio as legate to Rome. In May 1528 Wolsey obliquely suggested that Campeggio's delay in departing for England made him suspect of trying to appease the emperor, but he seems to have been confident from the beginning that Campeggio was not inclined toward the imperialist party in the king's matter and could be won over to the English point of view.[8] Later when the process had been bogged down in England, the English ambassadors in Rome attempted to divert pressure from themselves by emphasising Campeggio's supposed imperialist preferences; but there is little evidence that they had much insisted on it beforehand. Even in 1529 Henry VIII discounted their suspicions. Despite his much later claim to the contrary, as early as 13 January 1528 Casale recommended Campeggio as the most suitable cardinal. In March Gardiner and Foxe assured Wolsey that Campeggio was one 'de cujus voluntate non dubitatur', for the pope had been urged by Campeggio in Rome to give credence to the king's letters and reasons.[9] Among alternative choices to Campeggio, Wolsey first considered de Cupis or Farnese, and as an afterthought Cesi, del Monte or Piccolomini. Cardinal Pucci's services were enlisted in Rome, but he was apparently never considered as a possible co-legate. Alone among the other cardinals Pietro Accolti seems to have been given serious consideration, and

[7] *LP* iv, 2857, 3038, 3062, 3072, 3074, 3114, 3253, 3155–66, 3422, 3424ff. and 3813; *Sp. Cal.* iii, ii, 259 and 262.

[8] *LP* iv, 3693 and 4288f.

[9] *LP* iv, 3802, 5213, 5427 and 5471; Pocock, *Records of the Reformation*, ii, 517–18.

then only if Campeggio's illness with gout should prevent his own coming.[10]

There were telling reasons for wanting Campeggio. He had lived for a year in England as legate in 1518–19, and that experience with him encouraged Wolsey to imagine him easy to dominate in conference and to dazzle with display and gifts. During the intervening years it was Campeggio rather than Wolsey who had shown the more enthusiasm for his continued relationship with England. He begged Wolsey for a bishopric as a dog might beg for a bone, and his extraordinary gratitude for the gift of Salisbury suggested other possibilities. Of all the cardinals Campeggio had the advantage of being the one whom Wolsey knew best, and whom by personal experience he felt sure he could manage. Just the previous year Cardinal Pietro Accolti, protector of Scotland, had acted as judge in the marriage suit of Henry VIII's sister, Queen Margaret of Scotland; and her marriage to the earl of Angus had been declared null. There was reason to think that Campeggio as protector of England, especially in England itself and with Wolsey as co-judge, could do as well. If the sack of Rome had placed the pope at the mercy of the emperor, it had also emphasised the steady loyalty of Henry VIII and had at the same time provided the justification for hearing the case in England. Both Henry and Wolsey could wistfully persuade themselves that on purely political grounds the private preference of both Clement VII, past protector of England, and Campeggio, present protector of England, should be for the king. If Campeggio had in the past been much associated with the Empire, this could now serve to give the trial in England as least the appearance of objectivity. Lastly, Campeggio possessed the qualification which properly should have been considered first: he was an experienced and learned canon lawyer and judge.

Although Clement VII at Orvieto had given assurance in January 1528 that he would send as co-legate whichever cardinal Wolsey might choose, provided he be a jurist and theologian, Campeggio was formally named to England and Farnese his replacement as legate to Rome only in the consistory of 8 June. However, both the king and Wolsey had enlisted Campeggio's aid, along with that of Giberti, Accolti, del Monte and Pucci, in

---

[10] *LP* IV, 3693, 3749, 3751, 3781, 3784, 3788, 3913, 3919f., 4120, 4167 (p. 1841), 4289f. and 4814f.

support of the mission of Gardiner, Foxe and the former nuncio Gambara. In February Casale wrote to Campeggio from Orvieto to ask whether he would go to England if there were occasion and, receiving a favourable reply, went to Rome to pursue the matter personally.[11] The joint commission for Wolsey and Campeggio was agreed to on 13 April, along with a far-reaching dispensation for a future marriage, if the king's present one should prove invalid. A month later there was open talk in Venice that Campeggio was going to England to annul the king's marriage; and Wolsey, already restless at his delay in setting out, was expressing gratitude for the pope's having chosen him.[12]

From the beginning the purely judicial and legal matter with which Campeggio and, lest it be forgotten, Wolsey were entrusted was deluged by the political considerations which surrounded it. If Clement VII was caught between Charles V and Henry VIII, Campeggio was the object of enormous pressures from all three. Rather than simply recount the already familiar unfolding of events during Campeggio's stay in England, it might be more useful for present purposes to attempt to analyse in turn some of these pressures on Campeggio, first from the pope, then from Henry VIII and Wolsey, and finally from Charles V.[13]

The pope had confidence both in Campeggio's ability and in his loyalty but could not bring himself to allow Campeggio freedom simply to hear the case with Wolsey and then decide it on its merits. Campeggio became a cloak for his own indecision and his instrument in a massive subterfuge. To satisfy the English he issued a bull empowering Campeggio and Wolsey to give

---

[11] S. Ehses (ed.), *Römische Dokumente zur Geschichte der Ehescheidung Heinrichs VIII. von England, 1527–1534*, Görres-Gesellschaft, Quellen und Forschungen aus dem Gebiete der Geschichte, II (Paderborn, 1893), p. 205; PRO 31/10/15, fol. 103; *LP* IV, 3802, 3910, 3921, 3970 and 3995. The Casale brothers, Gregorio, Gianbattista, Paolo and Vicenzo, were, like Campeggio, from Bologna.

[12] Ehses, *Römische Dokumente*, pp. 28–30 and 33–6; *Sp. Cal.* III, 427; *Ven. Cal.* IV, 292; and *LP* IV, 4167, 4249, 4288 and 4355.

[13] The best of the more recent accounts of the divorce are G. de C. Parmiter, *The King's Great Matter, a Study of Anglo-Papal Relations 1527–1534* (London, 1967); and J. J. Scarisbrick, ch. VII, 'The canon law of the divorce', and ch. VIII, 'The struggle for the divorce', *Henry VIII* (London, 1968), pp. 163–240. M. Albert, *The Divorce, a re-examination by an American of the Great Tudor Controversy* (London, 1966) is a popular account. H. A. Kelly promises a study of the divorce from the point of view of legal incest.

sentence together or even alone, if the other were unwilling or
unable to do so. From the beginning Campeggio suspected,
correctly, that Clement VII was not being completely frank.[14]
Beyond the famous secret decretal bull sent with Campeggio the
pope evidently made promises to the English ambassadors of
which Campeggio was not directly informed. Yet he commanded
Campeggio to delay matters in England as much as possible, to
work first at reconciling the king and queen, and not to allow the
case to come to trial without another explicit mandate. Salviati's
letters, written with the pope's full authority, continued to insist
upon these instructions.[15]

To satisfy the emperor, Clement VII emphasised that the
matter had been entrusted to Campeggio because he was a good
jurist, had experience of England, and was in the emperor's
confidence; he raised hopes that Campeggio might induce
Henry VIII to abandon the case altogether. By February 1529
Charles V in Spain had finally learned that, despite his assurance
to the contrary, Clement VII had issued the mandate for the case
actually to be tried in England, and in May the imperial ambassador in Rome was still protesting to Charles V that the commission
had been given without his knowledge.[16] However, as Wolsey
quickly discerned, Clement VII, for all his supposed terror of
Charles V, could not resist using Campeggio's coming to England
as a lever against the emperor in the hope of obtaining peace in
Italy. Such an occasion was even useful for the smaller purpose
of seeking the restitution of Ravenna and Cervia to the Papal
States from Venice. Clement VII, despite the repeated pressure
of Wolsey upon the Venetians and his own enlisting of French
aid, had specifically included this condition in Campeggio's
instructions, intimating that he would be ready to state his mind
about permitting Campeggio and Wolsey to bring the marriage
case to trial when Henry VIII had done his utmost to compel the
Venetians to restore the pope's territories.[17] In the flush of happi-

---

[14] Campeggio to his brother Tommaso, from Rome, 21 April 1528, 'Non la
intendo perho chiaramente, perche mi disse non seti vui stato avisato da
nostro Signore del tuto' (Bologna, AS, AMC, 3rd series, 22/545).

[15] Ehses, *Römische Dokumente*, pp. 40–6, 48, 55, 109 and 260; and also his
'Papst Klemens VII. in dem Scheidungsprozesse Heinrichs VIII.',
Historisches Jahrbuch, XIII (1892), 483; *LP* IV, 4721, 4736ff. and 5604.

[16] *Sp. Cal.* III, 537; *Ven. Cal.* IV, 299, 301 and 372; *LP* IV, 5301 and 5346.

[17] Ehses, *Römische Dokumente*, pp. 43 and 53; *LP* IV, 4898. On 8 December
1528 Henry VIII in the presence of Wolsey and Campeggio formally

ness at Clement VII's election in 1523 Clerk, intending a high compliment, had written to Wolsey that 'every man supposyth ther is as moche crafte and pollicye in hym as in any man lyving'.[18]

Whatever his personal loyalty and obligation to the pope, Campeggio's long and personally profitable relationship with Henry VIII and Wolsey raised in them a not unreasonable expectation of cooperation. But the intensity of Henry VIII's desire and the desperateness of Wolsey's position combined to generate a pressure on Campeggio beyond what even he must have foreseen. Wolsey set the tone by assuring Campeggio, even before the papal commission had been issued, that the king's matter was so plain as not to admit of discussion and too righteous to be brought into controversy. The king had set out his own case in a book to which Wolsey had appended a collection of learned opinions. After presenting the book to the pope in Orvieto, Stephen Gardiner brought it or a duplicate to Campeggio when he came to Rome in April 1528.[19] Wolsey advised Campeggio to inform the pope that the king fully expected not to be disappointed. Of this Campeggio was already keenly aware. He also knew the case could never be treated as the purely English affair which the king and Wolsey wished to make it.

Once it was decided that Campeggio was to come to England, Wolsey set in motion a bustle of activity between Rome and London designed to speed Campeggio's departure and ease his journey. He supposedly arranged to pay all Campeggio's expenses and sent elaborate instructions to Gardiner and Casale in Italy and to Clerk in France to provide for ships, changes of horses, a

---

directed the Venetian ambassador in London to write to the Signoria that neither he nor the king of France would tolerate a refusal (*Ven. Cal.* IV, 376). Gardiner had already made fruitless appeals in Venice itself (*LP* IV, 4430, 4436, 4553, 4920 and 5447).

[18] Br. Mus., Vitell. B. v, fol. 224ʳ (*LP* III, 3594).

[19] Campeggio to his brother Tommaso from the Castel Sant'Angelo, Rome, 21 April 1528, 'Mi ha dato Messer Stephano lo libro del re qual è molto copioso lo vado legendo. Quando venireti rasonaremo insieme. Mi par comprender che loro habino havuta la commissione al cardinale Eboracense et me, et sanno che la maestà regia non voglia aspetare tanto' (Bologna, AS, AMC, 3rd series, 22/545). Perhaps the content of this mysterious book is related to that of the carefully written presentation copy of a brief for the king's case, addressed to the legates and now in the Wren Library, Trinity College, Cambridge (MS B. 15. 19); a modern copy in Cambridge Univ. Lib., MS Mm. 1.41.

litter and even table wine for his gout-afflicted co-legate. To ensure that Campeggio should have comfortable and familiar lodging in London, Wolsey arranged for him once more to live in the bishop of Bath's London house 'without Temple-barre', the place in which he had been lodged in 1518–19, although as the dislodged and disgruntled Bishop Clerk of Bath protested, Wolsey's own Durham Place was available.[20] The exhausted and suffering Campeggio arrived privately in London by water on 8 October 1528. He was taken directly to Bath House and confined to bed. The next day Wolsey paid the first of a succession of calls upon him there and entered immediately and with full force into the reasons why the king's marriage must be declared invalid.[21]

Campeggio found the king's conviction unshakable and his pressure unrelenting. His first audience with the king, on 22 October, was followed by another session four hours long with him next day. The king had a profound knowledge of the theology and law connected with his case, and Campeggio thought that an angel descending from heaven could not persuade the king that his marriage was valid. Campeggio was even driven by the king and Wolsey to write a letter, which he later disclaimed, begging the pope to grant the king's wish.[22] Contrary reasons, he said, were without effect upon the English, and the least thing said was exaggerated and interpreted in their favour. At Bath House Campeggio, again acting under pressure, signed a three-point engagement that he had not and would not divulge either his own opinion or any of the king's secrets either to the pope or to anyone else; secondly, that should the king object to an advoca-

---

[20] *LP* iv, 3910, 3913, 3921, 4249, 4288, 4355, 4430, 4553, 4611, 4753f., 4768, 4789, 4795 and 4820; *Ven. Cal.* iv, 374; *Sp. Cal.* iii, 556. Archbishop Warham, pleading illness, excused himself from Wolsey's request that he meet Campeggio and accompany him to Rochester, and he permitted the use of his own litter for Campeggio only from Dover to Canterbury (*LP* iv, 4763 and 4788).

[21] Ehses, *Römische Dokumente*, pp. 47–8 (*LP* iv, 4857); and *LP* iv, 4851.

[22] Campeggio to Clement VII, 27 November 1528, giving as grounds 'satisfare a la conscientia sua, a la salute de la persona di S. M. et di questo regno et al stabilimento de la succession sua, et si provederà a molti scandali, che facilmente seguiranno' (Ehses, *Römische Dokumente*, p. 65). Another letter, of 18 February 1529, apparently freely written and also sympathetic with the king, is printed with introductory comment by Ehses in the *Römische Quartalschrift*, xiv (1900), 256–68; Ehses' own corrections in light of a better text are given in Pastor, *History of the Popes*, trans. Kerr, x, 267.

tion of the case to Rome, he would without reservation use all his efforts with the pope to prevent Queen Catherine from prosecuting the case there; and, thirdly, that, as a sworn councillor to the king, he would do his best to advance the king's interests and dignity.[23] As the case proceeded to trial Campeggio reported that the king and Wolsey were importuning him beyond measure.

The evidence makes it clear that this pressure on Campeggio was accompanied by what was in effect bribery, to which Campeggio had hitherto seemed to be so susceptible. Earlier Wolsey, who had never seen York, caustically suggested that Campeggio's coming to England might afford him the opportunity to visit his bishopric of Salisbury.[24] Gardiner and Foxe had been authorised to offer rewards to the legate selected; and on 23 May 1528 Wolsey brightly assured Casale that he was confident that Campeggio, knowing the reward awaiting him, would not refuse this opportunity to serve the king. The foremost reward was certainly the promise of a wealthier bishopric in exchange for the already impressively endowed Salisbury. Bishop Richard Fox of Winchester had died just before Campeggio's arrival in London from Dover; but rumours that this prize, one of the richest sees in Christendom, was to fall to Campeggio were mistaken. This Wolsey wanted for himself; and should he thereby be required to relinquish Durham, his first thought for a successor there had been his son Thomas Winter, chancellor of Campeggio's Salisbury. Subsequent developments, however, seem to substantiate the fact that Durham was promised to Campeggio. In his first letters despatched from England Campeggio urged Wolsey's provision to Winchester. Two weeks later he urged, using chiefly erroneous information, that Wolsey's exchange of Durham for Winchester be expedited as cheaply as possible, and specifically requested Salviati to inform Wolsey's agents in Rome that he had written

---

[23] PRO, SP 1/55, fol. 31 (*LP* iv, 5820). The date is missing but London, Bath House, and Campeggio's signature and seal are intact; this was Gardiner's work.

[24] *LP* iv, 3693. Evidently Campeggio had actually planned to visit Salisbury. An indulgence bull of Clement VII, designed for the occasion and issued at Viterbo on 6 June 1528, asserts that Campeggio 'ecclesiam ipsam suam visitare et in ea forsan etiam Missam in Pontificalibus celebrare intendat' (Bologna, AS, AMC, 2nd series, 55/292). In the same carton is another bull empowering Campeggio to publish a plenary indulgence immediately following any solemn mass he might celebrate in the king's presence.

warmly on his behalf. In December the French ambassador in London reported that Campeggio was to be given Durham; and when Wolsey was provided to Winchester in Consistory on 8 February 1529, Durham was allowed to remain enticingly vacant during the rest of Campeggio's stay in England. When Clement VII was thought to be dying, Wolsey even sent instructions to the English agents in Rome that they should strive to secure the election of Campeggio as pope if Wolsey's own candidacy were not successful.[25]

During the spring of 1529, when affairs in England were moving toward a climax, there were more reports of royal offers to Campeggio. Cardinal Salviati wrote from France to his father in Rome that Campeggio had been offered a bishopric, and Brian protested from Rome that Campeggio's supposed loyalty was governed by his desire to have Durham.[26] Chapuys, who replaced Mendoza as Charles V's ambassador in September 1529, wrote from London that, in addition, there had been the offer 'de l'argent une mirable somme'; Campeggio was supposed to have received plate worth 4000 ducats on arrival and a further 3000 ducats' worth before leaving. Campeggio's sixteenth-century biographer, Sigonio, claims that the king made a direct attempt to buy a favourable decision, but his mention of Winchester as the bishopric offered to Campeggio makes the accuracy of his entire statement suspect.[27]

According to Chapuys, Campeggio claimed to have withstood the king's offers of innumerable presents. Certainly whatever offers were in fact made, were upon the condition that Campeggio hand down a favourable sentence. On 12 May 1529 Campeggio insisted to Rome that he had sustained heavy expenses during the preceding five months in England and was much in need of his regular curial income. Eight days later he thanked Salviati for payment of the sums due to him, and on 29 May word was again sent that money was on its way to him. Unless Campeggio was working a devious scheme, this implies that the king and Wolsey did not, or were not permitted to pay his ordinary expenses as they had promised. In the end he complained of his mail being

25 *LP* IV, 3913 (p. 1741), 4289, 4824, 4857, 4898, 5063 and 5270.
26 Ehses, *Römische Dokumente*, p. 264; and *LP* IV, 5519.
27 Carlo Sigonio, *De vita Laurentii Campegii Cardinalis liber*, p. 70; *Sp. Cal.* IV, 182 and 241; *LP* V, pp. 311 and 315f.

intercepted and tampered with, and of his luggage being broken open and searched at his departure from England.[28] On 21 February 1530 Campeggio himself referred in Consistory the translation of Tunstall from London to Durham.

When the legates were first formally received by the king at Greenwich on 16 October 1528, the speeches, one of which was made by Campeggio's secretary Floriano Montini, emphasised all that Rome had recently suffered, especially from the sack by the imperial troops.[29] The king's present expectation of favour from the pope was based on his record of unswerving loyalty to Rome in the past; but, from the first, the dark threat was there that the pope's failure to grant the king's desire would mark the ruin of papal power in England. Eager as the king was to have the case tried in England, Wolsey rather ominously followed the letter of the English law and issued a royal licence under the great seal to himself and Campeggio, permitting them to execute their original commission to hear the case, and issued still another on 30 May 1529 just before the actual trial began. Wolsey's opening words of greeting to Campeggio in England were to explain the fact that many in England had insisted that no legate was necessary at all to try the case, and only with difficulty had he convinced the king otherwise. Campeggio's intransigence, Wolsey warned, could wreak havoc. In the event of Clement VII's death and the election of an imperialist pope, even Wolsey himself was prepared to withdraw his allegiance from Rome. The message got home to the Curia.[30]

As the king's patience grew thinner, not only did he send Gardiner to Rome to threaten that he was prepared to throw off papal allegiance, if Campeggio was not directed to proceed with the trial; but he even began to toy publicly with the threat to turn to Lutheranism. The imperial ambassador Mai jested to the English ambassadors in Rome that, in such a case, Henry's book on that very subject would have to be returned.[31] During an informal discussion with Campeggio, in the presence of Wolsey, the king raised supposedly theoretical objections to the wealth of

[28] Ehses, *Römische Dokumente*, pp. 82 and 264–5; *LP* iv, 5535, 5572, 5604, 5995 and 6026.

[29] *Sp. Cal.* iii, 586.

[30] Ehses, *Römische Dokumente*, pp. 48, 50 and 263; *LP* iv, 4346, 5611 and 5576.

[31] Ehses, *Römische Dokumente*, p. 263.

the Church and to the wickedness in the Curia. Campeggio's arguments in reply were those of a man who, while not himself corrupt, had learned to live among those who were. In advoking the case to Rome Clement VII made a special appeal to Wolsey that he try to keep the king well disposed toward the Holy See. Already there was talk of anti-papal feeling in the parliament which had been summoned; and during his last interview with the king before his departure from England, Campeggio alluded to the approaching parliament and earnestly warned the king against despoiling the Church. Henry left the ambiguous impression that he was very well disposed to do good, but parliament might prove to have a mind of their own.[32]

In addition to these conflicting pressures from the pope and from England, there were still others from Charles V, to whom through the years Campeggio had also become obliged. In a sense Charles V was faced with a dilemma of his own. If he supported his aunt too vigorously, he would simply sever relations with Henry VIII and strengthen the position of Francis I and the French. On the other hand, if he failed to support Catherine's cause, he stood to lose much more than a sense of family honour. His own numerous and diverse territories and titles were the fruit of successful Habsburg marriage alliances. His very Spanish-minded cousin, Princess Mary, was then the only legitimate child of Henry VIII; Queen Catherine's continued health and ripe middle age promised to preclude Henry VIII from having any other. At this point Charles V could not have readily foreseen that what he himself had yielded by jilting the Princess Mary in 1525, he would later possess through her marriage with his son Philip; but it was still important for him that Mary continue to be Henry's only direct heir. His first line of defence lay in the pope's assurances that Campeggio was not authorised to bring the case to trial in England, and on 1 September 1528 the emperor relayed the pope's written assurances to Queen Catherine that nothing would be done by Campeggio to her detriment.[33]

The emperor's ambassadors in London, first Iñigo de Mendoza and then Chapuys, could never hope unaided to counterbalance the pressure upon Campeggio from the king and Wolsey; but at least, before Clement VII's tactics exasperated much of England,

[32] *Sp. Cal.* IV, 160 and 168; *LP* IV, 5416, 5785 and 5995.
[33] *Sp. Cal.* III, 537.

public opinion in London openly favoured Queen Catherine. Mendoza was not invited to the reception of the legates at Greenwich and found it difficult even to gain access to Campeggio, still less to discover what his actual mandate was. In order to get information about Henry VIII's interview with Campeggio at Bath House, he bribed an Italian to eavesdrop from an adjoining room. When at last he obtained an interview, Mendoza prudently congratulated Campeggio on his coming to England and told him that the emperor was pleased at his appointment. In his turn Campeggio assured the ambassador that all England could not make him swerve from whatever proved the right, and that he would not move another step in the case until he had received replies to his letters to Rome. Although Mendoza told Campeggio that he trusted him, he did, however, cast doubt upon him to the emperor and, reporting a rumour that Campeggio was already supposed to have received upwards of 20,000 crowns from the king, added darkly that if the king had thought Campeggio incorruptible he would not have sent for him.[34] The emperor had already sent Mendoza a letter for Campeggio. King Ferdinand of Bohemia, the emperor's brother and personally acquainted with Campeggio, wrote twice from Vienna to advise that Campeggio use the utmost caution in safeguarding the honour of both pope and emperor.[35]

Even before Charles V had received authentic information about Campeggio's actual mandate, he advised Mendoza that the best protection for his dear aunt was to prevent the trial in England. Even if he were able to trust Campeggio's good will, the emperor could not believe that Campeggio could continue to withstand English pressure, once a trial began. When the king sent Gardiner off to Rome to obtain the pope's mandate to begin the trial, Mendoza reported that Campeggio was no more trustworthy than Wolsey. The imperial ambassador in Rome began insisting that among the many other reasons for calling the case

[34] *Sp. Cal.* III, 550, 570 and 586.
[35] Ferdinand to Campeggio, 25 October 1528 and 9 January 1529, in copy and a copy of an inhibition of 11 November 1529 to Wolsey and Campeggio (Vienna, HHSA, England, Varia, Karton 2). In the same archive, Rom, Hofcorrespondenz, Karton 1, is a letter from Campeggio to Ferdinand, dated at Viterbo, 1 July 1528, gently complaining of not having received a reply to his earlier letter from Rome touching on personal matters and congratulating him on the birth of a son, the future Maximilian II.

to Rome was the fact that both legates, especially Wolsey, were
very much suspect.[36]

Campeggio in England as legate and judge

Seen in the light of the conflicting pressures placed upon him by
the pope, the English and the emperor, Campeggio's conduct in
the years 1528–9 as legate in England becomes more understand-
able, and those efforts he made toward objectivity as a judge in
the marriage case become more praiseworthy. That in the end
Campeggio came out in favour of the validity of the marriage is
not so important as his grounds for doing so. Against his skill as a
jurist can be set his inclination to consider factors external to the
case, and probably Campeggio himself could not disentangle the
part eventually played by each. Before he was named legate,
Clement VII sent Charles V's special envoy, the Franciscan friar
general Quiñones, from Orvieto to Rome to seek Campeggio's
opinion on points of canon law involved in the marriage case just
broached in the Curia by William Knight. In an autograph reply,
written from the Castel Sant'Angelo on 14 December 1527, Campeggio informed the pope that if it were a question of the power
to give the dispensation, the marriage was clearly valid; but
supposing the relevant impediment had not been properly identified or an insufficient dispensation given, the marriage was not
valid. In the latter case, the marriage could still be validated,
provided that the pope granted the proper dispensation, and that
both parties persisted in their original consent. Although the pope
could annul any lower judicial decision that might be made, it
would not be appropriate to do so; and the wisest procedure
would be to summon the case to a papal court at once rather than
accept it on appeal from a lower church court. If it were then
found in closed trial that the marriage was illegitimate and invalid, the pope could avoid all scandal by granting a sufficient
dispensation and the marriage could be validated. If either or
both parties were unwilling to renew the contract, the pope had
no choice but to inform them that they were not married. Any
children born to the parties to such an invalid marriage would be
de jure legitimate, if the parties were in just ignorance; but a
papal dispensation permitting the validation of such a marriage

---

[36] *Sp. Cal.* III, 566 and 621; *LP* IV, 4535, 5063 and 5529; *Ven. Cal.* IV,
482.

could specifically declare legitimate any children born in it.[37]

As lawyer and judge-legate Campeggio continued to view the case in terms of these principles. His monstrous suggestion that the succession to the English throne be made secure by the marriage of the Princess Mary with her bastard half-brother Henry FitzRoy, duke of Richmond, illustrates the lengths to which he thought papal dispensing power might go. The English insistence that the dispensation involved divine law from which the pope could not dispense, he found irritating.[38] Campeggio's initial effort to resolve the crisis by attempting to persuade Queen Catherine to take religious vows seems likewise to be based on a striking extension of legal precedent, since in the past such a means for dissolving the marriage bond had been limited to a marriage that was unconsummated.[39] Had Queen Catherine established her claim to have been still a virgin when she entered the marriage with Henry, the case against the sufficiency of the original dispensation would have been much weakened; but Campeggio always considered the canonical proof for her claim insufficient.[40] Had the dispensation been made only in the form found in the English State Paper Office, he might have found grounds for declaring it insufficient. The case for Campeggio, then, hung heavily on the authenticity of the more amply and precisely phrased copy found in Spain, especially since the Spanish brief seemed to render insufficient the terms of the decretal commission issued to Campeggio and Wolsey for trying the case in England. If the brief's existing only in Spain and not in

---

[37] Ehses, *Römische Dokumente*, pp. 12–13. The specific charge of Quiñones was to reconcile the pope to Charles V in the wake of the outrageous sack of Rome by his Spanish and German troops; Quiñones was created cardinal on 10 January 1529.

[38] *LP* iv, 4881, 4942 and 5447.

[39] *LP* iv, 4874f., 4880, 4898 and 5681. The medieval legislation in the *Decretales* of Gregory IX (iii, xxxii, cc. 2 *Verum* and 14 *Ex parte*; iv, i, c. 16 *Commissum*) was taken over into the *Codex Juris Canonici* (Can. 1119) of 1918. Campeggio urged Queen Catherine to follow the example in this of the Blessed Jeanne de Valois, whose marriage with Louis XII was declared invalid before his accession.

[40] *LP* iv, 4875 and 6528. In Lambeth Palace, MSS 2341 and 2342, acquired by purchase in 1969, contain a number of documents, including the defence briefs of Bishop West of Ely (MS 2341) and of Bishop Fisher of Rochester (MS 2342, fols. 1ʳ–21ᵛ in an Italian hand, and another in an English hand, fols. 23ʳ–32ᵛ, both copies signed by Fisher). MS 2342, fols. 79ʳ–82ᵛ, contains numbered lists of arguments and notes on consanguinity, evidently in Campeggio's hand.

England opened its authenticity to suspicion, Ghinucci and Lee's confident report from Spain certifying it was spurious was also suspect on the same grounds. It was a windfall in the effort to slow the progress toward trial, but it was also basic to it.[41]

Possibly Campeggio's statement in November 1528 that he regarded the cases both for and against nullity as strong may be dismissed as an attempt to dissemble his private opinion in favour of the validity of the marriage. Wolsey, on the other hand, however carefully he may have informed himself of the case, made no real effort to assume the guise of a disinterested judge, objectively considering the evidence in terms of the relevant canon law. In contrast with Campeggio, Wolsey was not a trained canonist or even a lawyer. His only previous experience with any law had been his forthright but amateur hearing of cases as lord chancellor in the developing court of the Star Chamber. During their first term as co-legates in 1518–19, when Wolsey had chosen to play the part of senior legate, their chief concerns were of diplomacy, an art in which Wolsey was much practised. Campeggio's distracted complaints in June 1529 against Wolsey's ignorance of proper canonical procedure are enlightening.[42] Campeggio was moving with all deliberate slowness (*andar pesatamente*); but even had the case been one which Wolsey could have approached disinterestedly, Campeggio must have found him a trying colleague.

As the English steadily drove Campeggio toward the day of sentence, and as Clement VII continued to hesitate either to advoke the case to Rome or to permit sentence to be given in England, Campeggio's position became almost unbearable; and he exclaimed 'I pray God, that I do not have to remain forever in England!' ('Prego Dio, ch'io non habbia a restar per sempre in Anglia').[43] On 21 June 1529 he assured the pope that when he knew positively that the king was wrong, he would be ready to give sentence against him without fear, even if he were certain to die at that moment. Although Queen Catherine's refusal to co-operate in the trial provoked him, he was apparently already sure in his own mind on 25 June that sentence would have to be given against the king; and within a month he openly informed Wolsey

---

[41] *LP* IV, 3643, 4980, 5181, 5441, 5447, 5474, 5477, 5480 and 5535. See Scarisbrick, *Henry VIII*, pp. 217ff.

[42] *LP* IV, 4942, 5595, 5636, 5681 and 5713.

[43] Ehses, *Römische Dokumente*, p. 108.

that his voice was in favour of the validity of the marriage.[44]

Even if Campeggio's opinion that the marriage was valid was solidly rooted in an honest conviction as lawyer and judge, his own activities were not always calculated to convey this fact. His famous 'diplomatic gout', which had so considerably slowed his journey to England, has been considerably overemphasised. Campeggio had complained of these severe attacks of gout even before the sack of Rome and continued to do so after final sentence had been passed. His suffering during his journey was substantially genuine, and even the king was sure it was unfeigned.[45] Curiously, Campeggio's trip from Rome to London in 1528 was but a few days longer than the same trip ten years before; it simply seemed longer. As both Campeggio and Clement VII remembered only too well, Wolsey had sought to delay Campeggio's arrival in 1518 in order to achieve his own ends, as much as he sought, in different circumstances but again for his own ends, to speed Campeggio's arrival in 1528. When Campeggio stopped at Viterbo en route to England to receive the decretal and oral instructions from Clement VII, the pope's concern went far beyond mere questions of law and legal justice. During his audience with Francis I at Paris, Campeggio sought to sound out this king's opinion on the marriage case and his unwillingness to cooperate in forcing the Venetians to return Ravenna and Cervia to the pope. Such an approach suggests the wiles of the diplomat more than the reserve of a judge. Campeggio, who had also been specially commissioned for the purpose, was taking active part in Clement VII's campaign to arrange peace in Italy.[46]

Lorenzo Campeggio's ties with his sons and brothers were always very close, perhaps closer even than was characteristic of an Italian society which normally saw family solidarity as its one

---

[44] *LP* iv, 5713 and 5919; *Sp. Cal.* iv, 134.

[45] Campeggio to Wolsey, 28 April 1527, 'Podagra vehementer laboravi: neque adhuc satis recta utor valitudine' (Br. Mus., Vitell. B. ix, fol. 101^v; *LP* iv, 3072); *LP* iv, 4120, 4735, 4767, 4804 and 4894; *LP* vii, 1370; *Sp. Cal.* v, 104.

[46] The bull, addressed to Campeggio alone and issued at Viterbo on 8 June 1528, provides 'Ad prefatam Regem [Henricum]...et eius Regnum ac quecunque alia Regna et loca ad que te forsan declinare contigerit pro pace et aliorum negociorum huiusmodi expeditione nostrum et apostolice sedis legatum creamus et destinamus' (Bologna, AS, AMC, 2nd series, 55/292). Another bull, dated at Rome on 16 December 1528 and filed in the same carton, gives Campeggio wide, unspecified powers.

unfailing foundation. His legation of 1528–9 to England, like all his other legations and concerns, was family business as well; and in 1528 his kin were scattered abroad, busily engaged in assisting him. His brother Marcantonio, now bishop-elect of Grosseto, who customarily went to establish control of Campeggio's benefices and expedite the collection of their revenues, was in England with Wolsey. Their brother Tommaso, bishop of Feltre, had left Venice, where he had been acting as nuncio; and Campeggio's son Alessandro, bishop-elect of Bologna, had gone there, perhaps unofficially, to replace him. Tommaso himself joined the pope at Orvieto and acted as an informal, personal liaison with Campeggio, who was serving as legate to Rome from the Castel Sant'Angelo. Campeggio's son Rodolfo acted as courier between England and Italy. Floriano Montini, Campeggio's secretary and a prebendary of Salisbury, was engaged with Campeggi family business in his native Ferrara and elsewhere in Italy. Campeggio's chamberlain Giacomo, evidently in England with Marcantonio, was occupied in making various advance arrangements.[47]

The unusually confused state of Italy during 1527–8 affected the Campeggi very directly and encouraged them to exchange letters in cipher, which were evidently then destroyed. What survives of their unciphered correspondence reflects very little opinion of any kind. Campeggio had been aware of Henry's problem since 1527 and had been approached by Casale in Rome the following February. In the course of two long autograph letters of 26 and 28 March to his brother Tommaso from the Castel Sant'Angelo, Campeggio referred in passing to letters from Henry VIII and Wolsey about the king's 'matrimonial matter'. Tommaso was instructed to speak with the English ambassadors, evidently Gardiner and Foxe, and offer Campeggio's services.[48] In April Campeggio sent letters for Henry VIII and Wolsey to his brother Marcantonio, and Tommaso was again tersely instructed that Campeggio wished to do all he could in the king's matter.[49]

---

[47] Numerous family letters from 1528 are in Bologna, AS, AMC, 3rd series 22/545 and 27/549; see also *LP* IV, 4380 and 5769.

[48] Bologna, AS, AMC, 3rd series, 22/545; *LP* IV, 3910 and 3921.

[49] Lorenzo Campeggio to Tommaso, from the Castel Sant'Angelo, 18 April 1528, 'Circa la cosa del serenissimo re de Anglia io desidero quanto mi sia possibile per il debito mio servir sua maestà' (Bologna, AS, AMC, 3rd series, 22/545), and to Marcantonio in London, 10 April 1528 (AMC, 3rd series, 27/549).

From Venice Alessandro advised his uncle in London that Campeggio had been with the pope in Viterbo on 14 June, and that a galley had been hired from Andrea Doria to carry Campeggio to Marseilles.[50]

The overriding concern of the Campeggi that emerges from their letters is their effort to recover from the financial dislocation resulting from the sack of Rome, and to consolidate family control of various benefices. Campeggio was particularly concerned to ensure the future security of his kin by arranging for them to succeed to his benefices during his own lifetime. An effort was likewise made to have Tommaso, also a sometime lecturer in law in the University of Bologna, assume his brother's place in the Signatura Justitiae during the legation to England.[51] By special grace Clement VII issued a bull guaranteeing the enforcement of Campeggio's last will and testament, and exempting his estate from the third or whatever part usually collected in taxes.[52]

It is not possible to reconstruct the whole membership of Campeggio's party en route, but up to eleven others seem to have stayed with him at Bath House in London.[53] His brother Marcantonio was already in London, and his chamberlain Giacomo seems to have come from London to meet him at Canterbury. His son Rodolfo, who was knighted by the king at Greenwich during Christmastide, and his ubiquitous secretary, Floriano Montini, evidently travelled with him from Italy. At least two other Italians were Guglielmo Corvino Nucerno and a man called Molza, who was an acquaintance of the marchioness of Mantua.[54] Representing the Spanish party was an Aragonese canonist who had served upwards of thirty years as a clerk of the Rota, and whom Queen Catherine befriended.[55] Wolsey's original instructions to Rome directed Gardiner to accompany Campeggio

---

[50] Letter of 6 July 1528 (Bologna, AS, AMC, 3rd series, 27/549).

[51] Ovidio Bargelino to the Senate of Bologna, from Viterbo, 9 June 1528 (Bologna, AS, Archivio del Reggimento, Lettere dell'ambasciatore bolognese in Roma al Senato, volume for the years 1528–31). On 31 May he wrote from Orvieto that Campeggio was expected that week in court on his way to England.

[52] Issued at Viterbo, 8 July 1528 (Bologna, AS AMC, 2nd series, 55/292).

[53] The master of the Great Wardrobe delivered him bedding for twelve people (*LP* IV, app. 208).

[54] *LP* IV, 4803f. and 4858; *LP* VIII, 1096; *Ven. Cal.* IV, 374.

[55] *LP* IV, 5980 and 6660; *Sp. Cal.* IV, 177.

out of Italy. In Paris the party was met by Bishop John Clerk, whom Campeggio had long known, and by Francis Brian, king's chamberlain and a relative of Anne Boleyn.[56] In this respect Campeggio was the very model of balanced objectivity.

Taking example from Julius II and Clement VII, Campeggio arrived in England with a long, untrimmed beard, which he explained was worn in mourning for the unrestored losses of the Church. Even as judge his first duty was to attempt a reconciliation of the parties and to rectify the marriage, but it was clear from the start that his motives were as much diplomatic as moral. The king and Wolsey were well aware that Campeggio came to England in the form of a commissioned judge after English wishes, but that in reality he was an unfree agent bound by minute secret instructions from Clement VII. In a letter to Salviati from Paris Campeggio made a final rehearsal of his instructions and gave solemn assurances of his determination to be loyal to them. He was chiefly preoccupied with his diplomatic instructions but insisted that if it were impossible to change Henry's mind, it also seemed impossible to avoid a trial in England without giving the impression that he had come to England merely to hoodwink them. Despite Campeggio's continual insistence on the pope's good will, his refusal to allow his commission to fall into Wolsey's hands hardly inspired confidence in it. Henry VIII's reaction to Campeggio's effort to dissuade him from attacking his marriage was to ask the pope whether it was Campeggio's idea or his own and to say he resented it. Campeggio was realistic enough after his arrival in England to insist still again that it seemed impossible to avoid trial; but whether acting simply on the pope's instructions or not, Campeggio's steady refusal to be frank could only irritate Wolsey and the king. However devious their own methods might have been, they at least made their ends clear. Salviati's remark in May 1529 that Campeggio had hitherto sustained his role with great dexterity suggests the image of a master juggler in a marathon performance.[57] Campeggio's one great act of personal initiative, his proroguing of the trial on 23 July until October, was an act of desperation, evidently done in ignorance that, on the report of

---

[56] *LP* IV, 3913 (p. 1741), 4736 and app. 196.
[57] *Sp. Cal.* III, 304 and 570; *Ven. Cal.* IV, 372; *LP* IV, 4736, 4881, 4915, 5038, 5604 and 5928.

Cardinal Accolti, the advocation of the case to Rome had already been approved in Consistory seven days before.[58]

Campeggio was to spend three still more difficult months in England. In a letter to Salviati of 7 October from Canterbury he correctly surmised that his letters to Rome were being intercepted and indicated that the originals of the letters of 19 and 23 July from Rome halting the trial had never reached him.[59] The formal letters of advocation, inhibiting further action by the legatine court in England, were issued in Rome only on 29 August and 1 September and included an explanation by Clement VII that formalised threats of penalties and censures against the king within the text of previous letters on the subject were made without his knowledge and were null and void. The case was formally suspended until Christmas to allow the queen opportunity to make her appeal.[60] Wolsey and Campeggio, exiled from the royal presence, spent much of September together, possibly to shield Campeggio from contact with Queen Catherine and Chapuys, the newly arrived imperial ambassador. As Campeggio prepared to take his leave, Henry's sense of prudence partially checked his anger. Campeggio could still be of use in Rome or at least not be so provoked as to do the king's cause harm.[61] Letters of introduction of Campeggio to Francis I were prepared, and both legates were received by the king. Bishop Ghinucci, just returned from Spain, was ordered to Rome. Wolsey was making one last throw to maintain himself. Francis I and Campeggio were to intervene actively in an effort to transfer the case to some neutral place, possibly in France.[62]

---

[58] Ehses, *Römische Dokumente*, pp. 122–5 and 205. On 6 July Clement VII had summoned the English ambassadors and intimated the fact (*Ven. Cal.* IV, 485, 490ff. and 500); and *LP* IV, 5916f.

[59] Ehses, *Römische Dokumente*, p. 132 (*LP* IV, 5995). The last previous surviving letter from Campeggio to Rome is of 13 July. There are two copies of Clement VII's letter of 19 July to Wolsey, informing him of the advocation of the case to Rome and referring him to Campeggio. One of these is probably the duplicate which accompanied the duplicate Campeggio finally received (*LP* IV, 5785).

[60] Theiner, *Monumenta*, pp. 564–5 (*LP* IV, 5916). See Ehses, *Römische Dokumente*, pp. 125f.

[61] *LP* IV, 5936, 5945 and 5995; *Sp. Cal.* IV, 135, 152, 160 and 182.

[62] *LP* IV, 5949, 5953, 6003, 6008 and 6053. See Henry VIII to Clement VII, 30 September 1529 (Theiner, *Monumenta*, p. 564; *LP* IV, 5966). Francis I received Campeggio only after having spoken with the papal nuncio and with the English ambassadors.

This time when Campeggio withdrew from England, his Siamese twin in the legateship did not survive the separation. It has been too little emphasised that Wolsey's career as legate in England began when Campeggio crossed to England in July 1518 and ended in October 1529 as Campeggio waited at Dover to cross to France. Wolsey's double power as lord chancellor and legate had been built up through the articulation of royal and papal policy, to which Campeggio as protector of England had been a party until the end. The designs against Wolsey which brought him down were on foot even before Campeggio took leave of him.

It is not surprising that there should have been suspicion that Wolsey would attempt some secret practice with Campeggio in order to save himself. No one really knows what was being looked for when Campeggio's luggage was broken open and searched at Dover, but everyone including Campeggio himself connected it with a suspicion of collusion of some kind with Wolsey. The angered Campeggio protested to the king against the disrespect shown his episcopal dignity and the violation of his legatine authority. He declared he would not leave England until the calumny of collusion with Wolsey in the marriage case had been cleared up and satisfaction given for so atrocious a wrong. According to Chapuys' report of the incident, Campeggio claimed they had done great wrong to suppose he could be corrupted by Wolsey, when he had been proof against corruption by the king.[63] There is no indication that Campeggio's protest included mention of the wrongs suffered by the legate Wolsey, or that he laid his own wrongs to the charge of the king personally.

The king's reply to Campeggio, which exists in draft and was supposedly sent from Windsor on 22 October four days before Campeggio's crossing to Boulogne, threw to the winds the gracious restraint and assurance of good will that marked their final interview. The king saw the offence as minute and grossly exaggerated, and as one for which the official in charge alone was responsible. There was no violation of Campeggio's legatine authority, because it had ceased to exist with the termination of the trial; and Campeggio's claim still to use it was in violation of English law. As a bishop in England his ignorance of the law was as surprising as his failure to appreciate his oath to respect the

[63] *LP* iv, 5635 and 6026.

royal dignity and jurisdiction. Henry claimed that his subjects were not well pleased that the cause had come to no better conclusion, and that he had reason to doubt Campeggio's faith and the integrity of his friendship, when his words and professions so little agreed.[64]

In fact, there was nothing for Campeggio to gain from collusion with Wolsey, if as the search had demonstrated it were not in his baggage; but Campeggio had a great deal to lose in losing the friendship of the king. In Campeggio's next letter to Rome there is no report of this exchange of angry letters with the king or of the incident which provoked it. He blandly told Salviati that he did not cross the channel until 26 October because of 'various hindrances' which he encountered between London and Dover. Quite without regret he described the fall of Wolsey and remarked that so far as ecclesiastical affairs were concerned, Wolsey had done nothing in the past to merit such disgrace. With an equanimity remarkable in the circumstances, Campeggio reasoned that the king would not go to extremes but would act considerately in the matter as he was accustomed to do in his other actions.[65] This colouring of the facts in the king's favour was hinted at in Campeggio's earlier letter of 7 October from Canterbury. Until the end Campeggio would insist on the 'buon animo' of the king and lay responsibility for all that ran counter to it upon his evil councillors. As for Wolsey, neither he nor Clement VII raised a finger to save him or uttered a word of protest at his arrest and condemnation, although the utter violation of legatine authority involved in it made the searching of Campeggio's luggage seem the minute offence the king pronounced it to be. For all their years of intimate contact with Wolsey, there is no indication that either Clement VII or Campeggio felt any real friendship for him. When word of Wolsey's death reached Campeggio in Cologne on 21 December the following year, in writing Salviati of it next day he laconically offered two clichés as his epitaph, 'Cuius anima requiescat in pace, et sic transit gloria mundi.'[66]

---

[64] PRO, SP 1/55, fol. 218 (*LP* IV, 6016). The opening section of the king's letter summarises that of Campeggio, which is apparently lost.

[65] Ehses, *Römische Dokumente*, p. 136f. (*LP* IV, 6050); and *Sp. Cal.* IV, 160.

[66] Campeggio to Salviati, 22 December 1530, 'Heri sera ricevei uno altro pachetto d'Anglia, . . .et intendera la morte del Rmo. Eboracensis' (Arch. Vat., Lettere di Principi XI, fol. 54ᵛ and fol. 60ʳ). This is the only reference

The protector of England in the company of Charles V

The final sentence in the marriage case in Rome and the first Act
of Supremacy in England came only in 1534, but both evolved
from attitudes already evident when Campeggio left England.
Unless new evidence appeared, there was little likelihood that
Campeggio's opinion, which was in favour of the queen when he
was in England, would shift to the king once he came under the
direct influence of the pope and the emperor. The king's main
chance of success was gone; the best he could hope for was to
maintain Campeggio in an attitude of loyal neutrality, until he
could gain new leverage against the pope. Grasping at straws,
'Uncle' Henry continued his diplomatic correspondence with
'good nephew' Charles V and sent Wiltshire himself off to him at
Bologna to explain the marriage case.[67] For Clement VII the
problem was chiefly one of finding the opportune time and means
to pronounce the marriage valid without provoking the dire
reprisal to papal authority in England that the king had so clearly
threatened. His main hope was that Henry VIII would not really
go so far. Regardless how matters went Campeggio would remain
a central figure to them.

The next months held little to encourage Henry VIII or his
particular cause. By the treaty of Cambrai of 3 August 1529
Francis I again renounced his claims to Italy; and Charles V, who
had landed at Monaco on 6 August, swept all before him as he
made his deliberate progress through Italy to Bologna, where at
the emperor's request Clement VII had come to meet him.
Cardinal Campeggio had just arrived in Paris when Charles V
made his formal entry into Bologna on 5 November; but evidently
it was his twenty-five-year-old son Alessandro, bishop-elect of
Bologna and future cardinal, who met the emperor at the city
gates.[68] During four months the pope and emperor lived next
door to each other in the Palazzo Pubblico and had regular
private conversations over topics which the young Charles care-

to Wolsey in an otherwise long and secret letter in which Campeggio
could have felt free to speak his mind.

[67] There are numerous letters, in French, in the correspondence between
Charles V and Henry VIII in Vienna, HHSA, England, Hofcorrespondenz,
Karton 1ff. Henry VIII continued to sign himself 'bon oncle' until the
marriage with Anne Boleyn; Charles V still addressed Henry as 'bel oncle'
even after the death of Catherine of Aragon.

[68] Ehses, *Römische Dokumente*, p. 135 (*LP* IV, 6050).

fully prepared beforehand. Clement VII's most vivid memories of Bologna hitherto were from his journey there in 1516 with Leo X for a similar encounter with the then youthful Francis I. On that occasion, to the discomfiture of England, Giulio de'Medici had accepted the protectorship of France. Now with the emperor, as in 1512 with the French, another restoration of the de'Medici to Florence was to be arranged; and Henry VIII could hope for little good from the surrounding negotiations.

It is not clear when it was that Campeggio arrived in Bologna from Paris. He gave no impression of rushing the return trip. After having taken from 5 October until 4 November to get from London to Paris, he spent six days there. In addition to business with Francis I in the name of Henry VIII and on written instruction from Salviati, he arranged with Francis I to resign as abbot *in commendam* of Orbais in favour of his son Alessandro, whose future he was especially eager to make secure.[69] Complaining of the bad road and his physical weakness, he set out for Bologna on 10 November. Still carried on a litter, he arrived just before Christmas or shortly after. As a sign of special recognition from pope and emperor, Clement VII made over to Campeggio and his heirs the castle of Dozza near Bologna, and in terms of the gift Charles V took Campeggio and all his possessions under his protection.[70]

There is little reliable information about what Campeggio actually said about the marriage once he was in Bologna, but the general presumption of all was that he favoured Queen Catherine. Chapuys, who had become more militant on the queen's behalf than was her nephew, advised the emperor from London that Campeggio should report in Consistory in the presence of theologians and canonists from Bologna and Rome. Since both the interests of the queen and the authority of the Apostolic See were seriously compromised, the matter should be settled quickly. Chapuys was pessimistic about the English attitude but was sure

---

[69] Three bulls, all dated at Bologna on 28 March 1530, issued without tax and effecting the transfer from father to son with an annual pension of 25 Tours pounds reserved to the father, are in Bologna, AS, AMC, 2nd series, 55/292; Campeggio had himself been provided to Orbais on 5 October 1525. See also Müller, *Legation Lorenzo Campeggios*, ɪ, 85; and *LP* ɪᴠ, 6003 and 6053.

[70] Ehses, *Römische Dokumente*, p. 138 (*LP* ɪᴠ, 6053); *LP* ɪᴠ, 6280; and Müller, *Legation Lorenzo Campeggios*, ɪ, lxviiiff.

that Campeggio and Mendoza, the former imperial ambassador in London, were two excellent witnesses for the imperial point of view. Bishop Ghinucci, who had returned to his post as auditor of the Chamber in Rome and as an avowed support of Henry VIII in the marriage case, advised the king of reports that Campeggio was occupied with the king's cause and often had himself carried to the pope and was occasionally with the emperor.[71] On 16 February Campeggio requested in Consistory that the provision of Durham be expedited at the reduced rate permitted on the two previous occasions and five days later referred the translation of Tunstall from London to the bishopric which supposedly had earlier been offered himself. To mollify John Stokesley and the earl of Wiltshire, father of Anne Boleyn, both of whom were in Bologna as English envoys to Charles V, Campeggio referred Stokesley's provision to London on 28 March without the personal fifteen per cent service charge due him; and shortly afterwards Campeggio, in writing to Salviati, recommended Stokesley as a man of good intention.[72] But Richard Croke, who had accompanied Stokesley to Italy, reported that Campeggio was actively seeking all the friends he could for the queen against the king, and that he had won over from the king's side numerous English Franciscans who Ghinucci had assured him would support the king.

Even in early February there were rumours that Campeggio was to go as legate to the Imperial Diet at Augsburg with the emperor, but that he had not yet accepted. On 22 and 24 February Campeggio, as senior cardinal priest, took part in the coronation ceremonies of Charles V. The official commission of Campeggio as legate was made on 16 March, and six days later Charles V returned to Bologna to accompany him to Germany.[73] Clement VII wrote to Henry VIII on 26 March 1530 concerning Wiltshire's and Stokesley's mission to the emperor and himself, but he made no mention of his interviews with Campeggio.[74] Thereafter, until the emergence of Cromwell, the real centre of indecision was

[71] Br. Mus., Vitell. B. xiii, fol. 15 (*LP* IV, 6158); *Sp. Cal.* iv, 228 and 252.

[72] PRO 31/10/15, fol. 107 (Arch. Vat., Arch. Cons., Acta Cancel. 2, fol. 164); Arch. Vat., Lettere di Principi xi, fols. 112ᵛ–113ʳ; and Ehses, *Römische Dokumente*, pp. 277–8.

[73] The bulls and numerous papal letters connected with the legation are in Bologna, AS, ACM, 2nd series, 55/292.

[74] *LP* iv, 6280 and 6288; Ehses, *Römische Dokumente*, pp. 140–2.

Henry VIII, as is evident in his ambivalent relations with Cardinal Protector Campeggio.

In April 1530 Campeggio travelled, usually with the emperor, from Bologna by way of Mantua to Germany. They spent May and early June in Innsbruck in conference with the cardinals of Salzburg and of Trent, and the dukes of Saxony and Bavaria in preparation for the confrontation with the Protestants at Augsburg. Travelling by way of Munich, Campeggio arrived in Augsburg on 15 June and remained there throughout July. In December 1530 he was in Cologne and spent the year 1531 in Belgium. Passing by way of Nuremberg, he arrived in Regensburg in March and remained there until mid-August. During all this time in the Empire he was in regular contact with Charles V, whose general itinerary he followed. In late August Campeggio returned to Italy to wait at Bologna for the emperor's arrival.[75]

During these almost three years the main object of common interest between Campeggio and the emperor was their opposition to the growth of Protestantism. When Campeggio's brother Tommaso was sent as legate to Germany in 1540 after the cardinal's death, Charles V recalled that Campeggio's intentions at Augsburg had been good, but that he had not obtained from the Imperial Diet all that he might have. Yet the emperor and Cardinal Campeggio seem to have got on well enough together, and the emperor's ambassador in Rome was concerned to find an adequate substitute for Campeggio there.[76]

Over Spanish protest Charles V gave Campeggio the bishopric of Huesca and Jaca in 1530, for which he had first been mentioned in 1527, but reserved one quarter of the annual income of 4000 ducats for his own purposes. There was delay until Campeggio sent on his consent to these pensions. Then after he was provided on 2 September 1530, objection was raised that there had been a Spanish coadjutor provided with right of succession in 1517; and Campeggio sent off his brother Marcantonio to take possession. The best Marcantonio could obtain from the recalcitrant clergy

[75] Ehses, 'Kardinal Lorenzo Campeggio auf dem Reichstage von Augsburg 1530', *Römische Quartalschrift*, xvii (1903), 383–406; and his *Römische Dokumente*, pp. 145–200; Pocock, *Records of the Reformation*, ii, 125–364; G. Müller, 'Kardinal Lorenzo Campeggio, die römische Kurie und der Augsburger Reichstag von 1530', *Niederlands Archief voor Kerkgeschiedenis*, lii (1972), 133–52.
[76] *Sp. Cal.* iv, 322 and 367; *Sp. Cal.* vi, 137.

seems to have been the disputed promise of a subsidy, and even from this they appealed to the metropolitan at Zaragoza.[77] Despite an Act of the Cortes attempting to prevent foreigners from possessing Spanish bishoprics, he seems to have held it until 8 June 1534, when he resigned it shortly before being provided to the poorer bishopric of Crete.[78] In 1532 the emperor gave the bishopric of Mallorca to Campeggio for his son Gianbattista, then twenty-five, with the reservation of the administration to the father.[79] A report in Italy, apparently garbled, said that Campeggio had made an exchange of his Spanish bishopric at a gain of about 5000 florins.[80] On 6 June 1533 Campeggio also became administrator of the modest bishopric of Parenzo in Istria, upon the resignation of Girolamo Campeggio, who had held it since 1516.[81] All this new income, in so far as he succeeded in collecting

---

[77] Juan Pérez to Charles V, from Rome, 2 September 1527 (Madrid, Real Academia de la Historia, Collección Salazar, A-4, fols. 155–7). There is a copy of a legal instrument executed in the presence of Marcantonio Campeggio, JUD, in Jaca on 30 October 1531 in Bologna, AS, AMC, 2nd series, 57/294; in 55/292 there is a description of the case in Huesca and the appeal.

[78] *Sp. Cal.* iv, 558. An editor's note in *Sp. Cal.* iv, p. 999, says that Campeggio was compelled to exchange Huesca-Jaca in 1532 for Mallorca, and in 1534 was moved to Tarragona. But this does not accord with the evidence in Eubel, *Hierarchia*, iii, 233, 250, 264 and 308, where Campeggio is not shown as ever having held Tarragona; nor was there any other provision to Tarragona at this time to which a reserved pension for Campeggio could have been attached. Campeggio obtained the bishopric of Crete through Venetian influence; he resigned it on 28 January 1536 in favour of Pietro Lando, aged eighteen, with the reservation of the income and rights of administration to himself until Lando should be twenty-seven (Eubel, iii, 181).

[79] Campeggio, writing to Gianbattista from Regensburg, 30 July 1532, describes it as 'neque honore, neque censu Bononiensi inferiore' (Bologna, AS, AMC, 3rd series, 23/546). There were difficulties, first because the son's age had been given as twenty-six in place of twenty-five, and then about the payment of taxes, which Campeggio wished waived in virtue of his own position as a curial cardinal. Although Gianbattista held the bishopric from 25 September 1532 until resigning it on 19 September 1561, he had on 28 February 1541 sought postponement of priestly orders until 21 April 1547.

[80] Fabrizio Peregrino to the marquis of Mantua, 19 July 1532, 'Campeggio ha permutato in Ispagna una sua chiesa e vi ha avantaggiato circa mille V' (cited by Chambers, 'English representation at the court of Rome', from Mantua Archivio di Stato, Gonzaga, Busta 881). This is part of what Chambers, pp. 588ff., plainly calls the duplicity of Campeggio in being friend to both Henry VIII and Charles V, and to which he gives special attention.

[81] Campeggio resigned on 27 May 1537 in favour of his nephew Giovanni

it, served to relieve Campeggio of the charge of being pre-
disposed to favour Henry VIII because of his English bishopric
of Salisbury; but this was a charge no longer being heard. Before
leaving Bologna with Charles V in 1530 Campeggio had offered
his services to Francis I as well, but the offer seems not to have
been accepted.[82]

In the light of Campeggio's constant company with the
emperor and his growing income, Henry VIII could not help but
be apprehensive about what was being said about the marriage
case. Yet if Campeggio was really actively working against
Henry VIII, there is no really incriminating evidence of it in his
secret correspondence with Salviati in Rome; but it is incontest-
ably clear, on the other hand, that he did nothing to help him.
Both from Mantua in April and from Innsbruck in May Campeggio wrote in false optimism that the duke of Norfolk had plans
to marry his eldest son to the Princess Mary, who must therefore
not be thought so illegitimate after all, and that the Boleyns were
less confident of success than before. He was hopeful that this
new system of marriages would lead to the dropping of the
marriage case. He remarked upon the king's good will and seemed
sure he would remain obedient to the pope. In Rome hope still
lay in delay, and Campeggio was instructed to explain the reasons
for it to the emperor. Campeggio unfolded his own optimistic
theories to the emperor, but on 26 June he reported from Augsburg that the emperor and Granvella were still dissatisfied at the
delay, which to his own mind was most expedient. Two days
later, in fulfilment of his promise in an earlier letter, Campeggio
wrote to Henry VIII a cheerful account of the first developments
in the Imperial Diet at Augsburg. He praised the piety of Charles
V and Ferdinand as well as Henry's action against heresy in
England as sources of encouragement. Of the marriage case he
made no mention whatever.[83]

Campeggio, then twenty-four, but reserved administration to himself until
Giovanni should be twenty-seven (Eubel, *Hierarchia*, III, 270).

[82] Gramont to Francis I from Bologna, 27 March 1530 (*LP* IV, 6290).

[83] Müller, *Legation Lorenzo Campeggios*, I, 24f. and 60; Ehses, *Römische
Dokumente*, pp. 145 and 149ff.; *Sp. Cal.* IV, 394; *LP* IV, 6480, summarises
Campeggio's letter of 28 June from Augsburg; H. Jedin, 'Der Quellen-
apparat der Konzilsgeschichte Pallavicinis', *Miscellanea Historiae
Pontificiae*, IV (Rome, 1940), 99–104, prints three other letters supposedly
sent by Campeggio to Henry VIII, from Innsbruck, 1 June 1530, and
from Augsburg, 13 and 30 August 1530. In the last he warmly recom-

Autumn 1530 brought a renewed effort by the English to have the case transferred to a neutral place such as Cambrai, to which the pope, king and emperor would send plenipotentiaries. Henry VIII had been fuming to the papal nuncio in England, baron de Burgo, that the pope and Rota were suspect, and that he wanted the case committed to the archbishop of Canterbury or to the chapter of Canterbury. Henry claimed that many persons of worth in England were saying that he should take the matter into his own hands. The nuncio made it clear that Henry VIII was ready to begin the work of isolating the English clergy from Rome.[84] Even though Francis I had guardedly come out in favour of delay, Campeggio was unable to assuage the emperor's impatience or his suspicion of the French cardinals Gramont and Duprat. At the end of November 1530 Salviati informed Campeggio that Clement VII could no longer withstand the emperor's pressure to get the Roman trial moving, but that the pope declined all responsibility for the evil consequences which would follow upon the completion of it.[85] Even with this virtual assurance that sentence would be given in favour of the queen, Charles V refused to countenance delay. In December 1530 baron de Burgo appealed to Campeggio from England to give support to the effort to induce the pope to transfer the trial to a neutral place. Campeggio, who was in close contact with England at the time, merely passed on the appeal together with one part of the nuncio's letters for the pope. He refused to espouse the king's plan or to urge it on the emperor without permission from the pope. Convinced that the emperor would never permit the trial to leave Rome, he privately advised Salviati against the English proposal as an impractical last resort. In effect Campeggio refused to assume a responsible role in bringing the matter to a conclusion and voluntarily sought to hide himself behind Clement VII, whose indecision had already made Campeggio's life so difficult. As it became more and more evident that Henry VIII's threat to carry England into schism was not an empty one, the English proposal to transfer the trial to some neutral place became Clement VII's new resort in the tactics of delay. On 6 June 1531

mends the baron de Burgo who he hears is being sent to England as papal nuncio.

[84] Ehses, *Römische Dokumente*, pp. 164–6.

[85] Müller, *Legation Lorenzo Campeggios*, ɪ, 176f. and 191; Ehses, *Römische Dokumente*, pp. 166f.

Salviati, aroused at last, urgently requested Campeggio to broach the possibility of Cambrai to the emperor.[86] Queen Catherine, increasingly aware of her deteriorating position in England, chose to lay blame for it on doubts raised to the justice of her case by the pope's long delay in deciding it. The emperor, urged on by the adamant queen, opposed the transfer from Rome. Campeggio reported the fact to Salviati from Brussels and claimed that many in England were confident that Henry VIII would patiently submit to a sentence passed in Rome.[87]

The refusal of Campeggio to take the initiative at Henry VIII's request, a not unreasonable thing to ask of a cardinal protector, had again brought the king's rage down upon him. Wild accusations were raised in England that Charles V was even intriguing to make Campeggio pope by force.[88] In January 1531 the clergy of the Canterbury Convocation gathered to purchase their pardon from the king for having participated in Wolsey's illegal abuses of his legatine powers. The Protector Campeggio was informed in Ghent of his share as bishop of Salisbury of the seven annual payments of the £100,000 voted the king by the province of Canterbury and, at the same time, of his dismissal as cardinal protector of England.[89]

After Campeggio reported it to Salviati on 20 May 1531, his dismissal from the protectorship became a matter of public knowledge.[90] Agostino Agostini, Wolsey's former physician now in Campeggio's entourage, whom Norfolk and Cromwell had hired to report on his master's activities, wrote to Norfolk on 3 June that Campeggio had taken it badly and laid blame either on coloured reports of him or on the suggestion of the Casales in

[86] Müller, I, 199 and 242; Ehses, pp. 175ff.; Simancas, Estado, Legajo 854, fol. 163.

[87] Müller, I, 263, 336–7 and 417; II, 487 and 501; Ehses, p. 179. The minutes of Campeggio's conversation with the emperor at Brussels on 10 October 1531 are in Simancas, Patronato Real, Legajo 21, doc. 58.

[88] Chapuys to Charles V from London, 23 January 1531 (*LP* v, 62); *LP* v, 887.

[89] Campeggio to Salviati from Ghent, 20 May 1531, 'Il serenissimo re de Angleterra me ha levata la prottetione de Anglia et oltre che per la imposition general al clero per anni sette mi toccarà una bonna summa. Temo di peggio' (Arch. Vat., Lettere di Principi XI, fol. 66ʳ; cited by Müller, *Legation Lorenzo Campeggios*, I, 239 n. 66.

[90] Mai to Cobos from Rome, 3 July 1531, 'Los Angleses han revocado la protecion de aquel Reyno que tenia el Campeggio y ha stagora no la han dado a otro' (Simancas, Estado, Legajo 853, fol. 68; *Sp. Cal.* IV, ii, 758).

Rome. Since then, he said, Campeggio had twice spoken with the emperor and had had a long interview with him. Unburdening himself to Agostini, Campeggio wondered whether he should make some appeal to the emperor on behalf of the case and declared himself convinced that the emperor's mind was wholly disposed toward justice. Agostini suspected that Campeggio's protestations that he would be the king's most devoted and faithful servant were designed to regain the king's confidence.[91] On 21 June the Milanese ambassador at Rome reported that it was not yet known whether Henry VIII would give the protectorship to someone else or keep it to himself, because he did not reckon to have much business at the Curia.[92]

In fact Henry VIII had dismissed Campeggio without having any prepared plan for seeking a successor. By March 1532 Cardinal de Cupis had emerged as an active candidate for the protectorship either of England or of France and attempted to use French influence with Henry VIII to obtain the English one.[93] The king himself had chosen Cardinal Farnese for the office. On 21 March the English ambassadors in Rome were instructed from England to offer it either to del Monte or to de Cupis, if Farnese had either refused or not been permitted to accept it. The king considered it particularly necessary, since it was certain to him that Campeggio would stand with the emperor and the pope.[94]

Ghinucci, Benet and Casale jointly replied from Rome that the times were such that the king could not afford to alienate anyone in the Curia. If Farnese were offered the protectorship, they feared that del Monte and de Cupis would take it badly, and it was evident that Campeggio and Cesi would think themselves wronged.[95] There is a suggestion that rivalry or, more likely, fraternal solidarity among the cardinals, perhaps influenced in the latter case by the stated pleasure of Clement VII, had prevented the replacement of Campeggio. Clement VII had neatly evaded the issue the previous October when Lee and Gardiner,

---

[91] Agostino Agostini to Norfolk from Ghent, 3 June 1531 (Pocock, *Records of the Reformation*, II, 129; *LP* v, 283). This is the first of thirteen letters written to Norfolk or Cromwell from Agostino (Pocock, II, between pages 125 and 364).

[92] *LP* v, 319; *Sp. Cal.* IV, 758 and 760; *Mil. Cal.* 867.

[93] *LP* v, 880 and 1110.

[94] *LP* v, 886. Farnese became Pope Paul III in 1534.

[95] *State Papers of Henry VIII*, VII, 368 (*LP* v, 971).

both very active supporters of the king's marriage hopes, were provided to York and Winchester, made vacant by Wolsey's death, by referring the king's nominations himself.[96] By Campeggio's account the expedition had been entrusted to him by letters from the king, and he had in turn delegated it to his substitute in Rome. Writing to Salviati from Tournai on 30 November 1531, he demanded his fair share of the taxes paid and protested against his meagre past income as protector from referring English provisions as inconsonant with the generous practice of other great princes.[97] The three English provisions made in 1532 were referred by Cardinal Cesi, Campeggio's regular substitute.

For Henry VIII's efforts of 1531 to outflank the pope by collecting the opinions of universities, and to stir up war against the emperor, Campeggio had only disapproval. By August he had seen the book listing the decisions of the universities and presumed that Clement VII had seen it as well. He advised Salviati that it was as important to the pope as to the queen to get some good theologian and lawyer to prepare a reasoned reply.[98] Perhaps Campeggio did not know that the empress, at the emperor's bidding, had already begun such consultation in Spain the year before in the hope of finding support for the queen's side.[99] Of the treatise arguing for the queen written by a canon of Padua and sent to him in Belgium with his son Alessandro, he made no mention.[100] At Salviati's instruction Campeggio consulted with Charles V at Enghien in November about the English effort to induce Francis I to renew the war.[101]

The continuing policy of assiduous delay in Rome had taken on

---

[96] Ehses, *Römische Dokument*, pp. 183–4 and 207. See Henry VIII to Clement VII, 12 September 1531 (Br. Mus., Add. MS 15387, fols. 240ʳ–242ʳ).

[97] Arch. Vat., Lettere di Principi x, fols. 112ʳ–113ᵛ; printed in Müller, *Legation Lorenzo Campeggios*, I, 441f. n. 122.

[98] Müller, *Legation Lorenzo Campeggios*, I, 274ff.; *LP* v, 366. See H. Thieme, *Die Ehescheidung Heinrichs VIII, und die europäischen Universitäten* (Karlsruhe, 1957), 23 pages.

[99] K. Brandi, *The Emperor Charles V*, trans. C. V. Wedgwood (London, 1968), p. 304. There are statements from Vicenza of 8 May 1530, Salamanca of 19 September 1530 and the Colegio de San Bartolemé in the University of Salamanca of 7 December 1530 in Simancas. Patronato Real, Legajo 53, docs. 93, 90 and 108; see also docs. 96 and 97.

[100] *LP* v, 281.

[101] Ehses, *Römische Dokumente*, pp. 186f. and 189; *LP* v, 1071.

a different purpose. In a new firmness of policy coinciding with Cromwell's admission to the inner ring of the king's council, the king in parliament began dismantling papal authority in England and subjecting the church to himself. In November 1531 Campeggio had sounded out Charles V's willingness to use force to protect the liberty of the church in England should Henry VIII take England into schism rather than accept an adverse decision. Charles V now had the confidence which Campeggio was beginning to lose that Henry would not go so far; but he proclaimed himself ready to enforce a sentence in favour of the queen, if need arose.[102] As Queen Catherine's complaints of ill treatment continued to come to the emperor, he expressed almost wistful worries to Campeggio that she would not live to see the end of the trial. Campeggio, who had hoped two years earlier to see Anne Boleyn withdraw, dared to reply that should it please God to give Catherine the paradise she deserved, it would provide an escape from a problem that could only get worse.[103]

To English chagrin, the pope and the emperor spent the winter of 1532–3, like that three years before, in Campeggio's Bologna. Campeggio himself arrived in September, before the pope had even definitely decided to come to Bologna. In October he received Gregorio Casale, who was on his way from Rome to England. Clement VII and many of the cardinals arrived from Rome on 8 December, and Charles V arrived on 12 December from Mantua. When the emperor entered the great church of San Petronio and was making his way toward the altar in procession, he saw Campeggio seated among the cardinals and broke out of the procession to go over to him and embrace him. Agostino Agostini, still in Campeggio's service and still employed to report on his activities, made careful report of the fact to Cromwell. Henry VIII was told of it by still another informer.[104]

The widening rift between England and the papacy[105]

In the circumstances Clement VII and Campeggio felt pressed to

---

[102] Müller, *Legation Lorenzo Campeggios*, I, 420, and II, 124; *LP* v, 604.

[103] Ehses, *Römische Dokumente*, p. 199.

[104] Hawkins to Henry VIII, 24 December 1532, 'Themperour hath given Campegius a Bishoprike and at his cumming now to Bononi, came to him sitting among the Cardinals, and did him greate honor and reverence' (*State Papers of Henry VIII*, VII, 404; Pocock, *Records of the Reformation*, II, 336 and 359.

[105] The late Edward Surtz, who had just finished writing a book on the

make some concession to Henry VIII, and that was the provision
of Thomas Cranmer as archbishop of Canterbury on 21 February
1533. Probably Campeggio did not yet know that Henry VIII had
secretly married the pregnant Anne Boleyn on 25 January; but he
did know that the king had continued to agitate to have the case
decided, with papal permission, by the archbishop of Canterbury.
Surely he must also have known that it had been Cranmer who
had suggested the consultation of the universities and gathering
their opinions into the book of which Campeggio had so sternly
disapproved. Indeed, it may have been Cranmer himself who
showed him the book. He was in Brussels as Henry VIII's ambassador at the very moment Campeggio made his objection, and like
Campeggio he moved with the emperor into Germany and
remained with him until after the legate had left for Italy. The
only thing of which Campeggio seems to have made an issue was
his receiving the *propina* of fifteen per cent, a handsome 1500
ducats. On 6 March he wrote his effusive thanks to the king from
Bologna for having restored him to royal favour and trust.[106]

Despite the fact that Cranmer had already emerged as no
partisan of the pope, Campeggio on 27 August referred the provision of a Premonstratensian abbot, Christopher Lord, as his
suffragan on 27 August. Cardinal de Cupis had seen to the quash-
ing of the election of a nominee to the bishopric of Kilmacduagh
in the province of Tuam and on 4 August had referred the provision of Malachy O Molony as bishop instead. On 3 September
Campeggio, acting at the express request of Henry VIII, had
O Molony's provision set aside and Christopher Bodkin provided
in his place. Four years later Bodkin as king's appointee to the
archbishopric of Tuam would lead the struggle to wrest that
western province from papal control.

Clement VII was closing the stable door too late, but even then
Henry was eager for whatever approval or acquiescence he could
wring from Rome. The king knew that Campeggio would figure

Roman aspects of the divorce before his death, was kind enough to read
this section and offer me the benefit of his criticisms.
[106] Campeggio to Henry VIII from Bologna, 6 March 1533, 'Posteaquam
sapiente sue lumine omnem illam suspicionis nebulam, quam temporum
...induxerat, disjectam intelligo, qua nisi illud unum nunc effari libet,
neque tempora neque homines unquam mihi erepturos quod meae erga
Majestatem Vestram fidei et observantie conscientia perpetuo fruar'
(*State Papers of Henry VIII*, vii, 437–8; *LP* vi, 207); *LP* vi, 177.

largely in the final sentence about to be given, and his renewed cordiality toward his protector in the Curia lasted just long enough to give Campeggio one final opportunity to show himself truly the king's man. In Holy Week 1533 Clement VII set up a committee which itself or through a succession of committees continued to function on into the summer. The membership is given variously by ambassadors reporting events in Rome, but the two members consistently present in every list were Cardinals del Monte and Campeggio.[107] On Good Friday, 11 April, Campeggio, following good canonical form, sent a copy of the objections of Henry's advocates to the defence lawyers for Catherine. Concerned for the growing rift with England, Cardinals del Monte, Campeggio and Cesi brought to Consistory a committee report recommending delay in attempting to constrain Henry VIII to return to Queen Catherine. Nicholas Schönberg likewise let it be known that Clement VII considered it necessary to proceed reservedly.[108] In fact, Archbishop Cranmer in England had already in April taken the first steps in resolving the marriage case in England; then on 23 May, after a formal trial of thirteen days, and citing the support of the universities and of Convocation, he pronounced the king's first marriage null and void. When word of the king's latest coup reached Rome, the reaction was a strong one. On 14 June William Benet reported from Rome, without giving his source of information, that del Monte like all the rest was very sore at Cranmer's proceedings, but that he had spoken in Consistory in earnest defence of the king and 'schewed hym rather your protector than otherwyse, where Campegius your protector dyd it not so earnestly'.[109] He urged Henry to use his influence to get del Monte some benefice in France. In July, five

---

[107] Ortiz to Charles V, 14 April 1533, gives the original committee as Cardinals del Monte and Campeggio together with Simonetta and Capisucchi, both auditors of the Rota (*LP* VI, 341). *LP* VI, 365 and 808, both give these four and add the datary (Giberti?). *LP* VI, 654, speaks of a committee of Cardinals del Monte, Campeggio and Cesi. *Ven Cal.* IV, 929, gives these same three but adds the datary. *LP* VI, 656 (*Sp. Cal.* IV, 1083) groups del Monte, Campeggio and Cesarini. *LP* VI, 663 (*Sp. Cal.* IV, 1129) mentions the same three. *Sp. Cal.* V, 76, lists del Monte, Campeggio, Simonetta, Capisucchi, and the datary, but the date given is 1534, when del Monte was already dead. It is possible that a formal tribunal was supplemented by a series of informal committees. Del Monte's actual family name was Ciocchi.

[108] *Ven. Cal.* IV, 877 and 887; *LP* IV, 654, 656 and 663; *LP* VI, 341.

[109] *State Papers of Henry VIII*, VII, 472 (*LP* VI, 643).

and a half years after the issue had first been raised, decisive steps were taken in Rome at last. The cardinals voted in Consistory, apparently secretly, that the pope did have power to dispense a man to marry his brother's widow. A papal sentence of excommunication, suspended until September, proscribed Henry VIII's divorce and his marriage with Anne Boleyn as a direct violation of the authority of the papal court in which the case was still under consideration.[110]

These developments and further reports from Rome unfavourable to Campeggio ended the short period of reconciliation. In a letter supposedly sent to Edmund Bonner during the summer of 1533, probably before the king had even learned of the threatened excommunication, he once again fulminated against Campeggio's dismissal:

An where, as ye write in your said letters, ye be secretly enformed of the unkinde and ingrate dealing and proceding of Cardinal Campegius against Us, who of good congruence and in maner as the cace standeth, of dieuty, ought not, of al other to be our adversarie, aswel for that he hath been of long tyme in visage countenaunce and demonstrucion our frende, and hath been promoted and beneficed by [Us], as specially for that he is our Protectour, whereby he indueth as it wer our owne Person, for the defence of Us and our Realme in al matiers, to be there treated touching the same; and contrary wise, of the benevolence and friendship which in al thinges that may helpe to the advauncement of our cases ye finde in the Cardinal de Monte, and that there canne no man be more ernest in speking and doing for Us, thenne he is: Ye shal undrestande that in like maner as remembring with Ourself the gratuitie and kindnesse in dedes hetherto shewed on our behaulf to the said Campegius with his unkinde and unfaithful demeanour again towardes Us, specially in the desire of the office of our Protectorship, by the same, as we maye wel of his dedes judge, to have the more auctoritie to annoye and displease [Us, wh]ich We be constrayned to have to harte, as the gravitie and importance of our cause doth enforce Us, and therfor resolved not to mynistre any longer wepon to our

---

[110] *Ven. Cal.* IV, 939; *LP* VI, 807. Ortiz learned of the vote only in March of 1534 (*LP* VI, 286).

enemye, wherwith he maybe the more hable to grieve Us, be
mynded to discharge hym of the said office of Protectorship
like as by these precentes our pleasure and commaundement
is, that in our name, according to the custume and maner used
in that behaulf ye utterly, without further respect, discharge
him of the said rome and office. . .[111]

It is unlikely that Cardinal del Monte ever actually became
protector of England, for he died on 20 September.

Striking where he knew it would hurt Campeggio most, the
king in August 1533 ordered Richard Hilley, Campeggio's vicar
general for Salisbury, to stay the revenues of the bishopric until
his further pleasure be known.[112] After Wolsey's fall and death
the bishopric and the city of Salisbury had continued to be
administered in Campeggio's name, but it was Cromwell who
had emerged as the effective force in setting policy.[113] When
Hilley died on 1 September, the king, possibly prompted by
Cromwell, seized the occasion to make an unusual assertion of
authority and claimed by commission from Campeggio the power
and authority to name the vicar general himself. Through a royal
letter copied into Campeggio's register at Salisbury the king,
acting in Campeggio's name, again instituted Thomas Benet,
Hilley's predecessor as vicar general.[114] The Salisbury prebend of

111 Corrected draft from about July 1533 (*State Papers of Henry VIII*, vii,
485–6; *LP* vi, 806).
112 Hilley to Cromwell from Salisbury, 7 August 1533 (*LP* vi, 951); *Ven. Cal.*
iv, 971.
113 A commission of gaol delivery of 20 March 1532 (PRO, E 135/25/25)
and a commission of the peace of 23 December 1532 (PRO, E 135/8/38;
LP v, 1656) were issued at Salisbury in Campeggio's name; see also
LP v, 627 (xxx and xxxi). On 6 April 1531 the Salisbury Corporation
begged Cromwell for commissions of gaol delivery which were to have
been brought from London by Benet (*LP* v, 182). On 2 January 1530 a
mercer of Salisbury had proposed to Cromwell that Cromwell himself
appoint a mayor (*LP* iv, 6136); normally this was the bishop's right. On
28 March 1533 the prioress of Wilton complained to Cromwell against
Hilley (*LP* vi, 285 and 737, x).
114 'Tenor vero huius commissionis sic incipit: Henricus octavus dei gratia
Anglie et Francie Rex, fidei defensor et dominus Hibernie, dilecto nobis
Thome Benet, legum doctor, canonico residentiario ecclesie nostro
cathedralis Sarisburiensis et capellano nostro salutem. Cum Reverendissimus in Christo pater, Laurentius miseratione divina tituli sancte marie
trans tyberem sacrosancte romane ecclesie presbyter cardinalis, Sarum
episcopus, in suis litteris commissionialibus sive procuratoriis nobis factis
inter cetera dederit et concesserit nobis potestatem et auctoritatem ac

Chisenbury and Chute, just voided by the death of Campeggio's secretary Floriano Montini, was by Cromwell's influence given to Benet as well.[115]

Campeggio, it seems clear, had long known that the marriage case would eventually have to be decided in the queen's favour. The chief question apart from when, was whether the decision would be made in the Rota or in Consistory. With his habitual discretion and even loyalty he resisted action against Henry VIII himself; but there is evidence, apart from the king's angry re-action, that by June of 1533 Campeggio had acceded at last to the overtures of the emperor and agreed to exert his influence to bring the case to its inevitable and long-delayed conclusion. Charles V's special instructions, both written and those relayed through his spokesman Rodrigo Davalos, were communicated to Cardinals del Monte, Campeggio and Cesi. Dr Ortiz reported to the emperor from Rome that Cardinal del Monte, whose words in Consistory on Henry's behalf William Benet had praised, and Cardinal Campeggio were both concerned to bring the case itself to a decision. Although further effort and delay could be expected, the English appeals had been denied; and the case was moving toward definitive sentence.[116] In July Campeggio, acknowledging his contact with Davalos who was returning to Charles V in Spain, assured the emperor of his devoted service in the marriage case and expressed hope that results would soon prove Campeggio faithful to his word. The favourable report from Davalos and Charles V's subsequent letter encouraged Campeggio to make a still guarded but clear commitment to the emperor in Septem-ber.[117] The ambassador Cifuentes from Italy implied that there

---

facultatem sufficientem nominandi, deputandi, proficiendi et constituendi vice et nomine suis vicarium in spiritualibus generalem ac officialem principalem...' The commission was issued under seal at Greenwich on 15 September 1533; the formal record of its presentation at Salisbury, from which the word 'pape' has been erased, is dated 26 September 1533 (Salisbury, Diocesan Registry, Register Campegii, fol. 40^{r-v}).

[115] William Benet to Cromwell from Rome, 18 May 1533, announcing that Floriano had died on 13 May, and asking Cromwell to obtain the prebend for his brother (*LP* vi, 501); and *LP* vi, 549. Thomas Benet surrendered the lesser prebend of Axford.

[116] Simancas, Estado, Legajo 860, fols. 29^v and 29*bis*.

[117] Campeggio to Charles V from Rome, 9 September 1533, '...Et per l'altera [lettera] dimostrando haver grato l'officio che per il debito de la servitù mia feci con quella per mezo del S. Roderico Davalo, commenda li servitii miei maxime circa la causa de la serenissima Reina l'Inghilterra,

was solid foundation for Henry VIII's suspicions and Charles V's expectations by suggesting to the emperor that he recompense Campeggio for the loss of his English income.[118]

Bishop Ghinucci of Worcester, auditor of the Chamber in the Curia and an avowed supporter of Henry's cause in Rome, had hitherto enjoyed immunity from Henry's growing dissatisfaction, and the king had even sought to have him created cardinal.[119] As the case moved forward during the summer of 1533, however, even Ghinucci began to lose favour. After the king sequestered the revenues of Worcester, Archbishop Cranmer took over the see and undertook to allow the absentee bishop only a free subsidy. Thomas Bagard, Ghinucci's vicar general, turned for direction to Cranmer and Cromwell in cooperation.[120]

Even this tenuous hold of Campeggio and Ghinucci on their English sees was soon lost. A bill of deprivation, directed specifically at the two of them, was drafted by Cromwell himself or at his direction for the fifth session of the Reformation Parliament (15 January to 30 March 1534).[121] It noted the existing statutes requiring residence and those forbidding both the appointment of aliens to benefices and the export of revenues without royal licence. It argued rather ingenuously that 'the Kynges Highnes beyng a Prynce of great benygnyte and liberalite, havyng no knowledge nor other due informacion or instruccion of the same Lawes Statutes and Provysions, heretofore hath nominated preferred and promoted Laurence Campegius Bisshopp of Sarum, beyng an Estraugier borne oute of this the Kynges Realme and all other his Dominions . . .' and Bishop Ghinucci to Worcester. The House of Lords returned the bill to the Commons with an amendment meant to protect all other persons 'holding offices, fees, annuities or grants from said bishiprics'. The House of Commons accepted this amendment and returned the bill to the Lords with an amendment of their own which allowed the two

et mi exhorta a perseverare nel medesimo offitio. . .Poi li prometto che in tutti li servitii di vestra Cesarea Maestà et de li suoi farò sempre quello offitio et usarò quella fede et diligentia che a bono et fidele servitore si conviene, il che desidero che quella connosca più presto da li effetti che da le mie parole. . .' (Simancas, Estado, Legajo 860, fol. 141); see also Campeggio to Charles V, 16 July 1533 (*ibid.* fol. 139).

118 *LP* vi, 1166; and Simancas, Guerra Antigua, Legajo 3, doc. 367.
119 Ehses, *Römische Dokumente*, p. 205; PRO 31/9/62, fol. 194.
120 *LP* vi, 1510; *LP* vii, 722, 922(v) and 923.
121 Cromwell's remembrances (*LP* vii, 50).

bishops four months' grace following Easter 1534 to come to England and be sworn to the king.[122] After final passage in the House of Lords, only nine legislative days after they had first received it from the Commons, the bill became law on 21 March 1534. The only bishops present on the several days when the bill came under consideration were Cranmer, Stokesley, Gardiner, Longland and Clerk. Bishop de Athequa of Llandaff, the Spanish Dominican who was confessor to Queen Catherine, had attended on four other days of the session but was prudently absent from these discussions.[123] Thomas Benet was given a new commission as vicar general of the vacant see of Salisbury, and Thomas Bagard as vicar general of Worcester.[124]

The long delay in deciding the marriage case in Rome provided both the motive and the opportunity for a propaganda campaign against the papacy in England. In the circumstances it was easy to emphasise the burdens rather than the advantages of union with Rome. Popular opinion, at first openly favourable to Queen Catherine, was increasingly defied by the furious king, who saw himself as the victim of papal politics. The years of cooperation from both popes and cardinal protectors had taught a wilful Henry VIII to expect to have his way over the church in England.

So long as the course of Anglo-papal relations ran smoothly and Wolsey was lord chancellor and legate, much of the routine exercise of royal and papal power was centred in Wolsey personally. Neither the clergy of England nor the Roman Curia regretted the king's ungracious destruction of his faithful minister. Short of granting the divorce, the apprehensive Clement VII was willing to make all concessions possible to mollify the king. Henry VIII could even bully the Convocations of Canterbury and of York into buying pardon for having cooperated in Wolsey's exercise of a legatine power which the king had encouraged and they had resented.

But the fall of Wolsey did not make Henry VIII the supreme

---

[122] 25 Henry VIII c. 27, *Statutes of the Realm*, III (1818), 483–4. The statute asserts that £3000 at least were taken out of England yearly.

[123] *Journals of the House of Lords*, I (London, 1888), 76[a-b], 77[a], 77[b], 78[b], 79[a] and 80[a]; S. Lehmberg, *The Reformation Parliament, 1529–1536* (Cambridge, 1970), pp. 185 and 257.

[124] Salisbury, Diocesan Registry, Register Campegii, fol. 49[r]; *LP* VII, 922(v) and *LP* VIII, 149 (lxi). The new commission was on 7 December 1534 for Benet.

head of the church in England, it merely left a vacuum. The long-standing Statute of Praemunire contradicted papal jurisdiction; it did not abolish it. When eventually the king's anger subsided, that vacuum might have been filled in a number of ways, including a return to something like the state of things before Wolsey. Until Archbishop Warham's death, there were even signs of this. Instead, Cromwell and parliament filled the vacuum with the king, and the king was pleased. What was once regularly but tortuously accomplished through legatine bulls, diplomatic haggling, mutual favours, papal acquiescence and the payment of annates was to be done directly by the king as part of his prerogative.

While Cromwell was cutting England's legal ties with Rome by statute, Henry was further isolating England diplomatically, at just the moment when he might have gained new leverage against Charles V. During 1533 Clement VII was once again occupied in the dangerous game of constructing a counterpoise to imperial power in Italy through negotiations with Francis I. The climax to them was a conference of more than four weeks between the pope and the French king at Marseilles in October and November. The chief result was the marriage of Catherine de'Medici and Francis I's second son and, as it later proved, his heir, Henry duke of Orléans. Certainly Francis I had never in the past offered Henry any substantial reason to trust him, but on this occasion the French king seems to have been faithful to his word and made effective efforts to stay promulgation of the sentence of excommunication with which Henry was threatened. Rather than exploit this new alliance of France with Florence and the de'Medici pope, Henry VIII allowed himself in the end to be overcome by suspicion and anger. When he failed to stop the meeting at Marseilles altogether, he recalled Norfolk from Lyons, where he awaited instructions, and terminated the commissions of his ambassadors in Rome.[125]

Matters in England and in Rome were now set upon a course so definite that the end game lost all semblance of moves and countermoves. Despite his bad health Campeggio appeared in Consistory on 23 March 1534 for the final, unanimous decision in favour of validity. In what were in effect victory letters sent out by the imperialists in Rome to Charles V, Campeggio was men-

125 Scarisbrick, *Henry VIII*, pp. 316–21.

tioned among those deserving of reward.[126] Campeggio could not have known that just two days before he had been deprived of his English bishopric by parliamentary statute. In England the Convocation of Canterbury denied the existence of papal authority on 31 March, Tuesday of Holy Week, by a vote of 34 to 4; and that of York did so unanimously. The Act of Supremacy was passed in parliament during November, but Clement VII did not live to hear of this finishing touch in the separation of England from Rome. After another extended illness, he died on 25 September.

In the end it could be said that Giulio de'Medici had exerted himself to the utmost to exchange the position of a great and influential cardinal for that of a miserable, despised pope.[127] Yet he cannot be accused of having deliberately, still less maliciously, occasioned the English schism. There was a Florentine flexibility that ran clean through de'Medici's character, but what seemed a want of principle was often only the want of decision or the desire to satisfy all parties to a dispute. Except for his adamant candidacy in the conclave which finally elected him pope, Clement VII lacked that force of character which is the mark of a true Machiavellian. He died regretting his personal breach with England but had really been incapable of doing much differently. From its jubilant beginning twenty years before, Giulio de'Medici's relationship with England had come to a pathetic end.

[126] Ortiz to Charles V, 24 March 1934 (*LP* vii, 370; and *Sp. Cal.* v, 29); *LP* vii, 367ff. Campeggio was one of a series of cardinals to whom Ferdinand wrote letters of thanks from Prague on 15 April 1534 (Vienna, HHSA, Rom, Hofcorrespondenz, Karton 1). Cardinals Farnese (30 May), Pucci (31 May) and others acknowledged the emperor's thanks (Simancas, Estado, Legajo 861, fols. 79–84).

[127] 'Giulio...duro una gran fatica per diventare, di grande e reputato Cardinale, piccolo e poco stimato Papa' (F. Vettori, 'Storia d'Italia dal 1511 al 1527, sommario per cura di Alfredo Reumont', *Archivio storico italiano, Appendice*, vi [1848], 348).

7

CAMPEGGIO AND THE FAILURE OF RECONCILIATION, 1534–9

The last appeal to Charles V

In the conclave following the death of Clement VII Campeggio was a cardinal who might have been seriously considered as a candidate for the papacy had not Cardinal Farnese's election been universally favoured. Just before the conclave Gregorio Casale approached Farnese to remind him, falsely, that in 1529 when Clement VII was thought to be dying, the kings of England and France had sent his brother Vicenzo to Rome with letters supporting Farnese's candidacy over that of even Wolsey or Campeggio. He also reminded Farnese that he had been offered the protectorship of England after the first dismissal of Campeggio. When, as Casale reported to Cromwell, he explained the king's surprise that after these marks of good will Farnese should have opposed the king's cause, Farnese attempted to excuse himself and threw the blame on Clement VII.[1] Despite the protest of Campeggio, Farnese's proposal to the cardinals in Conclave on 12 October that the voting should not be secret was accepted. In the single scrutiny, taken next day, Campeggio joined the rest in voting for Farnese. According to Casale, all the cardinals venerated the newly elected Paul III and kissed his feet except Campeggio, who took ill. Campeggio had indeed suffered a great loss in the death of Clement VII, but the implication that Campeggio was bitter toward Clement's successor required better evidence than that offered.[2]

Campeggio, having lost two of his career-long patrons, Henry

---

[1] *LP* vii, 1255; Pocock, *Records of the Reformation*, ii, 590–602 (*LP* iv, 5270).

[2] *LP* vii, 1262; there was bitterness between Casale and Campeggio. In 1535 Campeggio and Simonetta acted as judges in a suit in the Rota involving the estate of the late Clement VII (Florence, AS, Carte Strozziani, 1st series, xviii).

VIII and Clement VII, turned to the one still left, Charles V. Campeggio certainly had not sold his vote in the marriage case; but in the time-honoured tradition of diplomacy, once his decision was made, he anticipated that the winner would make good the losses he had sustained from the loser. To Campeggio's complaint in 1534 at what he had suffered solely for having served justice and the emperor, Charles V soothingly promised such liberal recompense that he might live out the rest of his days in honour and comfort. Once final sentence was actually given, however, the emperor's generosity waned. The persistent Campeggio appealed personally for support to Cardinal Merino of Jaén and the imperial ambassador, Cifuentes.[3] When the ambassador returned to Charles V in Spain during November 1534, Campeggio gave him a letter to the emperor, reminding him of his pressing need and failing health. Campeggio was then just over sixty and had almost five more years to live, but it was the letter of a man profoundly saddened and waiting for death.[4]

Campeggio continued for the rest of his life to serve as protector of Germany.[5] The Spaniards had in the past resisted Charles V's penchant for rewarding clerical supporters of his imperial projects with benefices in Spain. This and Campeggio's continuing preoccupation with securing the future of his sons and brothers may explain the emperor's failure to make good his promises.

---

[3] Cardinal de Jaén to Charles V from Rome, 5 and 6 November 1534 (Simancas, Estado, Legajo 861, fols. 34, 63 and 67).

[4] 'Già sono alcuni mesi, ch'io hebbi una lettera di vestra Cesarea Maestà piena de la solita sua benignità et gratia verso di me: per la quale rispondendo ad un'altra mia sopra l'aggravio et danno seguitomi ne le cose mie di Inghilterre, solo per havere io servito alla justitia et a lei: mi dava certissima speranza di provedermi de la liberalità sua...Io hormai dal peso de li anni, et parte da questa mia continua infirmità sono aggravato tanto... Già mi sento caminare verso il fine...Con tutto il core supplico humilmente alla Cesarea Maestà vestra che per sua innata clementia si degni havere a core la fidele mia servitù, et la presente necessità mia, et con la gratia sua consolare a tempo questa mia stanca vecchiezza' (Simancas, Estado, Legajo 861, fol. 85; copy in Br. Mus., Add. MS 28587, fols. 100–1; *LP* vii, 1370; *Sp. Cal.* v, 104).

[5] Charles V to Campeggio, 4 November 1538, draft, asking his assistance with a number of problems because 'pro Germanicarum rerum cura et protectione apud istam sanctam sedem praecipue demandata est' (Vienna, HHSA, Rom, Hofcorrespondenz, Fasz. 2). When an effort was being made to name Campeggio's successor as protector, it was recalled that Campeggio had insisted that the protectorship of Germany included that of 'Flanders' as well (Aguilar to Charles V from Rome, 21 October 1539, Simancas, Estado, Legajo 868, fol. 15).

Among the benefices vacated by the death in August 1535 of Cardinal Ippolito de'Medici, vice-chancellor of the Church, was the Sicilian bishopric of Monreale. Against the chance of better success in obtaining it than a Spanish bishopric, Campeggio wrote to Charles V, who was also king of Naples, the day after Ippolito's death to ask for it for himself or his son Gianbattista, bishop-elect of Mallorca. The emperor had promised, he reminded him, to remedy the 'misfortune of his affairs in England' on the first occasion. The bishopric could still console and sustain his poor and infirm old age, while he yet had a little time to live. He claimed his need was such that not only could he not provide for his sons, but he did not even have enough from one year to the next to cover the ordinary expenses of his household.[6]

During his visit of 1536 to Rome Charles V himself gave Monreale to Paul III's sixteen-year-old grandson and namesake, Cardinal Alessandro Farnese, now vice-chancellor of the Church.[7] Possibly to offset the unpleasant memories of the sack of Rome nine years before, the emperor made generous gifts to the cardinals which they were still struggling to apportion among themselves nine months later; Campeggio was but one among the many.[8] In June 1537 he sharply rebuked his son Rodolfo, then at Padua, for living beyond his father's means. Not only was the family without his English income; but, because of the renewed Franco-imperial war, his income from France and Lombardy was cut off as well.[9] Even the bishopric of Mallorca was insecurely held, and Bishop Marcantonio was sent there to sort out difficulties.[10] The ties binding the Campeggi to the Habsburgs wore thin, but they did not break.

[6] Campeggio to Charles V from Rome, 11 August 1535 (Simancas, Estado, Legajo 863, fol. 109); partially printed in Müller, *Legation Lorenzo Campeggios*, i, lxxif. n .166.

[7] Alessandro Farnese to Charles V from Rome, 19 May 1536 (Simancas, Estado, Legajo 856, fol. 122). Farnese was born on 7 October 1520; Ippolito de'Medici had died at the age of twenty-six.

[8] Alessandro Campeggio from Rome to his brother Rodolfo in Bologna, 3 February 1537, in which he speaks of his own debts and complains that it will be six more months before 'questa beata distribution' of the emperor will be finished with (Bologna, AS, AMC, 3rd series, 5/529).

[9] Lorenzo Campeggio to his son Rodolfo, 4 June 1537 (Bologna, AS, AMC, 3rd series, 23/546); the top half of the first page of the letter has been carefully cut away (!).

[10] Marcantonio Campeggio to Lorenzo from Mallorca, 30 July 1539 and to Tommaso, 31 July 1540 (Bologna, AS, AMC, 3rd series, 29/551).

The failure of reconciliation with Henry VIII

In Rome, the English schism was not yet considered beyond facile healing. The election of the wise and aged Farnese as Paul III in 1534 raised hopes of a restoration which Campeggio shared, and which renewed his hopes of recovering his still vacant English bishopric. Polydore Vergil had come to Basle in 1533 to arrange for the first printing of his *Anglica Historia* and then came on to Rome. Although Campeggio had probably asked him to intercede with the king, it was Thomas Cromwell with whom Vergil came into contact on his return to England. Cromwell, as was his nature, gave polite assurances of assistance which Vergil relayed to Rome. Writing on 14 January 1535, and giving a new twist to a familiar term, Campeggio begged Cromwell never to desist from 'the protection of me and my affairs'. Although his opinion in the marriage case differed from 'some', he insisted that he always had and always would be the king's loyal and faithful servant. He also asked Cromwell to take a favourable opportunity to intercede for him with the king.[11]

Campeggio mistook Cromwell's courtesy for cooperation. On the very day he had written to Cromwell from Rome, Chapuys wrote to Charles V from London that the king had just given away the bishoprics of Campeggio and Ghinucci, and that sermons and public ridicule against papal authority continued daily as much as ever. Cromwell's campaign to enforce the reformation was fully in motion.[12] By a kind of perverse aptness of the sort the king could appreciate, Salisbury was given to Cranmer's 'old acquainted friend', Nicholas Shaxton, the heretical almoner of the, for the moment, triumphant Queen Anne. In each step of the formal procedure of institution which followed, the fact of Campeggio's deprivation had prominent mention. Conservative Salisbury, conditioned by a generation of experience with the aged Audley and then the absentee Campeggio, resisted its new bishop and his too active interest in exercising his rights over the Salisbury Corporation.[13] Four years later both Shaxton and Hugh

---

[11] *State Papers of Henry VIII*, VI, 583–4 (*LP* VII, 51); *LP* IV, 737(v).

[12] *LP* VIII, 48 (p. 17).

[13] *LP* VIII, 149 (xxvi), 632(i), 766 and 1158(ii); *LP* XII, 52, 308, 389f., 756 and 1114; *LP* XIV, 1217; *LP* add. I, i, 439f.; Thomas Cranmer, *Miscellaneous Writings and Letters*, ed. J. Cox, The Parker Society, vol. 16 (Cambridge, 1844), p. 309. In 1533 Shaxton had been instituted to East Foulestone in the diocese of Salisbury by the king as patron during a

Latimer, who had been given Ghinucci's Worcester, would resign under pressure of accusations of heresy.

In the face of Henry VIII's continued defiance, Paul III felt obliged to make certain rumbling noises in Rome but cushioned them with delay. As a maladroit gesture of conciliation he particularly favoured England in a creation of cardinals on 21 May 1535. For Charles V he included Schönberg; for Francis I, du Bellay; and for Henry VIII, both Fisher and Ghinucci.[14] It was too late for Ghinucci to be of much service to the king, and the king correctly understood the inclusion of the imprisoned Fisher as an effort to save his life. When Casale intimated to the pope the king's displeasure at Fisher's elevation, the pope justified himself by appealing to the esteem in which his books were held in Germany and Italy, and how Campeggio and others had praised him, hardly reasons of a sort to convince the king.[15]

The execution of Cardinal Fisher aroused the pope to wrath and moved him to promulgate the excommunication and deposition of Henry VIII. In writing to Ferdinand I in Vienna in search of support, the pope compared the king's action with Henry II's involvement in the murder of Thomas of Canterbury and openly admitted to having created Fisher cardinal in the hope of saving his life.[16] The matter was taken under study by a committee of three cardinals, Campeggio, Cesi and the newly created Simonetta.[17] From the beginning it was clear that any hope of success in such a venture depended on firm cooperation from both Charles V and Francis I. The French had used the difficulties between Henry VIII and Charles V to form an alliance with England, but one which had begun to prove more embarras-

vacancy at the abbey of Wilton, in whose gift it was (Salisbury, Diocesan Registry, Register Campegii, fol. 5ᵛ).

14 See Ghinucci to Cromwell, 28 June 1535, announcing his creation as cardinal, and requesting payment of his subsidy from Worcester (*LP* viii, 940). Shortly before his elevation Ghinucci had assisted the *custos* of the English Hospice in Rome in having a member who had spoken treasonably against the king sent to the galleys (*LP* viii, 763).

15 Casale to Cromwell, 29 May 1535 (*LP* viii, 777); and Cromwell to Casale (*LP* ix, 240).

16 Paul III to Ferdinand I, 26 July 1535 (Vienna, HHSA, Rom, Hof-correspondenz, Fasz. 1).

17 Campeggio's copy of the monitorium and excommunication is with the family papers but mislabelled by a later hand as that of Clement VII rather than of Paul III (Bologna, AS, AMC, 2nd series, 55/292); another copy is in Arch. Vat., A. A. Arm. i–xviii, no. 5240.

sing than useful. The imperialist Ortiz insinuated that the French would not be so much interested in depriving Henry VIII of his kingdom as in depriving him of Calais, and of his empty but irritating claim to be king of France. Campeggio astutely raised objection to the deposition on the ground that it would injure princes allied with Henry VIII, especially the king of France. Cardinal du Bellay thanked Campeggio for his new-found concern for the interests of Francis I and interpreted Campeggio's comment as implying that there was something in the treaties of Francis I with Henry VIII to the prejudice of the papacy.[18] But Campeggio's disinclination to second Cardinal Schönberg, an avowed imperial, in pressing for an immediate sentence of deposition suggests that his remarks may well have been an effort to use Franco-imperial differences to thwart the whole project, or at least to demonstrate that it could not succeed. Then the death of Catherine of Aragon on 7 January 1536, coupled with the renewal of war between Francis I and Charles V, not only assured Henry VIII's safety but made him a prize again to be courted. Continued militant talk of Henry's deposition was mixed with contrary talk of a possible voluntary reconciliation with Rome.

After Henry VIII's gigantic effort to have Anne Boleyn as his wife, his sudden repudiation of both her and the validity of their marriage might have made him the laughing stock of Europe had there not been so much at stake. The execution of Anne Boleyn on 19 May 1536, which followed only four months after the death of Catherine of Aragon, tidily disposed of the past and left the king free for a wholly fresh start. Francis I piously let it be known that he desired the honour of bringing Henry VIII back into the fold; and Pio Rodolfo de Carpi, the nuncio in France, wrote to Rome of the happy prospect on the very day that Queen Anne went to the block.[19] Charles V was even quicker off the mark. In acknowledging the letter of his ambassador in London reporting the death of his aunt Catherine, he indicated willingness to negotiate a new understanding with his uncle Henry.[20] There

---

[18] *LP* ix, 249, 269 and 1007.

[19] *LP* x, 922. The letters sent to Rome by de Carpi in 1536 are in Arch. Vat., A. A. Arm. i–xviii, no. 6529; many of them are calendared in *LP* x and xi.

[20] K. Lanz (ed.), *Correspondenz des Kaisers Karl V* (Leipzig, 1845), ii, 212–213; Cromwell to Gardiner and Wallop in France, 8 January 1536, citing the instructions of the king, 'themperour having none other cause or querele to the kinges highnes will of grete lightlywod by all weyes and

were wistful reports even in March that Bishop Gardiner of Winchester, known in Rome for his able and zealous efforts earlier as a lawyer on behalf of the king's cause, was urging the king to reconcile himself with the pope. At the end of May the pope summoned Casale and discussed arrangements for sending an unofficial envoy to the king.

The fall of Anne Boleyn made it likely that her almoner, Nicholas Shaxton, already under attack in England for heresy and unpopular in Salisbury, would not long outlast her.[21] It is not clear just how much Campeggio knew about Shaxton and current conditions in Salisbury, but he fully sensed the possibilities of the moment. With the king's matrimonial problems resolved, all that had stood between the king and his former protector in the Roman Curia was supposedly cleared away. Campeggio saw a golden opportunity to effect the double 'reintegration' of himself with his bishopric, and of Henry VIII with papal authority. As his agent for this delicate task, he chose his brother, Bishop Marcantonio of Grosseto, then in France, who was already well known in England, and who had gone on numerous other missions on the cardinal's behalf. Apparently this was a private venture of Campeggio's. He was certainly responding to attitudes expressed by the pope and the emperor; but if he was acting in explicit cooperation with either or both of them, there was no indication of it in his correspondence with his brother.

On 6 June 1536 he launched the project through a long, rambling letter to Marcantonio.[22] Necessary money for expenses was to be taken out of pension funds due from the abbey at Orbais in the diocese of Soissons or, failing that, from Giovanni Buongulielmo at Lyons with arrangements for repayment from Orbais or from Rome. He was to go to Boulogne and obtain a safe conduct to England from the deputy at Calais or, better, send a messenger to London for it. Since Marcantonio had no one suitable for the purpose among his servants, Campeggio recommended Gérard Boncourt, a canon of Liège once in his service,

meanes seke for the kinges highnes amytie' (R. Merriman, *Life and Letters of Thomas Cromwell* [Oxford, 1902], II, 2; *LP* x, 54).

[21] *LP* XIII, i, 572.

[22] Campeggio to his brother Marcantonio, 6 June 1536, Italian original (Br. Mus., Vitell. B. XIV, fols. 222–3); Latin original, apparently in the possession of Cranmer (Lambeth Palace, MS 2002, fols. 1–2); copy of the Latin original by Piero Vannes (PRO, SP 1/104, fols. 127–30); *LP* x, 1077.

who was fluent in English, and who could make advance arrangements as well as obtain the safe conduct. Riccardo del Bene in Paris, whom the Campeggi had long known and with whom Marcantonio was in contact, could introduce the two.

Campeggio did not anticipate a thoroughly enthusiastic welcome for Marcantonio in England. If possible he was to obtain an interview with the king, offer Campeggio's services, and present his letters of credence. Then, or failing that, he should contact the most important of the king's councillors and go into the particulars of his mission. Further, or that also failing, he was to arrange unobtrusive contacts with the councillors when they were at church functions or at recreation. At any point when he met a strongly negative reaction he should hold off pressing business until a more opportune moment; but if he encountered a willing ear, he should put the other foot forward.

Marcantonio's first object of business was to arrange for the payment of past and future revenues of the bishopric of Salisbury or, failing that, at least to have them held by his bailiffs. Should it be necessary, Polydore Vergil, who could advise him further, already had a mandate in due legal form as Campeggio's procurator for the collection of this income. Secondly, he was to mention the general council of the Church to be held at Mantua and the importance of maintaining English influence and interests at it by the naming of someone of experience and influence to act as protector, a title with which the king had once adorned Campeggio, and which he would be happy to assume on this occasion. Thirdly, although the pretext of the mission was Campeggio's personal affairs, Marcantonio was to urge the reintegration of Henry with the Apostolic See both for the welfare of souls endangered by the continued spread of heresy in England and for the peace of Christendom. He was to raise examples of difficulties between Henry's predecessors and past popes which had ended happily with the humble submission of the king and a reconciliation which redounded to the royal credit. Once the pope and Henry were again at peace with each other, the two of them could arrange the peace between Francis I and Charles V, and Henry could resume his accustomed place as the arbiter and superarbiter of European affairs. This was especially urgent should the Turks make peace with the Persians and renew their attacks in the West. Marcantonio was to offer Campeggio's services in arranging the reconciliation, the proper function of a protector. Should the king show sign of his willingness, then it could be arranged for a formal commission for this purpose to be given to Campeggio either alone or in cooperation with a special envoy from England. 'The reducing of His Majesty to devotion to the Apostolic See' was a matter of greater concern to Campeggio than the recovery of any bishopric; for the second would follow *ipso facto* from the first.

In Campeggio's view both he and the king were innocent of wrong in all that had happened. The occasion for the mission, which Campeggio would like to have been able to undertake personally, had been provided by the prudence and good will shown in Henry's extricating himself from bad counsels and his greater readiness to listen to the truth. Despite what detractors had said, Marcantonio was to assert constantly and everywhere that, except for having given his vote freely in the marriage case contrary to the example of Henry's flatterers, Campeggio had always upheld the king's honour and dignity, ascribing every evil effect to perverse ministers and councillors. Among the councillors themselves Marcantonio was to emphasise Campeggio's eagerness to have use made of his services so that his loyalty and zeal might indicate that he still remembered the king's hospitality and generosity in the past.

There were five royal councillors whom Campeggio recommended to his brother as his special friends and as men whom he trusted: the dukes of Norfolk and Suffolk, and Bishops Clerk, Tunstall and Gardiner. All five were men that he knew personally. Perhaps the letters of credence which Campeggio wrote on 5 June to Suffolk and Tunstall are simply the chance survivors of a set, but certainly Campeggio knew that Norfolk and Gardiner had been the more deeply involved in making Anne Boleyn queen. The two short letters read much the same, but Suffolk was informed that Marcantonio had been sent to explain 'certain matters' on Campeggio's behalf; to Tunstall, Marcantonio was to 'reveal the whole purpose' of his mission.[23] Conspicuously absent from Campeggio's list were Archbishop Cranmer and Thomas Cromwell, both of whom seem to have come into possession of

---

[23] Campeggio to Tunstall, 5 June 1536 (PRO, SP 1/104, fol. 121; *LP* x, 1067); the letter to Suffolk is printed in the *State Papers of Henry VIII*, vii, 657 (*LP* x, 1068).

copies of his original instructions to Marcantonio. His appeal was being made to those conservative members of the council who only four years later would have Cromwell's head.

In April 1536 Campeggio, lying ill at Rome with gout, offered a banquet reception for Charles V's ministers de los Cobos and Granvella, who spent two hours next day in audience with the pope.[24] Campeggio's fundamental loyalties to imperial interests were but poorly concealed in his instructions to Marcantonio, but there is no evidence to indicate that his approach to Henry VIII was as a covert agent of Charles V. To inform Marcantonio of the differences agitated between the Empire and France, Campeggio quite objectively sent along copies of the long discourse made before the papal court by Charles V in person during Easter week in April, and the reply made for Francis I on Ascension day in May. However, he advised Marcantonio to acquaint himself with the past difficulties between kings and popes by reading especially Polydore Vergil's *Anglica Historia* and Paolo Emilio's *De Rebus Gestis Francorum*.[25] Campeggio, much practised in the difficulties of sending secret diplomatic correspondence, sent his brother his seal for writing letters in his name and a cipher. Marcantonio's letters to Campeggio were to be sent in duplicate or triplicate by way of France, of Flanders, or in care of the regent of the Netherlands. In them he was not to indicate that he was acting as Campeggio's agent nor present Campeggio as being partial to either France or the Empire. Letters were to be despatched by means of the emperor's ambassador in London, the Venetian ambassador, or with merchants. Campeggio's mistrust of the French and reliance on the imperialists is evident. Yet Chapuys' innocent report from London to Granvella on 12 August 1536 noted only on the basis of hearsay that Marcantonio was on his way.

What the ambassador Chapuys had remarked was the presence in London of Marcantonio's servant sent from Paris to obtain the

[24] *LP* x, 670 (p. 271).
[25] The first edition of Vergil's history, up to 1509, was printed in Basle in 1534; only in the third Basle edition, that of 1555, the year of Vergil's death in his native Urbino, was the reign of Henry VIII up to 1538 included (D. Hay, *Polydore Vergil, Renaissance Historian and Man of Letters* [Oxford, 1952], p. 79). Vergil had not forgotten that Campeggio had been promised Salisbury as a reward for cooperation with Wolsey in obtaining the deprivation of Vergil's patron, Cardinal Adriano Castellesi; but his sparse comments about Campeggio seem objective enough (*Anglica Historia*, ed. Hay, p. 252).

safe conduct. Antonio Bonvisio in London sent a letter dated 15 August back to Paris with this servant Lodovico, but a reply of 10 September from a French associate of Marcantonio suggested that there were difficulties and that Marcantonio had not yet departed from Paris. He expressed hope, however, that Campeggio as the king's protector in Rome would still be able to act as the king's mediator.[26]

Marcantonio's own letter to Campeggio, written in Paris, evidently in cipher, on 4 September 1536, was far less sanguine.[27] The servant Lodovico, who had gone off to England when Campeggio's son Gianbattista had arrived from Rome with the instructions, had returned with an oral message from Cromwell, who was polite but more apparently than actually helpful. The instructions originally made by Campeggio from Rome were in the circumstances unworkable. Marcantonio reported that Polydore Vergil, Bishop Clerk and Bishop Gardiner were away; Suffolk was banished; and Norfolk, whose brother was under sentence of death, could be of little use. All negotiation had to be done through Cromwell, who was first secretary and, since June, keeper of the privy seal. In spite of Cromwell's great courtesy, Marcantonio sensed that he would not prove sympathetic to Campeggio's purposes.[28] All foreigners who had held English benefices had been required to appear within a specified time or forfeit them. Marcantonio had been told that Salisbury was now held by a 'German' bishop (*episcopo todesco*), and Ghinucci's Worcester was reportedly given away as well. On Cromwell's proposal more than three hundred monasteries had already been

[26] *LP* xi, 286 and 438.

[27] Bologna, AS, AMC, 3rd series, 15/538; the letter is an unsigned contemporary copy of three pages, possibly from a ciphered original.

[28] 'Ludovico, che andò al jongere de Jo: Baptista, è ritornato con risposta a boccha da Milord Cremuel primo secretario che tiene el privasigel de comissione del Re, che andasse ad ogni mio piacere, che sempre seria il ben andato. . . .Governando solo il sopradetto, et nessuno altro. Il Polidoro, Bada, Vintoniensis sono fora. Sofoles sta bandito. Norfoch è in corte, et tene un fratello condemnato a morte, ne ardisse fare moto per lui: Et se ben vi fosseno, non serviriano de nulla: perché non se volono ingerire de cosa alcuna: per forza si convien negotiare tutto con il detto Cremuel. Lo quale referisseno essere Gentilissima persona, ma non scio come se dimostrarà alla nostra intentione' (Marcantonio Campeggio to his brother Lorenzo from Paris, 4 September 1536; Bologna, AS, AMC, 3rd series, 15/538). Cromwell had become keeper of the Privy Seal in succession to Thomas Boleyn, earl of Wiltshire, who himself had been named in January 1530 in succession to Campeggio's friend, Bishop Tunstall.

pulled down (*trecente abbatie sono abbatute*), and more were in the process of being destroyed. The archbishop of Canterbury (Cranmer) and the bishops of Rochester (Hilsey) and Salisbury (Shaxton) were persisting in their errors, and a major effort was under way to promulgate and enforce the new statutes of parliament. Piero Vannes and Antonio Bonvisio had seen Lodovico in London and inquired whether Campeggio in Rome was informed of these occurrences in England. Marcantonio thought their effort would be in vain but awaited Campeggio's adjusted instructions. He closed with the news that the new queen was well loved and to be crowned on 29 September, that Princess Mary had again been returned to favour, and that Henry FitzRoy, duke of Richmond, had died.

Eventually Marcantonio did arrive in London; but, as he had foreseen, his diligent efforts met with little success. Campeggio's reply of 27 January 1537 to his report from England made still another attempt to answer charges of disloyalty. Again he insisted that his vote in Consistory for the validity of the king's marriage was the one exception in his otherwise faithful service to the king. He was pleased that the 'tumults' in England had halted themselves, and he hoped that parliament would be able to end the matter. As a cardinal bound to reside in the papal court, he argued that it was necessary and permissible for him to govern his see *in absentia*. He recalled how he had succeeded Clement VII as protector when the latter was elected pope, and he wished to resume his service to the king.[29]

Gianbattista, still bishop-elect of Mallorca, and acting as courier between his father in Rome and his uncle in England, had carried off an earlier letter of Campeggio's to which Marcantonio replied on 3 February from London. Neither the Irish rebellion led by 'Silken Thomas' in 1534–5, nor the rebellion in the north of England had tempted the Campeggi away from their dedication to Henry VIII. Marcantonio remarked a jealous unwillingness of the populace to follow the leadership of the nobles in the uprising at York, but attributed the total extinction of the rebellion to the prudence and dexterity of the king. He noted with approval the

[29] Campeggio to his brother Marcantonio, 27 January 1537, '[Re]cordo della protettione mia di detto regno, la quale però mi fu data dalle felice memoria di [Clemente VII] secondo che si usa, essendo lui prima ante promotionem ad Papatum protettore' (badly burnt; the fragmentary text is printed entire in *LP* xii, 255).

king's diplomatic approaches to Scotland and France in order to control the rebellion, and also the governmental reform that was in fact the reorganisation of the Council of the North. The execution that day of an important Irish nobleman and his five relatives after fifteen months' imprisonment in the Tower was noted without judgment; the nobleman in fact was 'Silken Thomas' Fitz-Gerald, Lord Offaly, executed with his five Geraldine uncles. One of the eleven prisoners from the uprising at Lincoln was supposed to have died in the Tower. Marcantonio closed with the observation that at present things were tranquil, and that Campeggio's matters stood as usual.[30]

Marcantonio evidently stayed on in London until the end of March, but it was clear that Campeggio's undertaking was doomed to failure before ever Marcantonio crossed the Channel.[31] Cromwell was far more solidly placed in power than Campeggio must have realised at the outset. By July 1536 Paul III, moved by news of the dissolution of the monasteries and the Pilgrimage of Grace, had decided that Henry VIII had no intention of repenting. He gave vent to rage against the king and against Cromwell, who had become a kind of anti-papal, lay Wolsey.[32] The man in Italy to whom the pope turned was Reginald Pole, who had

---

[30] 'Al presente le cose stanno in quiete. Le cose di V. S. Reverendissima stanno al solito' (Bologna, AS, AMC, 3rd series, 24/546); the letter, a small folio, is a copy and headed 'De Mons. di Grossetto, da Londra alli 3. di Feb. del 1537'. Another letter in the same carton from Alessandro Campeggio in Rome to his brother Rodolfo in Padua, dated 13 March 1537, notes that he encloses a copy of a letter recently received from England.

[31] George Lord Cobham to Cromwell from Cobham Hall in Kent, 21 March 1537, explaining that a Gullyam Tremoyle had brought three coffers and other items from London to Rochester and, after waiting four days 'for one Campagious who is yet at London', returned taking his chamber key; he asked Cromwell's wishes (*LP* XII, i, 691); *LP* XII, 166, 414 and 563. Possibly a search was made of Marcantonio's luggage and his correspondence seized. This and the fact that Lord Cobham was governor of Calais and a kinsman of Cranmer might explain the presence of Campeggio's letters to Marcantonio in Lambeth Palace (reacquired in 1963). My thanks to Miss Barber, assistant archivist at Lambeth Palace, for having drawn my attention to MS 2002 there.

[32] N. Raince to Cardinal du Bellay, 27 July 1536, 'Mgr. Nre. dict S. P. me parla du Roy dangleterre ansi comme jescript au Roy en bien grosse colere et se attache continuellement contre Cramouel' (cited in P. Friedman, *Anne Boleyn, a Chapter of English History, 1527–1536* [London, 1884], II, 307n.). Friedmann claims that Marcantonio was the pope's as well as Campeggio's agent and that this sharp change in the pope's attitude

already done his tactless bit to bring the king round. Taking the
death of Anne Boleyn as a suitable occasion, he sent his *De
Unitate Ecclesiae* to the king. The Venetian Gasparo Contarini,
created cardinal on the same day as Fisher and already Pole's
curial patron, wrote to him in February that he had written too
bitterly about Henry VIII; and Pole replied that flattery had been
the cause of all the evil. After a brief interlude of subdued
optimism about affairs in England, Pole returned to an attitude of
harshness in July, just prior to the pope's doing so.[33] As the rising
in the north of England gathered momentum during 1536, Pole's
harsher counsels gained the ascendant with the pope, who created
him cardinal on 22 December along with other men of the new
militant spirit, like Caraffa, who was familiar with England from
his days as resident nuncio there. Moves to revive the Franco-
Scottish alliance by the marriage of James V and Mary of Lorraine
were actively encouraged by the pope, and Count Gianantonio
Campeggio was sent off to Scotland in January 1537 with the
sword and cap of maintenance.[34] On 7 February Cardinal Pole
was commissioned as 'legate to England' and went off with
Gianmatteo Giberti to France and the Netherlands to urge on a
revolt whose power was already spent through its leaders' mis-
placed trust in the king's promises. The arrival in England of
Campeggio's letter of 27 January found all hope of reconciliation
vanished.

Campeggio and Pole
Tedious as it is to relate, the consistorial provision of bishops for
this period moved in interesting counterpoint to Campeggio's
claims to have remained loyal to the king. The last provision
made by royal supplication, that of Christopher Bodkin to
Kilmacduagh, had been referred by Campeggio on 3 September
1533. The next year Edmund O Gallchobhar was provided as
bishop of Raphoe on the pretext that there had been a vacancy of
about seventeen years' standing without a royal nomination; but

against Henry was presumably occasioned by negative reports received
from Marcantonio in England. In fact, Marcantonio did not even arrive in
England until autumn at the earliest.
[33] Pole's letters of 4 March to 27 July 1536 are calendared in *LP* x, 420;
426, 441, 619, 974, 1093 and 1197; *LP* xi, 91, 98 and 173.
[34] *LP* xi, 1173; *LP* xii, i, 166, 414 and 563; Scarisbrick, *Henry VIII*, pp.
335f., refers in passing to Campeggio's undertaking of 1536–7.

it was in fact in challenge to Cornelius O Cathain, whose provision had been referred by Cardinal Bainbridge in 1513, and who was now actively supported by the king. Significantly, it was not Campeggio but Andrea della Valle who referred it.[35]

After the election of Paul III and the Act of Supremacy there was evidently a check made through the consistorial records at Rome to establish which of the provisions made under the last three popes were at direct royal supplication.[36] During Campeggio's lifetime, however, no attempt was made to provide a bishop to any of the thirteen vacancies which occurred in England. In 1535 Hugh O Cearbhallain was provided to Clogher in Ireland but at the referral of Cardinal Pisano. In May 1536, when there was hope of reconciliation with Henry VIII, Campeggio referred the provision of the Cistercian James FitzMaurice, of illegitimate birth and twenty-five years old, as bishop of Ardfert, and of the Dominican Quinton O Quigley to Dromore. There was no royal nomination, at least no formal one, made in either case; but the king who had made George Browne archbishop of Dublin in March 1536 without papal provision, named no bishops to challenge the claims of FitzMaurice and O Quigley. The hardening of royal and papal positions in 1537–8 was reflected in an avowed struggle to gain control of the Irish church. It began in earnest in February 1537, when the king made Bishop Christopher Bodkin of Kilmacduagh also archbishop of the vacant see of Tuam, and the pope countered next year by providing Art O Friel, who was in Rome at the time.[37] Although Campeggio regularly referred German provisions from 1533 until his death, he took no part in the papal struggle for Ireland against the king. This role was assumed by the deprived bishop of Worcester, Cardinal Ghinucci.[38]

The last two years of Campeggio's life were chiefly occupied

---

[35] 'Ob non nominationem regis et vacavit ab annis XVII citra, fuit provisum de persona Odemundi Ogalembays' (PRO 31/10/14, fol. 99, from Arch. Vat., Arch. Cons., Acta Cam. 3, fol. 69ᵛ); Gwynn, *Medieval Province of Armagh*, pp. 232ff. There were local circumstances involved.

[36] Excepting the deprived Ghinucci, there were at Campeggio's death in 1539 only eight diocesan ordinaries left in England from among those papally provided before 1534: Archbishops Cranmer and Lee, and Bishops Clerk, Gardiner, Longland, Stokesley, Tunstall and Vesey.

[37] Gwynn, *Medieval Province of Armagh*, pp. 223–48.

[38] Wodka, *Protektorate der Kardinäle*, pp. 17n., 20n., 48 and 120.

with plans for the general council of the Church, to which he had hoped to go as Henry's special protector. He was one of nine cardinals named on 7 January 1538 to the commission for a council to be held at Vicenza, rather than at Mantua as planned earlier; and his advice was sought on the position to be taken with regard to the 'grievances of the German nation'. On 20 March, as Cromwell learned from an informer in Rome, Campeggio was named with Simonetta and Aleander as legate to Vicenza.[39] Because of Campeggio's slow progress en route and late arrival, the legates made their formal entry into the city only in May and then returned to Rome, when the council failed to materialise. In the spring of 1539 Campeggio again served on a committee of eight cardinals named to discuss reform. In Consistory Cardinal Caraffa made a resounding condemnation of pluralism among the cardinals, to which Campeggio objected, only to find himself opposed by Pole, Contarini and Quiñones. On 21 April Campeggio, Simonetta and Aleander were reconfirmed as legates for Vicenza; but Campeggio was already ill and dying and had to withdraw.[40]

Although the mind of the Curia continued to associate Campeggio with England as well as with the Empire, there is little reason to believe that he was ever on very close terms with Pole.[41] In September 1538 a government campaign was launched in England to destroy the religious shrines. In Consistory on 25 October the angry pope announced the spitefully thorough destruction of the shrine of St Thomas of Canterbury and appointed a committee of five cardinals, Campeggio, Ghinucci, Contarini, Caraffa and Pole, to find the ways and means to punish the 'ribaldo, sacrilego, heretico, scelerato' who was king of England.[42] Had Campeggio moderately insisted that it was not

---

[39] Guido Giannetto to Cromwell, April 1538 (*LP* xiii, i 886); and *LP* xiii, i, 51.

[40] H. Jedin, *A History of the Council of Trent*, trans. E. Graf (London, 1957,) i, 336ff. and 345; Pastor, *History of the Popes*, trans. Kerr. xi, 188f.

[41] *LP* xii, ii, 1026; *LP* xiv, ii, 54.

[42] PRO 31/10/14, fol. 86 (Arch. Vat., Arch. Cons., Acta Cam. 2, fol. 75ᵛ) and fol. 103 (Arch. Vat., Arch. Cons., Acta Cancel. 3, fol. 136) omit Ghinucci; PRO 31/10/15, fol. 136 (Arch. Vat., Arch. Cons., Acta Cancel. 4, fol. 68) and *LP* xiii, ii, 684, omit Pole. The list is complete in Giovanni Bianchetto to Cardinal Aleander, 28 October 1538 (Pastor, *History of the Popes*, trans. Kerr, xi, 575). Bianchetto, a former servant of Cranmer, was in the service of Ghinucci in Rome and an official of the Secretariat of

only the king but also his councillor Cromwell who was responsible, he would not have been far wrong. The fanatical excess did
not bear the stamp of Cromwell, but the quietly persistent policy
behind it did.

The English colony in Rome, centred in the Hospice of St
Thomas of Canterbury, had continued to remain loyal to Henry
even after the Act of Supremacy. This ended when Cardinal Pole
and the English exiles took control of the Hospice and were
formally confirmed in possession on 8 March 1538 by Paul III.[43]
It was by way of exception that Anthony Budgewood, an escapee
and fortune seeker from England, called on Campeggio in
December 1538 after having been put off by Pole.[44]

When Campeggio died in Rome in July 1539,[45] religious
differences had polarised politics in England and abroad. It was
Thomas Cromwell and Cardinal Pole who represented the two
aspects of the changed situation in England. Cromwell's role as
Henry VIII's viceregent for ecclesiastical affairs was directly
influenced by his service under Wolsey and gave him the leverage
by which he made Henry VIII pope in England. Pole became
leader of the party whose object was to restore papal authority as
it had existed. In 1539 Cromwell was under pressure from a
conservative reaction but by July had, for the most part, been
able to recover his political strength. Cardinal Pole was just com-
pleting a second tour as legate in the effort to stir up Charles V,
Francis I and James V to impose by force the decree of excommunication and deposition against Henry VIII. In their exchange
of epithets Cromwell referred to 'the traytour Pole', and for Pole

Briefs; in September 1536 he wrote to Cranmer with a report of Pole's
relationship with Paul III (Cranmer, *Miscellaneous Writings and Letters*,
pp. 330–2).

[43] Newns, 'The Hospice of St. Thomas and the English crown', *English
Hospice in Rome*, p. 175; the brief of Paul III is printed, pp. 185–7.

[44] *LP* xiv, i, 1.

[45] The day of Campeggio's death in July 1539 has in the past been given
variously (see the extended note 166 in Müller, *Legation Lorenzo
Campeggios*, i, lxxiif.). Müller does not cite the notice of 20 July 1539
from Rome which says that Campeggio died 'questa notte alle vj. hore'
(Bologna, AS, Archivio del Reggimento, Lettere dell'ambasciatore
bolognese in Roma al Senato, vol. for the year 1539). The inscription
added in 1868 to the now empty tomb of Lorenzo Campeggio and his son
Alessandro in the entry of S. Maria in Trastevere, Rome, plainly states,
however, that Lorenzo died on 25 July 1539 at the age of sixty-seven,
making 1472 and not 1474, as is more commonly accepted, the year of
his birth. The bodies had been transferred to Bologna in 1571.

Cromwell was 'Satanae Nuncius'.[46] Campeggio's world of comfortable compromise seemed gone for ever.

For twenty-two years of his life Campeggio had been a cardinal and at the centre of power in the church. His role, however, was more that of a servant to the leaders of Europe than that of a leader himself. For all his brilliance as a lawyer and diplomat, he participated in momentous events without shaping them or even seeming to catch their real significance. As a widower deeply concerned for the future of his children and his relatives, Campeggio continued to harbour a curial and legalistic notion of nepotism, and a sincere preoccupation with money. He had neither the zeal of a true reformer nor the panache of a genuine Renaissance cardinal-prince. His homely honesty was obscured by his constant opportunism.

Campeggio built his career chiefly from his two legations to England and his two in the Empire. Yet for all his experience with rising Lutheranism in Germany and his later support for the idea of a general council of the Church, he seems never to have caught the spirit which finally produced the Council of Trent. After his departure from England in 1529 he failed to grasp the radical changes which had taken place there in the years that followed. With the fall of Anne Boleyn in 1536 he genuinely hoped for a return to the state of 1518–19, when papal cooperation with Henry VIII was personified in Wolsey's arranging of the peace of Europe. To the end Campeggio saw in Henry VIII's break with the papacy an unthinkable isolation of England from the centre of European diplomacy. Actually, Wolsey's aggressive and flexible foreign policy, together with his involvement of England in Italian affairs, had done a great deal for Wolsey as servant of his king, but little for England. So long as the traditional Anglo-imperial alliance was in force, Cardinal Campeggio, like Cardinals Piccolomini and Castellesi before him, could without difficulty serve both Germany and England. Twice in Wolsey's time the Anglo-imperial alliance was abandoned and a shift was made toward France. Bainbridge was the first victim of Wolsey's and de'Medici's flexible diplomacy; Campeggio was the last.

Because Campeggio had died in the Roman Curia, Paul III could in theory invoke the right to name the successor to the see of Salisbury without seeming to reject the tradition of royal

[46] Merriman, *Thomas Cromwell*, I, 91–2; II, 55, 58, 87, 193 and 204.

nomination from England. For the first time since 1534 he made the empty gesture of providing a bishop to a vacancy in England. It is a mark of triumph of Pole and the policy of militancy over Campeggio's spirit of patchwork compromise that Pole, son of the imprisoned countess of Salisbury, should have been offered the title to the bishopric there. Writing to Contarini on 18 August 1539 to explain his refusal, Pole reasoned that should things in England be restored, he could not fail to get a bishopric except by his own fault; and if things remained the same, there was no more advantage in that of Salisbury than that of Antioch or Alexandria. He would have but a dry bone of which his adversaries would be eating the flesh.[47] Pole had the satisfaction of hearing of Cromwell's fall and execution the next year. In 1554 he had the further satisfaction of returning to England to 'restore things' under his cousin Queen Mary I; and he received the archbishopric of Canterbury, both bone and flesh.

Loyalty to the pope was not dead in England, but it never again became identified with the national interest. When Queen Mary, at the urging of the pope and contrary to Pole's wise counsel, had gone ahead with the marriage to King Philip II of Spain, the papal restoration in England was doomed even before it was accomplished. In 1555 the formal, short-lived reconciliation of England with the pope, now Pole's friend Caraffa as Paul IV, was made in Rome; but the new cardinal protector was named by the pope rather than the queen. When even Cardinal Pole and the cardinal protector, Giovanni Morone, were attacked by Paul IV in 1558, it became really clear how far England and the papacy had drifted apart. Cardinal Campeggio was in the unhappy position of being the last cardinal protector of England chosen by the crown.[48]

---

[47] R. Pole, *Epistolae*, ed. A. Quirini (Brixon, 1744–58), II, 186 (*LP* XIV, ii, 54). Contarini, who had been named Campeggio's successor as protector of the Benedictine Congregation of St Justin, had been give 'administration' of Salisbury in Consistory on 23 July 1539 and continued to hold the empty title until his death, when another successor was again provided (*LP* XIV, ii, 1308). There is no reason to suppose that the Curia was aware that Shaxton had resigned in July 1539, so that by coincidence the see was absolutely vacant for the moment. A similar empty provision was made to Worcester when Ghinucci died in 1541.

[48] Wodka, *Protektorate der Kardinäle*, p. 14n. Cardinal Giovanni Morone was a close personal friend of Pole. Charles V had much difficulty in naming a successor to Campeggio as protector of Germany. Cardinal Manriquez, his immediate successor, died on 7 October 1540. Cardinal

In Ireland, on the other hand, the continuing struggle for national independence from English domination became identified with loyalty to the pope. It was not the royally nominated hierarchy of the church of Ireland, but the bishops gradually provided by the pope without royal nomination, who came to hold the vast majority of the Irish. To the existing sources of discord and diversity in the British Isles and within England itself were now added those of religion as well. In a sense, the cardinal protectors had assisted in the loss of England to the papacy, and Ireland remained loyal to the papacy in spite of them.

Alessandro Farnese, vice-chancellor and grandson of Paul III, made a bid for the position through the nuncio (letter cited by Wodka), and on 3 November 1540 Charles V instructed Aguilar in Rome to encourage Farnese without either giving him hopes or taking them away from him. In fact the emperor had already chosen Cardinal Quiñones, who died on 5 November 1540, evidently before he could accept the appointment (Simancas, Estado, Legajo 869, fol. 221; *Sp. Cal.* vi, 137). Wodka, p. 19n. and 49, who has not noticed this letter of Charles V, gives Cardinal Aleander as successor to Manriquez and leaves Farnese's position open to speculation.

LIST OF SOURCES
AND SELECT BIBLIOGRAPHY

ABBREVIATIONS

LP
Letters and Papers, Foreign and Domestic, of the Reign of Henry VIII,
ed. Brewer, Gairdner and Brodie.

Milan Cal.
Calendar of State Papers, Milan, ed. Hinds.

Sp. Cal.
Calendar of State Papers, Spanish, ed. Bergenroth, Gayangos and Hume,
with two supplements, ed. Bergenroth and Mattingly.

Ven. Cal.
Calendar of State Papers, Venetian, ed. Brown.

All references to these and other calendars are to numbers of
the documents summarised except where page numbers
are specifically noted. Other abbreviations are
clear from the bibliography which follows.

MANUSCRIPT SOURCES

Bologna, Archivio di Stato [AS]:
   Archivio del Reggimento,
      Lettere dell'ambasciatore bolognese in Roma al Senato.
   Archivio Malvezzi-Campeggi [AMC],
      2nd series, 26/263, 55/292, 56/293 and 57/294.
      3rd series, 5/529, 15/538, 22/545, 23/546, 24/546, 27/549 and 29/551.
Brussels, Archives Nationales:
   Papiers d'Etat et de l'Audience, no. 75.
Cambridge, the University Library:
   MS Mm. 1. 41, and Additional MSS 4874, 4878 and 4883.
Dublin, National Library:
   Microfilms p. 3075 and p. 3178 (extracts from Arch. Vat., Reg. Vat.,
      vols. 775–990).
   Microfilms p. 2975, p. 2966 and p. 2977 (extracts from Arch. Vat.,
      Reg. Lat., vols. 925–1026).
Florence, Archivio di Stato [AS]:
   Carte Strozziani, 1st series, vii, viii, x, xviii and cxxx.

Mediceo avanti il Principato, Filze xv, xli, xlv, xlvi, lxvi and cv–cxlv.
Otto di Practica, Responsive ii.
Signori Responsive, Filze xxxi–xli.
London,
  British Museum:
    Add. MSS 5847, 15385, 15386, 15387, 15388, 15399, 15400, 21519,
      25114, 25578, 28383, 28583, 28587 and 45131.
    Cotton MSS
      Cleopatra. E. iii.
      Vitellius. B. ii, iii, iv, v, vi, vii, viii, ix, x, xi, xii, xiii and xiv
      (originals of State Papers, Henry VIII).
    Royal MS 12. E. xvi.
  Lambeth Palace:
    MSS 2002, 2341 and 2342.
  Public Record Office [PRO]:
    E 135/8/38 and E 135/22/25.
    PRO 31/9/1, 2, 3, 5, 15, 52c, 62 and 63 (Stevenson Roman transcripts).
    PRO 31/10/8, 10, 14, 15, 17 and 40 (continuation of the
      Stevenson Roman transcripts).
    SP 1/7, 9, 11, 12, 13, 14, 15, 16, 17, 18, 19, 20, 21, 22, 23, 24, 25, 26,
      27, 28, 29, 30, 32, 33, 35, 36, 37, 38, 39, 47, 50, 53, 55, 74, 89
      and 104 (originals of State Papers, Henry VIII).
Madrid, Real Academia de la Historia:
  Colección Salazar, A-4, A-23, A-27, A-35 and A-39.
Nottingham, the University Library:
  Middleton MSS, Register of Abbot Thomas Felde.
Rome,
  Archives of the Venerable English College:
    Liber Instrumentorum i; and Libri 17, 18 and 232.
  Archivio Teatino (Sant'Andrea della Valle):
    Busta 1 (Misc. Piccolomini papers).
  Biblioteca Angelica:
    MS Codex 1077.
Salisbury, the Diocesan Registry:
  Register Campegii.
Siena, Archivio di Stato [AS]:
  Balia v, Copialettere 418.
  Balia vi, Carteggi, vols. 548–633.
  Consistorio ix, Carteggi, vols. 2071–88.
  Fondo Piccolomini, Filza 36.
  Signori Responsive, Filza 10.
Simancas, Archivo General:
  Estado, Legajos 853, 854, 860, 861, 863, 865 and 868.
  Guerra Antigua, Legajo 3.
  Patronato Real, Legajos 21 and 53.
Tournai, Archives de l'Evêché:
  Inventaire (the documents themselves were destroyed by World
    War II).

Vatican,
Archivio Segreto Vaticano:
A[rchivium] A[rcis], Arm[aria] i–xviii, nos. 1436, 1901, 2377, 2381,
 2383, 2782, 2783, 2784, 2785, 2786, 2787, 2788, 2789, 2793, 2804,
 2805, 2836, 2840, 2841, 2842, 2850, 2851, 2852, 2853, 2854, 2855,
 2856, 2857, 2858, 2859, 2860, 2861, 2862, 2863, 2864, 2865, 2866,
 2867, 2868, 2869, 2870, 2871, 2872, 2873, 2874, 2875, 2876, 2877,
 2878, 2879, 2880, 2881, 2954, 2955, 2958, 3020, 4025, 4028, 4030,
 4031, 4033, 4034, 4035, 4038, 4040, 4041, 4042, 4043, 4044, 4046,
 4063, 4544, 5250, 6521, 6528 and 6529.
Arm[aria] xxxix, cod. 22, 28; and xliv, cod. 5.
Archivio Consistoriale,
Acta Camerarii 1, 2 and 3; Acta Cancellarii 1, 2, 3 and 4; Camerarii
 Diversoria 63, 66 and 73; Miscellania 44; Obligationes 82 and 83
 (see PRO 31/10/14, 15, 40; and 31/9/52c).
Archivio della Rota,
Manualia Actorum et Citationum 27.
Lettere di Principi i, ii, iii, iv, v, vii, x and xi.
Registra Lateranensia 932, 933, 935, 938 and 950.
Registra Vaticana 847, 849, 857, 868, 873, 875, 876, 965, 984, 989,
 1195, 1196 and 1198.
Biblioteca Vaticana:
Cod. Barb. Lat. 2876 and 2932.
Cod. Vat. Lat. 10, 384, 639, 6210 and 10637.
Venice,
Archivio di Stato [AS]:
Collezione Podocataro, Busta vii.
Biblioteca di San Marco:
Collezione Podocataro, MSS Lat. 3621 and 3624.
Vienna, Das kaiserliche und königliche Haus-, Hof-, und Staatsarchiv
 [HHSA]:
Belgien, PA-101.
England, Hofcorrespondenz, Karton 1–8.
England, Varia, Karton 1, 2.
Rom, Hofcorrespondenz, Karton 1, Fasz. 1, 2.

PRINTED SOURCES

Burchard, Johann. *Diarium sive rerum urbanarum commentarii, 1483–1506.*
 Ed. I. Thuasne. 3 vols. Paris, 1883–5.
Burckard, Johann. *Liber Notarum ab anno M.CCCC.LXXXIII usque ad
 annum MDVI.* Ed. E. Celani. Rerum Italicarum Scriptores, xxxii.
 Vol. i (1483–96). Città di Castello, 1906.
Burnet, Gilbert. *History of the Reformation of the Church of England.*
 Rev. N. Pocock. Vol. vi, documents. Oxford, 1865.
Calendar of Patent Rolls, Henry VII. 2 vols. London, 1914–16.
Campbell, William (ed.). *Materials for a History of the Reign of Henry VII
 from Original Documents Preserved in the Public Record Office.*
 Rolls Series, 60. 2 vols. London, 1873–7.

Conti da Foligne, Sigismondo dei. *Le storie de' suoi tempi dal 1475 al 1510.*
Vol. II. Rome, 1883.

Cranmer, Thomas. *Miscellaneous Writings and Letters.* Ed. J. Cox.
The Parker Society, vol. 16. Cambridge, 1844.

Ehses, Stephan (ed.). *Römische Dokumente zur Geschichte der Ehescheidung
Heinrichs VIII. von England, 1527–1534.* Görres-Gesellschaft, Quellen
und Forschungen aus dem Gebiete der Geschichte, II. Paderborn,
1893.

Ellis, Henry (ed.). *Original Letters Illustrative of English History from
Autographs in the British Museum and Other Collections.* 1st series,
vol. I, London, 1824; 2nd series, vol. I, London, 1827; 3rd series, vol. I,
London, 1846.

Elton, G. R. (ed.). *The Tudor Constitution, Documents and Commentary.*
Cambridge, 1960.

'Extracts from the Fondo Borghese in the Vatican Archives', *Archivium
Hibernicum.* XXIII (1960), 19–64.

Gairdner, James (ed.). *Letters and Papers Illustrative of the Reigns of
Richard III and Henry VII.* Rolls Series, 24. 2 vols. London, 1861–3.

*Memorials of Henry the Seventh, Bernardi Andreae Tholosatis vita
Regis Henrici Septimi; necnon alia quaedam ad eundem Regem
spectantia.* Rolls Series, 10. One vol. London,
1858.

Guasti, C. (ed.). 'I manoscritti Torrigiani donati all'Archivio di Stato di
Firenze', *Archivio storico italiano,* 3rd series, XIX (1874), 56–76 and
221–53; XX (1874), 19–50, 228–55 and 367–408; XXIV (1876), 5–31;
XXV (1877), 369–403; and XXVI (1877), 177–203.

Laemmer, Hugo (ed.). *Monumenta vaticana historiam ecclesiasticam saeculi
XVI illustrantia.* Freiburg-im-Breisgau, 1861.

*Lettres du Roy Louis XII et du Cardinal Georges d'Amboise, avec plusieurs
autres lettres, écrites depuis 1504 jusques et compris 1514.* 4 vols.
Brussels, 1712.

Martène, E., and Durand, U. (eds.). *Veterum scriptorum et monumentorum
historicum, dogmaticorum, moralium amplissima collectio.* Vol. III.
Paris, 1724.

Merriman, Roger. *Life and Letters of Thomas Cromwell.* 2 vols. Oxford,
1902. Part of vol. I and all of vol. II contain the letters written by
Cromwell.

Müller, Gerhard (ed.). *Legation Lorenzo Campeggios 1530–1532 und
Nuntiatur Girolamo Aleanders 1531. Nuntiaturberichte aus Deutschland
nebst ergänzenden Aktenstücken,* supplementary vols. I and II.
Tübingen, 1963 and 1969.

Pocock, Nicholas (ed.). *Records of the Reformation: the Divorce, 1527–1533.*
2 vols. Oxford, 1870.

Pole, Reginald. *Epistolae.* Ed. A. Quirini. 5 vols. Brixon, 1744–58.

Rymer, Thomas (ed.). *Foedera, conventiones, litterae, et cujuscunque generis
acta publica inter reges Anglicae et alios quosvis imperatores, reges,
pontifices, principes, vel communitates.* Vols. XI, XII, XIII and XIV.
London, 1704–35.

State Papers during the Reign of Henry the Eighth. Vol. I, domestic
correspondence; vol. II, correspondence relating to Ireland; vols. VI
and VII, correspondence between England and foreign courts.
London, 1830–52.

Theiner, Augustinus (ed.). *Vetera monumenta Hibernorum et Scotorum
historiam illustrantia, quae ex Vaticani, Neapolis, ac Florentiae tabulariis
depromisit et ordine chronologico disposuit.* Rome, 1864.

Vergil, Polydore. *Anglica Historia.* Bks. XXIV and XXV. Ed. D. Hay. Camden
Third Series, vol. LXXIV. Camden Society, 1950.

Wilkins, David (ed.). *Concilia Magnae Britanniae et Hiberniae.* Vol. III.
London, 1737.

CALENDARS OF DOCUMENTS WITH
SUMMARIES IN ENGLISH

Calendar of Carew Manuscripts in the Lambeth Library. Ed. J. Brewer and
W. Bullen. Vol. I, 1515–74. London, 1867.

*Calendar of Entries in the Papal Registers Relating to Great Britain and
Ireland, Papal Letters.* Ed. J. Twemlow. Vols. XII, XIII and XIV.
London, 1933–61.

Calendar of Letters and Papers, Foreign and Domestic, Henry VIII.
Ed. J. Brewer, J. Gairdner and R. Brodie. 21 vols. with a vol. of
addenda; vol. I, 2nd ed., 1920. London, 1864–1920.

*Calendar of Letters, Despatches, and State Papers Relating to the
Negotiations between England and Spain, Preserved in the Archives
at Vienna, Brussels, Simancas and Elsewhere.* Ed. G. Bergenroth,
P. de Gayangos, M. Hume and G. Mattingly. Vols. I–V, with a
supplement and further supplement to vols. I–II. London, 1862–1947.

*Calendar of State Papers and Manuscripts Existing in the Archives and
Collections of Milan.* Ed. A. Hinds. One vol. London, 1912.

*Calendar of State Papers and Manuscripts Relating to English Affairs,
Existing in the Archives and Collections of Venice, and in Other
Libraries of Northern Italy.* Ed. R. Brown. Vols. I–V. London, 1864–73.

Calendar of State Papers Relating to Ireland. Ed. H. Hamilton. Vol. I.
London, 1860.

Hannay, R., and Hay, D. (eds.). [*Calendar of*] *the Letters of James V
[of Scotland, 1513–42].* One vol. Edinburgh, 1954.

Historical Manuscripts Commission, *Fourth Report,* 1874; *Fifth Report,* 1876;
Eighth Report, 1881, vol. I; *Tenth Report,* 1885; *Various Collections,*
vol. IV; *Report on the Manuscripts of Lord Middleton Preserved at
Wollaton Hall, Nottinghamshire,* ed. W. Stevenson, 1911.

REFERENCE WORKS AND LITERATURE

Behrens, B. 'Origins of the office of English resident ambassador in Rome',
English Historical Review, XXXIX (1934), 640–56.

Brady, W. Maziere. *The Episcopal Succession in England, Scotland, and Ireland, A.D. 1400 to 1875.* 3 vols. Rome, 1876.

Chambers, D. S. *Cardinal Bainbridge in the Court of Rome, 1509 to 1514.* Oxford Historical Series, 2nd. Oxford, 1965. Taken from the author's Oxford D.Phil. thesis, 1962, entitled 'English representation at the court of Rome in the early Tudor period'.

'Cardinal Wolsey and the papal tiara', *Bulletin of the Institute of Historical Research,* xxxviii (1965), 20–30.

Conway, Agnes. *Henry VII's Relations with Scotland and Ireland, 1485–1498,* with a chapter on the Acts of Poynings' Parliament, 1494–5, by E. Curtis. Cambridge, 1932.

Cruickshank, C. G. *The English Occupation of Tournai, 1513–1519.* Oxford, 1971.

Ehses, Stephan. 'Papst Klemens VII. in dem Scheidungsprozesse Heinrichs VIII', *Historisches Jahrbuch,* xii (1892), 470–88.

'Zur Ehescheidung Heinrichs VIII. von England', *Römische Quartalschrift für christliche Alterthumskunde und für Kirchengeschichte,* xiv (1900), 256–68.

Elton, G. R. 'King or minister? The man behind the Henrician Reformation', *History* (new series), xxxix (1954), 216–32.

Policy and Police, the Enforcement of the Reformation in the Age of Thomas Cromwell. Cambridge, 1972.

'Thomas Cromwell's decline and fall', *Cambridge Historical Journal,* x (1951), 150–85.

The Tudor Revolution in Government, Administrative Changes in the Reign of Henry VIII. Cambridge, 1953.

Eubel, Conrad. *Hierarchia Catholica Medii Aevi.* Vols. ii and iii. Münster, 1910–14.

Friedmann, Paul. *Anne Boleyn, a Chapter of English History, 1527–1536.* 2 vols. London, 1884.

Gwynn, Aubrey. *The Medieval Province of Armagh, 1470–1545.* Dundalk, 1946.

Kelly, Michael. 'Canterbury jurisdiction and influence during the episcopate of William Warham, 1503–1532'. Unpublished Cambridge Ph.D. dissertation, 1963. Cambridge University Library.

Lehmberg, Stanford. *The Reformation Parliament, 1529–1536.* Cambridge, 1970.

LeNeve, John. *Fasti Ecclesiae Anglicanae, 1300–1541.* 2nd ed., completely revised by H. King, J. Horn and B. Jones. Fasc. i–ix. London, 1962–5.

Lunt, William E. *Financial Relations of the Papacy with England.* Studies in Anglo-Papal Relations during the Middle Ages, ii, Mediaeval Academy of America. Vol. ii, 1327–1534. Cambridge, Mass., 1962.

Mattingly, Garrett. *Catherine of Aragon.* New York, 1942.

Newns, Brian. 'The Hospice of St. Thomas and the English crown 1474–1538', in *The English Hospice in Rome.* The Venerabile Sexcentenary Issue, xxi, 1962, pp. 145–92.

Parmiter, G. de C. *The King's Great Matter, a Study of Anglo-Papal Relations 1527–1534.* London, 1967.

246   *Bibliography*

Pastor, Ludwig von. *History of the Popes.* Trans. from the German by
F. Antrobus and R. Kerr. Vols. v–xi. London, 1898–1912.

Queller, D. *The Office of Ambassador in the Middle Ages.* Princeton, 1967.

Scarisbrick, J. J. *Henry VIII.* London, 1968.

Schlecht, Joseph. 'Pius III. und die deutsche Nation', in *Festschrift Georg
von Hertling.* Munich, 1913. Offprint with an appendix of unprinted
letters and the eulogy of Engelbert Funk, Munich, 1914.

Sigonio, Carlo. *De vita Laurentii Campegii Cardinalis liber ad Laurentium
Campegium apud Senatum Venetum Nuncium Apostolicum.* Bologna,
1581.

Strnad, Alfred A. 'Francesco Todeschini-Piccolomini, Politik und
Mäzenatentum in Quattrocento', *Römische Historische Mitteilungen,*
viii–ix (1964–6), 101–425.

Wernham, R. B. *Before the Armada, the Growth of English Foreign Policy,
1485–1588.* London, 1966.

Wodka, Joseph. 'Das Kardinalprotektorat deutscher Nation und die
Protektorate der deutschen nationalen Stiftungen in Rom', in *Zeitschrift
der Savigny-Stiftung für Rechtsgeschichte* (Kanonistische Abteilung,
xxxiii), lxiv (1944), 301–22.

*Zur Geschichte der nationalen Protektorate der Kardinäle an der
römischen Kurie.* Publikationen des österreichischen historischen
Instituts in Rom, vol. iv, pt. 1. Innsbruck, 1938.

INDEX

The following abbreviations are used: amb.=ambassador, archbp=archbishop, archbpric=archbishopric, bp=bishop, bpric=bishopric, card.=cardinal, k.=king, nom.=nominated, q.=queen.

Henry VIII, k. of England, the role
of the card. protectorship, 6, 11,
73; marriage to Catherine of
Aragon, 29, 74, 76–7, 191; and
Castellesi, 34, 45, 107, 108n;
correspondence with Sisto
della Rovere Garo, 36; and
Card. Protector Alidosi, 37–8;
relations with France, 43–5,
49–50, 86, 111; and Wolsey, 51–2,
51n, 83–4, 87–8, 116, 154, 157–8,
174, 198, 217; and Bainbridge,
40–3, 45, 47–8, 50, 52, 79; and
Card. Protector de'Medici, 31, 48,
73, 82–3, 94, 99, 103, 128, 134,
138–40, 142–3, 157, 161–4, 180;
the occupation of Tournai, 87–8,
91–3, 95–7; his sister Mary, q. of
France, 86–7, 100; his sister
Margaret, q. of Scotland, 96,
101–3, 180; and Scotland, 47,
97–100, 173–5, 173n; relations
with Card. Protector Campeggio,
77, 111–13, 112n, 114n, 119,
122–3, 124n, 131n, 135, 141–6,
144n, 149, 154, 170, 176–7, 179,
181–2, 188–9, 194, 194n, 196–9,
199n, 203, 204n, 205–8, 205n,
207n, 210–16, 220–1, 223–32,
234–5, 237; relations with
Charles V, 115–16, 118, 122–3,
123n, 129, 177–8, 188, 200, 200n,
237; Defender of the Faith, 122,
125n, 140, 159; opponent of
Lutheranism, 122–4, 142, 187; and
Adrian VI, 129, 136; the divorce,
1–2, 96, 179–80, 182–7, 183n,
201–2, 206, 209, 211–13, 217,
225; relations with Francis I, 87,
89n, 96, 115–16, 118, 188, 197,
209, 218, 225; his illegitimate son
Henry FitzRoy, 191, 231, 233;
nominations to English bprics, 53,
150–1, 158–9, 160, 171; and
Ireland, 73, 80, 161, 164, 166;
the papal golden rose, 41, 140,
169; the papal cap and sword, 47,
83, 100; anti-papalism, 158–9,
187–8, 200, 206–7, 210, 217–18,
232–3; and Cromwell, 202–3, 218,
236; criticised by Pole, 232–3;
also 15, 171 and references to
Henry VIII under Julius II and
Leo X
Hepburn, John, candidate for the
archbpric of St Andrews, 98, 103
Hereford, bpric of, 25, 54, 54n, 57,
59, 63, 75, 150–1, 150n
Hilley, Richard, Campeggio's vicar
general in Salisbury, 147, 147n,

214, 214n
Hilsey, John, king's appointee as bp
of Rochester, 231
Home, Alexander, lord chamberlain
to James V of Scotland, 103
Home, David, prior of Coldingham,
97
Houran, Nicholas, priest of Hereford,
in Rome, 162
Howard, Thomas, 2nd earl of Surrey,
3rd duke of Norfolk, 164–5, 205,
207, 228, 230, 230n
Huesca and Jaca, bpric of, and
Campeggio, 203–4
Hulle, William, of Worcester, 151
Hunne, John, and anti-clericalism,
158n
Huse, Peter, papal envoy in
England, 16

Impingham, John, Benedictine prior
of Coventry, 85
indulgences, papal, for England, 11,
60, 71, 79, 82, 99, 101, 113, 120,
120n, 170–1, 170n, 185n
Inge, Hugh, *custos* of the English
hospice in Rome, then bp of
Meath, then archbp of Dublin and
lord chancellor of Ireland, 31, 75,
77, 79, 163–4, 167
Innocent VIII (Gianbattista Cibò),
pope (1484–92), 9, 11, 14, 16–17,
54, 61, 64
Irish church, in general, 63–73,
75–80, 114, 161–8; *see also* the
various bprics, Achonry, Anna-
down, Ardagh, Ardfert, Armagh,
Cashel, Clogher, Clonmacnois,
Cork and Cloyne, Derry, Dromore,
Dublin, Elphin, Emly, Glendalough, Kildare, Kilfenora, Killala,
Killaloe, Kilmacduagh, Kilmore,
Leighlin, Limerick, Mayo, Meath,
Ossory, Raphoe, Ross and Tuam

James IV, k. of Scotland, 43, 44n,
96, 102
James V, k. of Scotland, 96, 173–5,
173n, 174n, 233, 236
Jane, Thomas, bp of Norwich, 24n,
57–8, 57n
Jeanne de Valois, Blessed, invalid
marriage to Louis XII, 191n
John XXIII (Angelo Roncalli), pope,
140n
Jouffroy, Jean, card. procurator of
France in Rome, 8
Joyce, William, *see* Seoighe
Julius II (Giuliano della Rovere,
q.v.), pope (1503–13), and card.